Ambivalence, Politics, and Public Policy

AMBIVALENCE, POLITICS, AND PUBLIC POLICY

EDITED BY

STEPHEN C. CRAIG

AND

MICHAEL D. MARTINEZ

AMBIVALENCE, POLITICS, AND PUBLIC POLICY

First published in 2005 by
PALGRAVE MACMILLAN™
175 Fifth Avenue, New York, N.Y. 10010 and
Houndmills, Basingstoke, Hampshire, England RG21 6XS
Companies and representatives throughout the world.

PALGRAVE MACMILLAN is the global academic imprint of the
Palgrave Macmillan division of St. Martin's Press, LLC and
of Palgrave Macmillan Ltd. Macmillan® is a registered trademark
in the United States, United Kingdom and other countries.
Palgrave is a registered trademark in the European
Union and other countries.

ISBN 1–4039–6572–2

A catalogue record for this book is available from the British Library.

Library of Congress Cataloging-in-Publication Data

Ambivalence, politics, and public policy / edited by Stephen C. Craig
and Michael D. Martinez.
    p. cm.
Includes bibliographical references and index.
ISBN 1–4039–6572–2
    1. Political psychology. 2. Ambivalence. 3. Policy sciences.
4. Voting. 5. Decision making. 6. Social choice. I. Craig, Stephen C.
II. Martinez, Michael D.

JA74.5.A43 2005
320.6′01′9—dc22   2004065492

Design by Newgen Imaging Systems (P) Ltd., Chennai, India.

First edition: August 2005

10 9 8 7 6 5 4 3 2 1

Printed in the United States of America.

For
Matthew and Kathryn
Jessica, Charlie, Nicole, Patrick,
Deena, Jarren, and Bryan

CONTENTS

List of Tables   ix

About the Contributors   xi

Preface   xv
Stephen C. Craig and Michael D. Martinez

1. Group Ambivalence and Electoral Decision-Making   1
    Howard Lavine and Marco Steenbergen

2. Ambivalence and Attitude Change in Vote Choice:
    Do Campaign Switchers Experience Internal Conflict?   27
    Patrick Fournier

3. What Happens When We Simultaneously Want
    Opposite Things? Ambivalence about Social Welfare   47
    Jason Gainous and Michael D. Martinez

4. Ambivalence and Value Conflict: A Test of Two Issues   63
    Michael D. Martinez, Stephen C. Craig, James G. Kane, and
    Jason Gainous

5. Education, Ideology, and Racial Ambivalence:
    Conflict Amplification or Conflict Resolution?   83
    Christopher M. Federico

6. Managing Voter Ambivalence in Growth and
    Conservation Campaigns   103
    Dennis Chong and Yael Wolinsky-Nahmias

7. Ambivalence and Attitudes toward Church–State Relations   127
    Ted G. Jelen

8. Attitudinal Ambivalence and Political Opinion:
   Review and Avenues for Further Research   145
   Christopher J. Armitage and Mark Conner

References   167

Index   185

LIST OF TABLES

1.1 Effects of group ambivalence on policy preferences, ideology, party identification, and presidential vote choice   15

1.2 Effects of group ambivalence on error variance in policy preferences, ideology, party identification, and presidential vote choice   17

1.3 Effects of group ambivalence on timing of vote decision, ticket-splitting, and turnout   19

1.4 Effects of group ambivalence on candidate evaluation and vote choice   21

2.1 Distribution of stable and unstable vote choice across panel waves   32

2.2 Determinants of attitude change, three measures of ambivalence   36

2.3 Determinants of attitude change, Canada   38

2.4 Determinants of attitude change, Britain   40

3.1 Frequency and intensity of ambivalence about social welfare   57

3.2 Correlations between independent variables and social welfare ambivalence   58

3.3 Multivariate model of social welfare ambivalence   59

4.1 Frequency and intensity of ambivalence on abortion and gay rights   69

4.2 A multivariate model of ambivalence about abortion: traumatic and elective dimensions   74

4.3 A multivariate model of ambivalence about gay rights: adult roles dimension   76

4.4 A multivariate model of ambivalence about gay rights: children/families dimension   77

5.1 Explaining racial ambivalence: conservatism, education, and their interaction   92

5.2 Explaining the two types of value conflict: conservatism, education, and their interaction   94

5.3 Explaining racial ambivalence: mediators of the interaction between conservatism and education   95

6.1 Evaluation of alternative arguments for and against the public purchase of land   108

6.2 Priorities in managing growth   113

6.3 Support for open-space programs by voter priorities   114

6.4 Alternative measures of support for CGMI   115

6.5 Support for Citizen's Growth Management Initiative (CGMI) against alternatives   117

7.1 Cross-tabulation of Church–State items   134

7.2 Multivariate models of Church–State ambivalence   138

7.3 Multivariate models of concrete Church–State issues   140

About the Contributors

CHRISTOPHER J. ARMITAGE received his Ph.D. in Psychology from the University of Leeds in 1998. After holding posts at the University of Manchester and the University of Essex, he is now Reader in Psychology in the Department of Psychology at the University of Sheffield. He has published more than forty articles and book chapters in the broad field of applied social psychology. In addition to research interests in attitudinal ambivalence, he has also published work in the areas of attitude theory, behavior change, and social cognition.

DENNIS CHONG is the John D. and Catherine T. MacArthur Professor of Political Science and a Research Fellow in the Institute for Policy Research at Northwestern University. He specializes in the study of public opinion and political psychology and is the author of *Rational Lives: Norms and Values in Politics and Society* (University of Chicago Press, 2000). His current research examines the growth of community participation in local referendums and initiatives on environmental issues.

MARK CONNER received his Ph.D. in Psychology from the University of Birmingham in 1988. He has been at the University of Leeds in the Institute of Psychology since 1990, and is currently Reader in Applied Social Psychology. His research interests focus on the impacts of attitudes on behavior, and he has published over one hundred journal articles and book chapters in this area.

STEPHEN C. CRAIG is Professor of Political Science at the University of Florida, as well as director of the university's Graduate Program in Political Campaigning. He is author of *The Malevolent Leaders: Popular Discontent in America* (1993), as well as numerous journal articles and book chapters dealing with attitude measurement, partisan change, campaign effects, and other aspects of contemporary public opinion and political behavior in the United States.

CHRISTOPHER M. FEDERICO is Assistant Professor of Psychology and Political Science at the University of Minnesota, Twin Cities. He completed his Ph.D. at the University of California, Los Angeles, and his research interests lie primarily in the areas of race and politics, the structure of belief systems, and political cognitions. His work has appeared in *Journal of Personality and Social Psychology*, *American Journal of Political Science*, and *Public Opinion Quarterly*.

PATRICK FOURNIER is Assistant Professor of Political Science at the Université de Montréal. He received his Ph.D. from the University of British Columbia, and his research interests include political behavior, political psychology, citizen competence, attitude change, voting, public opinion, survey research, and methodology. He was coinvestigator of the Canadian Election Study for the 2000 and 2004 elections. His work has been published in journals such as *Electoral Studies*, *Journal of Politics*, *Political Behavior*, and *Public Opinion Quarterly*.

JASON GAINOUS is Visiting Assistant Professor at the University of Southern Mississippi. His dissertation and research agenda focus on Americans' ambivalence about social welfare issues, and he has coauthored several conference papers and journal articles dealing with public opinion, voter behavior, and the psychology of political attitudes.

TED G. JELEN is Professor and former Chair of Political Science at the University of Nevada, Las Vegas. He has published extensively in the area of religion and political behavior, church–state relations, and the politics of abortion. He is former editor of the *Journal for the Scientific Study of Religion*, and is coauthor (with Clyde Wilcox) of *Public Attitudes toward Church and State*.

JAMES G. KANE is president of the *Florida Voter* polling organization, and an adjunct professor with the Graduate Program in Political Campaigning at the University of Florida. He has coauthored journal articles, book chapters, and conference papers dealing with various aspects of public opinion and voting behavior in the United States.

HOWARD LAVINE is Associate Professor of Political Science and Psychology at the State University of New York at Stony Brook, coeditor of the journal *Political Psychology*, and 2004 recipient of the Erik H. Erikson early career award from the International Society of Political Psychology. His work centers on the cognitive and motivational underpinnings of public opinion and political choice, threat and authoritarianism, and experimental methodology.

MICHAEL D. MARTINEZ is Associate Professor of Political Science at the University of Florida. His research on partisanship, voting behavior, ideology, and attitudinal ambivalence has appeared in numerous academic journals, including *American Journal of Political Science, Canadian Journal of Political Science, Political Behavior, Political Research Quarterly*, and others. He has been a Fulbright Scholar at the University of Calgary, and a Visiting Associate Professor at the University of British Columbia.

MARCO STEENBERGEN is Associate Professor of Political Science at the University of North Carolina at Chapel Hill. His research interests span the fields of political psychology, voting behavior, public opinion, West European politics, and political methodology. His published work includes studies on the cognitive and affective underpinnings of candidate evaluations, and he is currently writing a book-length manuscript (coauthored with Howard Lavine) examining the role of ambivalence in electoral behavior.

YAEL WOLINSKY-NAHMIAS teaches in the Department of Political Science at Northwestern University. She is coeditor of *Models, Numbers, and Cases: Methods for Studying International Relations* (University of Michigan Press, 2004), and is currently conducting research on state and local ballot measures dealing with environmental issues. She has written about game theory and international environmental policy making, and about the effects of electoral politics on international noncrisis bargaining.

PREFACE

Stephen C. Craig and Michael D. Martinez

Conflict is the root of politics. Often, when we think about political conflict, we think about the issues that divide northerners from southerners, haves from have-nots, moralists from secularists, minorities from majorities, and women from men. After all, as James Madison reminded us in *Federalist 10*, differences in interests, abilities, and lifestyles that give rise to conflicts *between* people are "sown in the nature of man." But, conflict also exists *within* individuals' own thought processes. Poor people are more likely than rich people to see and value the societal advantages that accrue from social welfare policies, yet many rich individuals and poor individuals alike might value *both* economic opportunity *and* a tightly woven social safety net. Environmentalists are more likely than local developers to prefer conservation measures to unbridled economic growth, but each side (and especially people on *neither* side) might see both the upsides *and* the downsides of government regulation of property. Even on the culturally divisive issue of abortion, many people feel torn between two "rights"—that of the woman to decide whether to abort, and that of the fetus whose fate rests with her decision. The chapters in this book help us to understand how *ambivalence* affects the electoral choices and the politics of key issues that face voters in contemporary democratic societies.

A companion volume published earlier, *Ambivalence and the Structure of Political Opinion* (see Craig and Martinez 2005), focused mainly on conceptualization and measurement of ambivalence, its origins, and the role that ambivalence plays in shaping people's general political outlooks. The essays presented here continue these same themes, but with a greater emphasis on the effects of ambivalence on voter decision making and its consequences for interpreting public opinion on many of the central public policy issues of our day. There is, for example, a consideration of the relationship between ideology and ambivalence (are liberals or conservatives more likely to be ambivalent?), the extent to which value conflict is a source of ambivalence, the effect of ambivalence on the structure of citizens' issue preferences, and the question of whether ambivalence moderates or mediates the effects of those preferences on voter choice.

To repeat, conflict among groups is at the root of political conflict. In chapter one, an analysis of the 2000 American National Election Study leads Howard Lavine and Marco Steenbergen to conclude that "group ambivalence" (similar levels of support for conservative and liberal groups) has more consistent effects than "candidate ambivalence" or "party ambivalence" on a variety of behaviors and attitudes. Most significantly, people who are most ambivalent about group evaluations tend to decide later whom to support for president, are more likely to split their ticket on election day (supporting one party for president and another for Congress), have less stable evaluations of presidential candidates, and are less likely to utilize their issue preferences in forming a presidential vote choice. When voters are ambivalent about the groups that define their political space, their choices appear to become significantly more difficult.

Whether elections are contested in an electoral space characterized by sharply defined partisan cleavages, or on the shifting sands of a dealigned and malleable electorate, campaigns seek to mobilize candidates' base constituencies while also perhaps changing a few minds among those favoring the opponent. Typically, only a handful of voters are converted in any given election—but even a small number can represent the balance of power in a hard-fought race. In chapter two, Patrick Fournier examines the factors that distinguish voters who shift their preferences over the course of a campaign from "standpatters," with specific attention to the effects of ambivalence on the stability of candidate preference. Fournier employs a measure of "actual ambivalence" in candidate preference, conceptually based on the well-known concept of *cross-pressures* (see Berelson, Lazarsfeld, and McPhee 1954) and constructed using responses to closed-ended questions similar to those that are asked in most standard election studies. Analyses of panel data from three presidential elections in the United States, three national elections in Canada, two national elections in Britain, and a provincial election in Ontario show that ambivalence is indeed related to the probability of changes in voter preferences; that is, voters who change their minds are likely to have had some reason to do so before the campaign even began.

The question of how to balance an individual's opportunity to succeed (or fail) and society's responsibility to provide a social safety net has been at the heart of democratic politics in industrial and postindustrial societies for at least the better part of a century. In chapter three, Jason Gainous and Michael Martinez examine data from a recent statewide survey in Florida and propose that conflict between individualism and egalitarianism, the relative importance of these two core values to the individual, and the person's policy preference each play a role in shaping ambivalence on social welfare policy. Moreover, Gainous and Martinez find (in contradistinction to Zaller and Feldman 1992) that voters who tend to have liberal dispositions are *less* rather than more ambivalent about social welfare issues.

Although social welfare remains a persistent issue, cultural issues such as abortion and gay rights also are central in defining the current political landscape in the United States. In chapter four, we (along with coauthors, James Kane and Jason Gainous) examine two statewide surveys and find a fair amount of ambivalence on these presumably "easy" issues in Florida. Notably, ambivalence regarding both abortion and gay rights appears to have multiple dimensions; that is, people who are ambivalent about one aspect of the issue are not necessarily ambivalent about other aspects as well. In addition, though we find that conflict among core values (including support for traditional lifestyles, traditional marriage roles, and egalitarianism) is a source of ambivalence on both dimensions of both issues, the evidence suggests that such conflict is far from the whole story.

Racial politics are often seen as "black and white," both as an erroneous description of the groups on either side of the American racial divide and as a depiction of the starkness of public opinion about racial issues. In chapter five, however, Christopher Federico offers evidence that many white Americans have conflicted views in their perceptions of blacks. Echoing Gainous and Martinez's findings with respect to social welfare, Federico's analysis of the 1991 National Race and Politics Study suggests that white conservatives are more ambivalent about race than are white liberals. Moreover, the relationship between ideology and racial ambivalence is amplified among whites by higher levels of education. Federico also shows value conflict (this time between humanitarian concerns and individualism) is at the root of educated whites' racial ambivalence, but that conflict is better conceptualized in race-specific terms than as a reflection of one's general, overarching principles.

The politics of growth management in our urban areas reflects the balance between respect for the environment and expanding opportunities for economic growth. In chapter six, Dennis Chong and Yael Wolinsky-Nahmias examine the precursors to the defeat of a November, 2000, ballot measure in Arizona that would have forced local communities to develop urban growth boundaries and comprehensive land use plans. Looking at a 1998 statewide survey, Chong and Wolinsky-Nahmias find relatively small blocs of "no growth" and "no restraint" voters, and conclude that it is the large group of citizens falling in between these two extremes who are most susceptible to campaign messages that frame the issues and, in this case, prime anxieties about such things as "special interests," local control, and the prospect of litigation. While most voters are sympathetic to protecting the environment in the abstract, widespread ambivalence about specific policy proposals can create an opening for opponents to exploit.

Americans are a religious people, perhaps surprisingly so considering the country's high level of economic development (Wald 2003: 9); however, as Ted Jelen shows in chapter seven, many citizens possess conflicted attitudes about the role of religion in politics. Specifically, a plurality of respondents in a Washington, DC-area survey endorsed both a "high wall of separation" between church and state *and* protection of our Judeo-Christian heritage. Jelen finds that liberals and less devout people tend to experience more attitude conflict, and concludes that this "symbolic" ambivalence moderates the impact that religious beliefs have on attitudes about the appropriateness of moments of silence in school (but not prayers at high school football games).

In chapter eight, Christopher Armitage and Mark Conner review the contributions presented in *Ambivalence and the Structure of Political Opinion* (Craig and Martinez 2005) as well as this volume, and discuss how they help to frame our conceptualization of attitudinal ambivalence and its consequences. Armitage and Conner point out that even though the different essays vary in their approaches to understanding the factors that under-lay ambivalence, important common themes about the consequences of ambivalence nevertheless do emerge. The authors conclude by outlining an agenda of unanswered questions related to ambivalence that are ripe for future research.

We hope that these two books together will help to raise awareness, among scholars and practicing politicians alike, that citizens' thoughts and feelings about contemporary issues are often complex and multifaceted. It would be a gross exaggeration for us to claim that all voters are ambivalent (as many clearly are not), but it is important to recognize that many people do have both positive and negative attitudes and feelings about some of the choices they must make. Taking ambivalence into account gives us a broader understanding of how a significant proportion of the public grapples with the tough political issues they face at election time, and in the course of their everyday lives.

CHAPTER ONE

GROUP AMBIVALENCE AND ELECTORAL DECISION-MAKING

Howard Lavine and Marco Steenbergen

Recent insights about attitude structure and process have spawned a new understanding of the nature and dynamics of mass opinion. On the structural side, there is mounting evidence that political opinions are more complex than the unidimensional summary statements (e.g., unfavorable or favorable, cold or warm, negative or positive) routinely used to measure them. On the processing side, opinions often are not directly retrieved from memory in summary form but, instead, are constructed episodically on the basis of an "on-the-spot" memory search using whatever considerations are momentarily salient (Tourangeau, Rips, and Rasinski 2000; Zaller and Feldman 1992; but see Lodge, McGraw, and Stroh 1989; Lodge, Steenbergen, and Brau 1995). Although political scientists have only recently begun to incorporate these insights into empirical models of political behavior, they have long recognized that opinions are infused with conflicting beliefs and feelings. The authors of *The American Voter* wrote, for example, that an individual voter's "system of partisan attitudes" could be consistently favorable toward one party, or that the elements of the system could be in conflict (Campbell *et al.* 1960; also see Free and Cantril 1967; Lazarsfeld, Berelson, and Gaudet 1944). Contemporary research suggests further that *ambivalence*— an internalized conflict about a specific political choice—is a prevalent characteristic of political belief systems, with important implications for how citizens make political decisions.

Earlier theories assumed that inconsistent and unstable opinions reflected either uncrystallized views (Converse 1964) or deficient measurement (Achen 1975). Analysts now believe that these phenomena may also reflect attempts at reconciling strongly held but conflicting principles and considerations simultaneously present in the political culture (Feldman and Zaller 1992). Whether because disputes activate widely shared but inherently incompatible

lvarez and Brehm 2002), because few citizens possess the political
hal to resist arguments counter to their values and interests (Zaller
because electoral contests provide ample amounts of positive and
negative information about each of the competing campaigns (Lavine
2001), *many citizens appear to embrace central elements of both sides of
political debates.* For example, Americans often express support for both
individualism and egalitarianism on questions of welfare spending and racial
policy (Feldman and Zaller 1992; Katz and Hass 1988); feminism and
religion on abortion (Alvarez and Brehm 2002; Craig, Kane, and Martinez
2002); and moral traditionalism and social tolerance on debates about gay
rights (Craig *et al.* 2005b). At a more general level, citizens frequently
express opposing beliefs about the proper role of government in society
(Cantril and Cantril 1999; Free and Cantril 1967). Finally, in the electoral
realm, as much as one-third of the voting public report having conflicted
reactions toward presidential candidates and the political parties (Basinger
and Lavine 2005; Lavine 2001; Meffert, Guge, and Lodge 2000). Taken
together, these findings imply that positive attitudes are not simply the dia-
metric opposite of negative attitudes, such that the more one likes a political
object the less one dislikes it. Instead, political attitudes are often simultaneously positive and negative, or ambivalent.[1]

Beyond the question of prevalence, research has shown that ambivalence
has important consequences for political judgment and choice. In the public
opinion realm, attitudes marked by ambivalence tend to be held with less
confidence and more difficult to retrieve (less cognitively accessible) than
relatively one-sided or "univalent" opinions (Bargh *et al.* 1992; Huckfeldt
and Sprague 2000; Lavine, Borgida, and Sullivan 2000); consequently,
they are less stable over time and more vulnerable to persuasion (Bassili
1996; Zaller and Feldman 1992; Craig, Martinez, and Kane 2005a). More
generally, ambivalence appears to render policy choice fundamentally difficult
and unreliable, and contextually dependent on temporarily salient considerations (Alvarez and Brehm 1995, 2002; Haddock 2003; Lavine *et al.*
1998; Tourangeau *et al.* 1989a). In their examination of abortion attitudes,
for example, Alvarez and Brehm (1995) found that respondents who valued
both women's rights *and* religion (the main underpinnings of pro-choice
and pro-life positions, respectively) revealed considerably greater error variance in their policy choices than did respondents who valued one of these
considerations to the relative exclusion of the other.

Ambivalence has also been shown to influence electoral decision-making
in presidential and congressional contests. Conflicted attitudes toward presidential candidates often produce unstable electoral judgments, and weaken
the effects of both personality assessments and issue proximity on vote choice
(Lavine 2001). In House elections, Basinger and Lavine (2005) found that

ambivalence can decrease the electoral relevance of one ingredient while increasing the relevance of others, and that the relative weights of these factors depend jointly on ambivalence and sophistication. They argued that when congressional voters hold clear-cut (i.e., univalent) attitudes toward the parties, partisan cues convey sufficient electoral confidence and the benefits of further thought (or information acquisition) are negligible. Accordingly, they found that voters with univalent partisan attitudes—strongly liking one party and strongly disliking the other—relied heavily on partisanship and only slightly on ideology in making their vote decisions in House races. However, reliance on party identification was sharply reduced among voters with highly ambivalent partisan attitudes. To take up the judgmental slack, highly informed ambivalent voters increased their reliance on ideological proximity, whereas uninformed ambivalent voters increased their reliance on the simpler devices of incumbency and judgments about the economy. Finally, ambivalence may moderate the basic cognitive strategies that voters use to form electoral impressions. McGraw and her colleagues (2003) learned that, compared to those who possess univalent candidate attitudes, ambivalent voters are more likely to rely on immediately accessible considerations regarding the candidates than on an online tally of candidate likes and dislikes. This is a key finding, as memory-based processing is particularly likely to foster ambivalence-based instability and context-dependent judgment.

In sum, research to date suggests that the public's political attitudes are often fraught with conflicting beliefs and feelings that may, in turn, have consequences for cognition and behavior. There are, however, two important limitations within the literature that we wish to address here. First, despite considerable methodological and substantive variation, all past studies rely (at least implicitly) on the idea that ambivalence is a psychological state experienced in relation to a *specific attitude object* (Alvarez and Brehm 2002; Steenbergen and Brewer 2000; Tetlock 1986). There is nothing inherently problematic in this assumption; to the contrary, object specificity characterizes most research that has been done on attitude structure and attitude strength (see Eagly and Chaiken 1993; Petty and Krosnick 1995). Yet we believe that approaches in which the competing considerations vary from one opinion domain to the next are incomplete. In particular, they preclude the possibility that there exists a more abstract and fundamental type of "ideological" ambivalence, one that produces a generalized split in the political mind affecting a wide range of political choices. Our first objective, then, is to identify and test several potential forms of generalized political ambivalence.

The second weakness in the literature runs deeper, pertaining to the conditions under which ambivalence is aroused and likely to influence

. In previous work, ambivalence has sometimes been used ngeably with "inconsistency," implying that people experience ogical conflict whenever they embrace opposing considerations about an a.. :ude object (e.g., Zaller 1992; Feldman and Zaller 1992). We view ambivalence in more circumscribed terms, occurring only under highly specific—and probably infrequently occurring—conditions. Thus, our second objective is to sharpen the definition of ambivalence, and to provide a set of empirical procedures for determining when ambivalence (of any type) is present.

In the next section, we describe a method that can be used to determine the conditions under which ambivalence is likely to occur. We then develop the basis for a generalized form of ambivalence, focusing specifically on affective conflict rooted in sympathies and resentments toward ideologically linked social groups. We also test two other potential forms of generalized ambivalence: conflict about the role of government, and conflict rooted in core values. Our empirical analysis yields three important findings: first, inconsistent beliefs do not necessarily lead to the psychological experience of ambivalence (Holbrook and Krosnick 2005). Second, inconsistency exerts important effects on political behavior only when it produces demonstrable internalized conflict; that is, inconsistency matters only when it leads to ambivalence. Third, of the various types of political objects that may engender ambivalence (e.g., candidates, parties, government, values, groups), conflict rooted in positive feelings toward social groups of both the left and the right yields the broadest, strongest, and most consistent effects on political behavior.

WHEN DOES AMBIVALENCE OCCUR?

Ambivalence is most often defined as the endorsement of inconsistent beliefs about an attitude object. This position is exemplified by Zaller and Feldman (1992), who, noting that "most people possess opposing considerations on most issues" (p. 585), elevate ambivalence to a first principle of public opinion. In contrast, Alvarez and Brehm take a more limited view of the construct, regarding inconsistency as a necessary though not sufficient condition for ambivalence to occur. In their view, ambivalence denotes an internalized attitudinal conflict involving unresolvable psychological tension—a tension for which, to put it starkly, "to accomplish one value requires annihilation of the other" (Alvarez and Brehm 2002: 59). For this to occur, the competing values must be truly incompatible, such that they cannot be reconciled by privileging one over the other. From this perspective, individuals may well see merit in both sides of a political debate, but experience little psychological tension in expressing their own opinions about it.

Under what conditions, then, do inconsistent beliefs or feelings induce a state of internalized conflict, or ambivalence? Short of taking physiological measurements of inconsistency-induced tension, we argue that ambivalence occurs only when three empirical conditions are satisfied. First, the competing considerations should be *equally relevant* or important to the political choice in question. If two opposing beliefs are perceived as impinging on the choice, but one is viewed as more relevant or important than the other, the attitudinal conflict can be effectively eliminated by privileging the dominant value (see also Alvarez and Brehm 2002; Steenbergen and Brewer 2000). Second, if cognitive or affective inconsistency is to result in ambivalence, the competing considerations should *dominate* the prediction of the political choice. If these considerations are overwhelmed by other factors, then ambivalence about the choice should not be strongly felt. For example, even if individualist and egalitarian beliefs exert equally relevant (and opposing) effects on racial policy choice, they should instigate little psychological tension if the choice is determined largely by self-interest or racial prejudice.[2]

If these two criteria are met—if competing considerations have an equal and dominant influence on a political choice—then support for both should increase the difficulty of making judgments and choices. Such difficulty can be operationalized in a number of ways. Here, we follow Alvarez and Brehm (2002) and focus on the reliability with which choice is expressed. In operational terms, survey responses should contain more error variance when the most influential choice bases imply opposing alternatives.[3] Given these rather stringent requirements, we expect that most citizens will experience little if any ambivalence in their political lives. In many cases, political preferences will simply reflect a single "top-of-the-head" belief (Zaller 1992) or perhaps an online tally (Lodge, Steenbergen, and Brau 1995). Even when multiple considerations are taken into account, chances are that they will either reinforce one another, or that one will be perceived as more relevant to the decision than the other. And even when two conflicting considerations exert equal force, they should produce little psychological tension if other factors weigh more heavily in the decision. In sum, true ambivalence should occur only when a political choice is dominated by opposing considerations of equal relevance, and when simultaneous support for the opposing considerations increases response variance. It is only under these limited circumstances that inconsistent beliefs or feelings should have a meaningful impact on political behavior.

ON THE PRIMACY OF GROUPS IN AMERICAN PUBLIC OPINION

What form might a generalized ambivalence take? One possibility is that citizens may embrace aspects of the philosophical underpinnings of both liberalism and conservatism (e.g., endorsing both government redistribution of wealth *and* laissez-faire capitalism). At first blush, this might seem unlikely given the evidence that most Americans are innocent of such abstractions (Converse 1964; for a review, see Kinder and Sears 1985). However, there are two less cognitively demanding versions of the argument, one rooted in conflicting views about the role of government and the other centering on conflict between core American values. In making a distinction between two levels of political debate—one rhetorical and symbolic, the other concrete and specific—Cantril and his colleagues (Cantril and Cantril 1999; Free and Cantril 1967) found that upward of half of those who see the government as being too powerful nevertheless support increased or sustained government spending on a wide range of public programs. For example, they discovered that many people simultaneously believe that the government "does too many things people could do better for themselves," *and* that the government should spend more money on everything from education, job training, and health care to worker safety and clean air. Thus, citizens' *general* (conservative) views about the power of government are frequently at odds with their *specific* (liberal) preferences about what government should do in practice (for a different interpretation, see Jacoby 2005).

A related form of generalized ambivalence can be couched in the language of core values. Theorists have argued that the American political culture, deriving from "classical liberalism," emphasizes the conflicting values of self-reliance, limited government, and individual freedom on the one hand, and equality on the other (Feldman 1988, 2003; Jacoby 2002; McClosky and Zaller 1984; Rokeach 1973). Both individualism and egalitarianism clearly enjoy widespread public support; in the context of many political debates, however, they have opposing political implications. Debates about government power and economic redistribution have long been at the heart of ideological and partisan debate in American politics. Conflicting beliefs about the role of government or support for conflicting core values should therefore be good candidates for creating ambivalence about a broad range of political choices.

As our data analysis will show, however, each of these formulations falters on empirical inspection. The psychological experience of ambivalence requires that competing considerations pull the individual strongly, and equally, in opposite directions. These requirements are simply not met for attitudinal conflict rooted in either general versus specific views about government or individualist versus egalitarian values. A third possibility is that mass political ideology can be understood at the level of root likes and dislikes toward *social groups* (Conover 1988; Conover and Feldman 1981; Converse 1964; Sniderman, Brody, and Tetlock 1991). Groups constitute an integral part of the American political landscape. The policy and electoral cleavages that divide racial, religious, and gender groups are well-documented (e.g., Kinder and Winter 2001). More importantly, there is strong evidence that public opinion in the United States is "group-centric" in that sympathies and resentments toward politically salient social groups—blacks, whites, liberals, conservatives, gays, Jews, poor people, big business, evangelical Christians, and various others—fundamentally shape a broad range of citizens' political views (Brady and Sniderman 1985; Campbell *et al.* 1960; Conover 1984; Conover and Feldman 1981; Converse 1964; Miller, Wlezien, and Hildreth 1991; Nelson and Kinder 1996; Sniderman, Brody, and Tetlock 1991; Weisberg, Haynes, and Krosnick 1995; Craig, Martinez, and Kane 1999).

In its strongest form, the group-centrism hypothesis holds that affects toward social groups are the central organizing elements of political belief systems, bringing order to what might otherwise be largely haphazard collections of cognitively isolated opinions. Brady and Sniderman (1985: 1061) exemplified this position when they asked,

> What is the glue that holds [political beliefs] together? What provides citizens with the means and motive to achieve a measure of coherence in their views about political issues, given how little attention they are likely to pay to politics and how little information about it they are likely to possess? . . . Citizens can accomplish this, we argue, by relying on their political affect, their likes and dislikes of politically strategic groups.

Brady and Sniderman asserted that absent an understanding of the ideological abstractions that simplify political conflict, citizens can manage to negotiate political choices by knowing which groups they like and which they dislike (and which candidates, parties, and policies are likely to provide benefits or deprivations to specific groups). In this sense, group affect can be seen as an efficient heuristic device for parsing the political world without having much detailed information about it.

Evidence for the central role of groups in mass politics was provided first and most forcefully by Converse (1964). In his analysis of the electorate's "levels of conceptualization," Converse found that a comparatively small portion of the public (no more than 12 percent) could be counted as *ideologues* or *near-ideologues*, that is, making active use of the concepts of liberalism and conservatism in evaluating presidential candidates and political parties; indeed, responses classified as *nature of the times* (in which candidates and parties were evaluated in terms of their association with broader social conditions of war or peace, prosperity or economic downturn) occurred twice as often. It was Converse's middle category, however, described in terms of their emphasis on *group interest*, that represented the modal (and near-majority) response to politics, eclipsing ideologues and near-ideologues by nearly fourfold and nature-of-the-times respondents by twofold. Citizens who emphasized group interest were said to evaluate

> parties and candidates in terms of their expected favorable or unfavorable treatment of different *social groupings* in the population. The Democratic Party might be disliked because "it's trying to help the Negroes too much," or the Republican Party might be endorsed because farm prices would be better with the Republicans in office. The more sophisticated of these group-interest responses reflected an awareness of conflict in interest between "big business" or "rich people," on the one hand, and "labor" or the "working man," on the other, and parties and candidates were located accordingly (Converse 1964: 216, italics added).

Subsequent work has repeatedly borne out the significance of social groups in political perception and evaluation. In addition to playing a role in policy attitude formation (Conover 1988; Nelson and Kinder 1996; Sears, Hensler, and Speer 1979; Sniderman, Brody, and Tetlock 1991), basic ideological and partisan predispositions appear to be strongly rooted in affect toward groups perceived to be associated with Democrats/liberals (e.g., blacks, feminists, homosexuals, labor unions) or with Republicans/ conservatives (e.g., the military, big business, fundamentalist Christians; see Conover and Feldman 1981; Miller, Wlezien, and Hildreth 1991; Weisberg, Haynes, and Krosnick 1995; Craig, Martinez, and Kane 1999). This is perhaps most clearly evident in Conover and Feldman's (1981) analysis of the origins and meaning of ideological labels, in which evaluations of liberals and conservatives—and, ultimately, ideological self-identification as well— were found to be more strongly predicted by group likes and dislikes than by issue preferences. Based on these findings, Conover and Feldman concluded that the psychological underpinnings of ideology in the mass public have largely symbolic meaning rooted in social differentiation and conflict.[4]

Group Ambivalence

Given the bipolar nature of political competition in the United States, one might expect that those who like liberal groups will dislike conservative groups, and vice versa, leaving little room for the possibility of ambivalence. The evidence on group bipolarity is, however, mixed. At one end of the spectrum are Conover and Feldman (1981; also see Weisberg 1980), who found that liking for the cognate groups liberals and conservatives is largely orthogonal. Relying on Kerlinger's (1967) theory of criterial referents, Conover and Feldman concluded that individuals rely on different considerations (in this case, different social groups) to evaluate liberals and conservatives and, consequently, feelings for the two groups need not be of opposite valence. Sniderman, Brody, and Tetlock (1991) and Weisberg, Haynes, and Krosnick (1995), taking a middle position, described group bipolarity as variable; the former maintained that the likelihood of holding bipolar views increases with education, the latter that it depends upon the degree of ideological polarity in the political environment. Finally, in sharp contrast to Conover and Feldman, Green (1988) argued that group affect, at least for ideological and partisan labels, is highly bipolar, but that typical estimates are downwardly biased by random and especially nonrandom error variance. In particular, individual differences in the use of thermometer ratings induce positive error covariation in feelings toward opposing groups.[5] When these errors of measurement were purged, Green found that ratings of opposing ideological and partisan groups became nearly perfectly bipolar.

Like Sniderman, Brody, and Tetlock (1991) and Weisberg, Haynes, and Krosnick (1995), we believe that the structure of group affect is variable, such that some voters like groups on one side of the spectrum and dislike groups on the other side, whereas other voters like some of the groups on each side. Thus, we disagree with Green's (1988) conclusion of strong, or at least monolithic, group bipolarity. We part company with Sniderman and his colleagues, however, in their view that group bipolarity depends primarily on education. Ambivalence toward candidates and parties is, in fact, only weakly related to cognitive ability (Basinger and Lavine 2005; Lavine 2001; McGraw, Hasecke, and Conger 2003).[6] We also break with prior research in our approach to measuring the structure of group affect. In particular, to overcome the problems associated with individual differences in thermometer scale usage (Brady 1985; Green 1988; Wilcox, Sigelmen, and Cook 1989; Winter and Berinsky 1999), and to generate individual-level estimates of bipolarity, we calculate *group ambivalence* in the following way: $1 - |L - C|$, where L represents the average of feelings toward liberal groups and C represents the average of feelings toward conservative groups, both measured on 0–1 scales.[7] Low scores represent polarized feelings (high bipolarity), such that the respondent holds more positive feelings about social groups on one side of the political spectrum than the other. High scores represent ambivalent feelings (low bipolarity), such that the respondent feels similarly, either positively or negatively, about the two types of groups. Importantly, by comparing feelings toward liberal and conservative groups *within* rather than *between* individuals, we are not vulnerable to the possibility that individual variation in scale usage produces nonrandom measurement error that artifactually induces bidimensionality in concepts that might otherwise be bipolar in structure. Moreover, our measure allows for individual-level variability in the similarity or polarization of feelings toward opposing political groups, rather than a single aggregate-level summary statistic in which this person-to-person variability is ignored.

Hypotheses

If Green's (1988) conclusion of unwavering bipolarity is correct, and if it extends beyond ideological and partisan groups to social groups (e.g., feminists, homosexuals, fundamentalists), then any variation in our measure of group ambivalence should represent nothing more than error variance. If, on the other hand, there are substantial numbers of citizens who hold positive feelings toward groups on both the right and the left, and if this tends to pull them strongly in opposite directions across a range of political choices, then our simple measure should provide an approximation of the generalized type of ambivalence that we seek to identify. In the present research, we address two major questions about the structure of group feelings. First, does inconsistency lead to internalized conflict about policy, ideological, partisan, and electoral choices? That is, do individuals who lack bipolar group feelings experience greater difficulty in responding to questions about their policy attitudes, ideology, and so forth? Second, does holding ideologically inconsistent group feelings influence other aspects of political attitudes and behavior, such as the stability of electoral attitudes, ticket-splitting, and turnout?

We examine several hypotheses about the influence of group ambivalence on electoral decision-making. Our initial hypotheses involve whether group-ambivalent voters experience more difficulty in settling on a preferred presidential candidate than voters with polarized group feelings. We examine this in two ways. First, if group ambivalence pulls voters in opposite directions, they should delay forming a firm voting intention; that is, they should report remaining uncommitted until later in the campaign than voters with more polarized group feelings. Second, group-ambivalent voters should exhibit greater instability over the course of the campaign in their evaluation of presidential candidates than should those with polarized group feelings. This prediction is based on the varying accessibility of voters' positive feelings toward the two opposing types of groups (Lavine 2001; Zaller and Feldman 1992). In particular, when liberal groups are more salient, candidate evaluations should lean to the left; when conservative groups are more salient, they should lean to the right.

Our next hypotheses involve an examination of two aspects of voting behavior: turnout and ticket-splitting. If group-ambivalent voters experience indecision throughout the campaign, they should be less likely to cast ballots than those with polarized group feelings, and more likely to support different parties for president and Congress if they do vote. The latter hypothesis is particularly intriguing, in that it provides a rare opportunity for voters with two-sided attitudes to split the difference in their overt behavior. Our final prediction is that group ambivalence will decrease citizens' reliance on policy attitudes in rendering vote decisions. This hypothesis is also predicated on the axiom of accessibility: if policy opinions are constructed episodically on the basis of whichever considerations are recently activated or are at the "top of the head," the momentary preferences of group-ambivalent voters should be relatively unstable, as attitudes at t_1 might be based on positive feelings toward conservative groups such as the military or big business, but at t_2 based on positive feelings toward groups with implications for rendering liberal political judgments, such as the poor or feminists. Thus, for group-ambivalent individuals, policy attitudes should depend critically on which groups are most salient at the moment they are expressed. This malleability should decrease the observed relation between voters' expressed policy preferences and their subsequent vote decisions.

DATA AND MEASURES

Data from the 2000 American National Election Study (ANES) were used to test our hypotheses. Beginning in 1964, the ANES has routinely assessed citizens' feelings toward a wide variety of societal groups using 101-point "feeling thermometers." Respondents are instructed that ratings between 50 and 100 degrees reflect a favorable (or warm) feeling toward a particular group, while ratings between 0 and 50 degrees reflect an unfavorable (or cool) feeling. An index of feelings toward *liberal* groups was derived by averaging the thermometer scores across the following ten groups: people on welfare, environmentalists, feminists, homosexuals, poor people, Jews, labor unions, liberals, blacks, and Democrats. An index of feelings toward *conservative* groups was derived by averaging the thermometer scores across the following six groups: big business, Christian fundamentalists, the military, Protestants, conservatives, and Republicans. In each case, a preference for liberals over conservatives was positively correlated with support for each of the liberal groups, and negatively correlated with support for each of the conservative groups ($p < .001$ in each instance). Theoretically, group ambivalence should be high to the extent that feelings toward the two types of groups are similar in valence (Alvarez and Brehm 2002; Thompson, Zanna, and Griffin 1995). As feelings toward the two opposing groups become polarized—for example, as affect toward conservative groups becomes more positive than affect toward liberal groups—ambivalence decreases. To measure group ambivalence, we used the similarity component of the frequently cited intensity–similarity formula suggested by Thompson and her colleagues (1995). As noted earlier, we subtracted the absolute value of the difference between averaged feelings toward liberal and conservative groups (L and C, respectively, in the formula below) from one. Specifically,

$$\text{Group Ambivalence} = 1 - |L - C|$$

where L and C are recoded to a 0 to 1 scale. Low scores represent polarized group feelings, such that $L > C$ or $C > L$. In contrast, high scores represent similar feelings toward the opposing groups, such that $L = C$.[8]

Control Variables

In estimating the unique effects of group ambivalence, we must bear two burdens of proof. First, we must control for other, related types of ambivalence. Second, we must control for other variables that might account for any observed effects of group ambivalence. On the first count, we control for four alternative types of ambivalence that have been found to influence public opinion and electoral choice: value conflict, and ambivalence toward presidential candidates, political parties, and the role of government. Ambivalence toward candidates has been shown to increase the difficulty of forming stable candidate evaluations, and to reduce voters' electoral reliance on issues (Lavine 2001); value conflict influences policy attitudes in a variety of aspects including stability, reliability, polarization, and structural complexity (Alvarez and Brehm 2002; Feldman and Zaller 1992; Liberman and Chaiken 1991; Steenbergen and Brewer 2000; Tetlock 1986). With respect to our hypotheses, it is possible that ambivalence along any of these lines could moderate the dynamics of electoral choice. Therefore, in estimating the impact of group ambivalence, we control for the effects of these related forms of attitudinal conflict.

To assess ambivalence toward parties and candidates, we use the ANES open-ended likes/dislikes questions.[9] These questions assess the extent to which respondents' reactions consistently favor one party (or candidate) over the other (e.g., strongly liking the Democrats and strongly disliking the Republicans), or are inconsistent such that they are favorable toward one party (or candidate) in some ways and favorable toward the other party (or candidate) in other ways. To construct an index that involves both parties (or candidates), let P_D and P_R represent the number of positive reactions to the Republican and Democratic parties (or candidates), respectively, and let N_D and N_R represent the number of negative reactions to the parties (or candidates); then define D as the average of the positive reactions to the Democrats and the negative reactions to the Republicans ($D = [P_D + N_R]/2$), and define R as the average of the positive reactions to the Republicans and the negative reactions to the Democrats ($R = [P_R + N_D]/2$). We modify the Thompson–Zanna–Griffin ambivalence formula by comparing the overall intensity of affect toward both parties (or candidates), corrected by the extent to which the respondent's reactions are uniformly favorable toward one party (or candidate), in the following way:

$$\text{Party/Candidate Ambivalence} = \frac{D+R}{2} - |D-R|$$

P_D, P_R, N_D, and N_R range from 0 to 5; therefore comparative partisan (or candidate) ambivalence scores range from a high of +5.0 when reactions to both parties (or candidates) are highly intense and ambivalent ($P_D = N_R = N_D = P_R = 5$), to a low of −2.5 when reactions to the parties (or candidates) are highly polarized (when one party or candidate is strongly liked and the other strongly disliked, e.g., $P_R = N_D = 5$, and $N_R = P_D = 0$).[10]

Conflict between the values of egalitarianism and individualism was assessed with ten items from the 2000 ANES; six of these measured egalitarianism (e.g., agree or disagree that "our society should do whatever is necessary to make sure that everyone has an equal opportunity to succeed") and four tapped individualism (e.g., which statement comes closer to the respondent's own views, "ONE, it is more important to be a cooperative person who works well with others; or TWO, it is more important to be a self-reliant person able to take care of oneself"). Our index of value conflict is $1 - |E - I|$, where E is support for egalitarianism and I is support for limited government (E and I terms were first recoded to a 0 to 1 scale). Low scores indicate greater support for one value over the other (low conflict); high scores indicate equivalent support for the two values (high conflict).

Finally, following Cantril and Cantril (1999), we measured conflicting beliefs about the role of government using four items that assessed preferences for government intervention in the abstract (e.g., which comes closer, "ONE, the less government the better; or TWO, there are more things that government should be doing"), and twelve items that captured preferences for more, sustained, or less spending on various government programs.[11] Our index of conflict about government is $1 - |A - C|$, where A is opposition to government in the abstract and C is support for specific government programs (as before, A and C terms were first recoded to a 0 to 1 scale). Low scores indicate consistent support or opposition to government (low conflict); high scores indicate conflicting views about government.

Beyond alternative types of ambivalence, we control for three additional types of variables: cognitive ability, political involvement, and the extremity of political predispositions. First, educated and informed citizens are better able to put their political beliefs together in a coherent manner than are their less educated or informed counterparts (Delli Carpini and Keeter 1996; Zaller 1992); therefore, it is important to separate any effects of ambivalence from those stemming from these two cognitive characteristics. Second, affective and cognitive inconsistency might simply reflect a lack of interest in or attention to politics; accordingly, we include measures of political interest and media exposure to politics. Finally, as previous research has shown (Lavine 2001; Meffert, Guge, and Lodge 2000; Thompson, Zanna, and Griffin 1995), ambivalence is negatively associated with the strength or extremity of political attitudes. In the present context, we suspect that individuals with ambivalent feelings toward political groups will express less extreme ideological and partisan identifications. Thus, in estimating the effects of group ambivalence, we include indicators of the extremity of these two political predispositions as controls.[12]

RESULTS

Does Group Ambivalence Exist?

Our first empirical task is to determine whether the constituent elements of our group ambivalence measure (i.e., affect toward liberal and conservative groups) satisfy the three conditions we have set for inferring the existence of ambivalence. Specifically, to create generalized attitudinal conflict, the two variables should exert an *equal* and *dominant* influence on a variety of political choices (e.g., vote choice, policy attitudes), and positive affect toward both liberal and conservative groups should heighten the error variance in those choices.[13] Table 1.1 presents regression models predicting four dependent variables: policy attitude direction, ideological self-identification, party identification, and vote choice for president. The measure of policy attitude direction is an additive index based on respondents' preferences toward nine policy issues (recoded 0 to 1; see note 12), such that conservative policy preferences reflect higher scores; ideology and party identification (PID) are the standard 7-point NES variables (recoded 0 to 1), and vote choice is a dichotomous self-report (0 = Gore; 1 = Bush). The vote choice analysis, shown in the column second from the right, includes the fullest set of predictors, including the constituent variables of four of our ambivalence measures: affect toward liberal and conservative groups (group ambivalence), egalitarianism and individualism (value conflict), reactions toward Bush and Gore (candidate ambivalence), and reactions toward the Republican and Democratic parties (party ambivalence). The model also includes other standard predictors of vote choice, including issue proximity, party identification, ideology, race, sex, and economic retrospections, as well as a measure of moral traditionalism.

The numbers in brackets in the vote choice column represent the change in predicted probability of voting Republican as each variable moves from its minimum to maximum value, holding other variables in the model at their means. Coefficients for issue proximity, party ID, and race—but not

Table 1.1 Effects of group ambivalence on policy preferences, ideology, party identification, and presidential vote choice

Variable	Policy preferences	Ideology	Party identification	Presidential vote choice	
Affect: liberal groups	−0.28**	−0.45**	−0.58**	−5.76**	[−0.86]
	(0.03)	(0.06)	(0.06)	(1.81)	
Affect: conservative groups	0.27**	0.59**	0.51**	5.90**	[0.90]
	(0.03)	(0.05)	(0.05)	(1.82)	
Egalitarianism	−0.14**	−0.09**	0.01	0.97	[0.22]
	(0.02)	(0.03)	(0.04)	(0.90)	
Individualism	0.10**	0.06**	0.16**	1.47**	[0.34]
	(0.01)	(0.02)	(0.02)	(0.51)	
Likes/dislikes: Democrats	n/a	n/a	−0.42**	−1.75	[0.55]
			(0.04)	(1.06)	
Likes/dislikes: Republicans	n/a	n/a	0.40**	2.45*	[0.59]
			(0.04)	(1.07)	
Likes/dislikes: Gore	n/a	n/a	n/a	−5.75**	[0.89]
				(0.91)	
Likes/dislikes: Bush	n/a	n/a	n/a	5.04**	[0.85]
				(0.92)	
Moral traditionalism	0.07**	0.20**	−0.09**	0.86	[0.10]
	(0.02)	(0.03)	(0.03)	(0.78)	
Party identification	0.02*	0.15**	n/a	3.51**	[0.87]
	(0.01)	(0.02)		(0.57)	
Ideology	0.06**	n/a	0.15**	−0.15	[0.09]
	(0.02)		(0.03)	(0.70)	
Constant	0.43**	0.30**	0.42**	−3.44	
	(0.03)	(0.05)	(0.06)	(1.58)	
Number of cases	1294	1324	1323	973	
R^2	0.49	0.42	0.56	n/a	
Percent correctly predicted	n/a	n/a	n/a	92.6	

Note: Data are from 2000 American National Election Study. Entries in the first three columns are unstandardized regression coefficients and associated standard errors (in parentheses); entries in column 4 are logit coefficients (with standard errors and, in brackets, change in predicted probability of voting Republican by moving from minimum to maximum value on the listed variable, holding all other variables at their means). Demographic traits such as race, gender, and income exerted small effects and are not shown. Issue proximity and economic retrospections also were included in the vote choice analysis; both were significant but are not shown here. All variables in the table are scored from 0 to 1.

**p ≤ .01; *p ≤ .05.

ideology, sex, and economic retrospection—reach statistical significance. Most importantly, as the change in probabilities show, the group affect terms easily meet the first two of our ambivalence criteria: affect toward liberal and conservative groups exert roughly equal effects on vote choice, and they exert the strongest effects of any of the variables in the model. The constituents of candidate ambivalence (evaluative reactions toward Bush and Gore) also pass the equal relevance and dominance of influence tests (ignoring sign, the change in predicted probabilities is .85 and .89, for attitudes toward Bush and

Gore, respectively). However, constituents of the party ambivalence and value conflict terms fare less well: evaluative reactions toward the Democratic and Republican parties exert relatively equal but considerably weaker effects, and the effect of egalitarianism is statistically unreliable and incorrectly signed.

For the policy and ideology equations, we included the constituents of only two of our ambivalence terms, group ambivalence and value conflict.[14] For the party identification equation, we added the partisan attitude variables. It is clear from an inspection of the coefficients in table 1.1 that only the constituents of the group ambivalence term survive the equal relevance and dominance of influence tests for all dependent variables. Consider the prediction of policy attitude direction: affects toward liberal and conservative groups exert nearly identical (absolute) effects, −.28 and .27, and are by far the strongest predictors in the model. By contrast, the values terms pass the equal relevance test but are comparatively weak in magnitude (failing the dominance test). The ideology analysis yields similar results: group affect terms dominate the prediction, although here the effect is somewhat larger for conservative than for liberal groups; the effects of both value terms, by contrast, are nearly equal but quite small. Finally, the group affect terms dominate the prediction of party identification, with affect toward liberal and conservative groups exerting approximately equal effects. Partisan attitude variables are also equal in magnitude and quite strong (−.42 and .40, for reactions toward the Democratic and Republican parties, respectively). However, the values terms fail both equality and dominance tests.[15]

In sum, these analyses demonstrate quite clearly (for all four political preferences) that group feelings pass the equality and dominance requirements for the occurrence of ambivalence. Therefore, we expect that individuals who hold nonpolarized group feelings, liking some of the groups on each side of the political spectrum, will exhibit greater error in rendering these decisions than those with highly polarized group feelings. The candidate attitude terms also satisfied both the equality and dominance requirements for the one analysis in which they were included (vote choice), as did the partisan attitude variables in the party identification equation (although they were outpredicted by the group affect terms) but not the vote choice equation. As a result, we anticipate that individuals with ambivalent candidate attitudes will exhibit greater error in their vote preferences, and that those with ambivalent partisan attitudes will exhibit greater error in their party preferences but not in their vote choices. Because egalitarianism and individualism exerted weak and/or unequal effects throughout, we do not expect value conflict to predict levels of error variance for any of the political choices.

Table 1.2 presents regression models of the error variance (squared residuals) from the equations in table 1.1. Four types of predictor variables are included: cognitive ability (information and education), political engagement

Table 1.2 Effects of group ambivalence on error variance in policy preferences, ideology, party identification, and presidential vote choice

Variable	Policy preferences	Ideology	Party identification	Presidential vote choice
Group ambivalence	0.01	0.21**	0.09**	0.05*
	(0.02)	(0.02)	(0.02)	(0.03)
Value conflict	0.01	0.01	0.02*	0.02
	(0.01)	(0.01)	(0.01)	(0.01)
Candidate ambivalence	n/a	n/a	n/a	0.15**
				(0.02)
Party ambivalence	n/a	n/a	0.11**	0.02
			(0.02)	(0.02)
Information	0.03**	−0.09**	−0.05*	−0.04**
	(0.01)	(0.01)	(0.01)	(0.02)
Education	0.03**	−0.02	−0.02*	0.01
	(0.01)	(0.01)	(0.01)	(0.01)
Political interest	0.00	−0.02	−0.01	−0.01
	(0.01)	(0.02)	(0.01)	(0.02)
Media exposure	0.00	0.04**	0.01	0.00
	(0.01)	(0.01)	(0.01)	(0.01)
Ideological extremity	0.00	0.27**	0.02	0.00
	(0.01)	(0.01)	(0.01)	(0.01)
Partisan extremity	0.01	0.01	0.13**	−0.05**
	(0.01)	(0.01)	(0.01)	(0.01)
Constant	0.08**	−0.18**	−0.10**	0.00
	(0.02)	(0.03)	(0.02)	(0.03)
Number of cases	1287	1324	1314	968
R^2	0.02	0.29	0.16	0.13

Note: Data are from 2000 American National Election Study. Table entries are unstandardized regression coefficients and associated standard errors (in parentheses). All variables are scored from 0 to 1.

**$p \leq .01$; *$p \leq .05$.

(media exposure and political interest), extremity of political predispositions, and ambivalence. In each case, positive coefficients indicate that increases in the predictor variable are associated with larger errors of prediction. The vote choice model is the most interesting, as it includes the most complete set of ambivalence terms. As can be seen, ambivalence toward both groups and candidates—but not toward parties or values—significantly increases error variance in vote choice. This is consistent with our earlier finding that only group feelings and candidate reactions satisfy the equality and dominance requirements for ambivalence. Moreover, along with political information and the extremity of party identification, both of which had negative effects, these two ambivalence terms exert the strongest effects in the model. In fact, the effect of group ambivalence is significant in three of the four equations, increasing the errors of prediction in ideology and party identification, as well as vote choice. In each of these instances, individuals with similar feelings for groups across the political spectrum held less reliable preferences than those with strongly bipolar group feelings. Based on the results in table 1.1, we also expected party ambivalence to heighten error variance in expressed party preferences. As can be seen in the third column of table 1.2, this effect emerged as well, as did a small and unexpected effect of value conflict.[16]

There are two noteworthy aspects of the analyses presented in table 1.2. First, the results bear out our contention that inconsistency should heighten error variance only when constituents of the inconsistency term (e.g., feelings toward liberal and conservative groups) exert an equal and dominant influence on the political choice in question. Thus, for example, conflicted partisan attitudes increase error variance in reports of party identification (where the partisan attitude variables exert strong effects in the choice model), but not in vote choice (where the partisan attitude variables are not among the dominant predictors). Second, nonpolarized group feelings heighten error variance for all but policy attitude direction; respondents who fail to organize their group feelings along ideological lines have more difficulty expressing their political preferences than do those with bipolar group feelings. Based on our results so far, we conclude that holding inconsistent group feelings does indeed tend to instigate a *generalized* form of ambivalence with regard to a range of political choices. In the next section, we examine whether individual variation in group ambivalence is consequential for the expression of political behavior.

The Consequences of Group Ambivalence

Our first hypothesis is that voters with ambivalent group feelings will experience more difficulty than those with polarized group feelings in deciding on a preferred presidential candidate. We examine this by looking at *when* during the 2000 campaign voters reported forming their voting intentions, and by the consistency of voters' candidate preferences during the campaign. The timing of vote intentions was assessed by asking respondents how long before the election they decided they were going to vote the way they did (answers ranging from "knew all along" to "on election day"; scores were recoded from 0 to 1). Estimated effects of the four types of variables used to predict error variance (cognitive ability, political engagement, strength of political predispositions, and ambivalence) are shown in the first column of table 1.3. As can be seen, strong partisans and those interested in politics were more likely to form crystallized voting intentions earlier in the campaign than weak partisans/independents and those reporting little political interest. As the analyses reported above indicated that only inconsistency toward groups and candidates led to ambivalence in vote choice, we anticipate that only these two forms of ambivalence will delay the formation

Table 1.3 Effects of group ambivalence on timing of vote decision, ticket-splitting, and turnout

Variable	Timing of vote decision	Ticket-splitting		Voting turnout	
Group ambivalence	0.25**	3.57**	[0.27]	−0.35	[−0.04]
	(0.07)	(0.88)		(0.64)	
Value conflict	0.01	0.37	[0.01]	0.08	[−0.04]
	(0.04)	(0.39)		(0.31)	
Candidate ambivalence	0.52**	0.76	[0.07]	−0.57	[−0.11]
	(0.06)	(0.61)		(0.60)	
Party ambivalence	−0.01	0.60	[0.15]	0.08	[−0.04]
	(0.06)	(0.61)		(0.63)	
Information	−0.05	−0.54	[−0.07]	2.13**	[0.24]
	(0.04)	(0.44)		(0.37)	
Education	0.01	0.38	[0.04]	1.34**	[0.19]
	(0.03)	(0.32)		(0.28)	
Political interest	−0.10*	1.03**	[0.13]	2.12**	[0.32]
	(0.04)	(0.44)		(0.25)	
Media exposure	−0.01	0.33	[0.05]	0.57	[0.06]
	(0.04)	(0.37)		(0.29)	
Ideological extremity	0.02	0.19	[0.01]	0.02	[0.02]
	(0.04)	(0.40)		(0.33)	
Partisan extremity	−0.19**	−0.89**	[−0.12]	0.58*	[0.07]
	(0.03)	(0.32)		(0.26)	
Constant	0.22**	−5.64**		−1.62*	
	(0.08)	(0.98)		(0.72)	
Number of cases	1024	769		1325	
R²	0.21	n/a		n/a	
Percent correctly predicted	n/a	81.1		82.6	

Note: Data are from 2000 American National Election Study. Entries in column 1 are unstandardized regression coefficients and associated standard errors (in parentheses); entries in columns 2 and 3 are logit coefficients (with standard errors and, in brackets, change in predicted probability of casting a split ballot or turning out to vote by moving from minimum to maximum value on the listed variable, holding all other variables at their means). All variables in the table are scored from 0 to 1.

**p ≤ 0.01; *p ≤ 0.05.

of voters' electoral intentions—and that is exactly what the results show (estimates for both party ambivalence and value conflict being approximately zero). Moreover, the effect of group ambivalence is stronger than that of partisan strength, suggesting that ideologically consistent group cues provide more powerful electoral guides than even strong partisanship.

Next, to examine the consistency of voters' candidate preferences over the course of the campaign, we analyzed post-election comparative candidate evaluations (Bush thermometer rating minus Gore thermometer rating, recoded 0 to 1) as a function of pre-election evaluations. To determine whether ambivalent group feelings promoted instability, a pre-election comparative candidate evaluation × group ambivalence interaction term was included, along with five other interaction terms (separately multiplying pre-election candidate evaluation scores by candidate ambivalence, party ambivalence, value conflict, information, and extremity of ideology). These additional interactions allow us to separate any unique moderating effects of group ambivalence from other forms of ambivalence, and from political information and ideological extremity. As in the prior analysis, we expect both group and candidate ambivalence to cause instability; thus the interaction terms involving only those two forms of ambivalence should exert a significant impact on post-election candidate evaluations.

Estimates are shown in the first column of table 1.4. While the strongest effect on post-election candidate evaluations is exerted by pre-election evaluations, the observed effects of party ID, ideology, issue proximity, and race also are significant. Moreover, group ambivalence exerts a significant conditional "first-order" effect as well, indicating that (among those who preferred Gore and Bush equally in the pre-election survey, i.e., pre-election candidate evaluation = 0) those with ambivalent group feelings were more likely to prefer Gore than those with bipolar group feelings. The table also shows that only one variable significantly moderates the effect of pre-election candidate evaluations: group ambivalence. As the negative sign of the pre-election candidate evaluation × group ambivalence interaction term indicates, consistency between pre- and post-election evaluations declines as group ambivalence increases. Specifically, the effect of pre-election candidate evaluations is .862 when group ambivalence is at its minimum, but falls to .616—a reduction of nearly a third—when group ambivalence reaches its maximum. The interactions involving candidate and party ambivalence were of the correct (negative) sign but not significant, and other interactions were both incorrectly signed and nonsignificant.

In sum, across these two analyses we find strong support for the influence of group ambivalence in creating uncertainty and instability in presidential candidate preferences. Even when rigorously controlling for individual differences in political information, ideological and partisan extremity, and a variety of other types of inconsistency, voters who fail to organize their feelings about social groups along ideological lines appear to have difficulty both forming and maintaining consistent candidate preferences.

Let us now assess whether group ambivalence conditioned voters' reliance on policy considerations in making vote choices. We constructed a measure of overall issue proximity from nine policy questions in the 2000 ANES that asked respondents to indicate their perceptions of the candidates' positions (see note 12); this score was multiplied by group ambivalence to create the focal interaction. The usual interaction controls are also included in the model, including several terms that allow us to isolate any unique moderating effects of group ambivalence on voters' reliance on issues. Estimates shown

Table 1.4 Effects of group ambivalence on candidate evaluation and vote choice

Variable	Post-election candidate evaluation	Presidential vote choice	
Pre-election candidate evaluation (CE)	0.66** (0.03)	n/a	
Party identification	0.15** (0.02)	5.86** (0.46)	[0.89]
Ideology	0.03* (0.02)	0.11 (0.07)	[0.03]
Race	−0.04** (0.01)	−0.62* (0.33)	[−0.16]
Group ambivalence	−0.05* (0.03)	−3.56** (1.25)	[−0.57]
Candidate ambivalence	0.01 (0.02)	1.33 (0.79)	[0.30]
Party ambivalence	0.03 (0.02)	0.70 (0.84)	[0.17]
Value conflict	0.02 (0.01)	0.16 (0.51)	[0.04]
Information	0.00 (0.02)	−0.21 (0.51)	[−0.04]
Ideological extremity	0.01 (0.02)	−0.02 (0.50)	[0.00]
Issue proximity (IP)	0.06** (0.02)	4.49** (0.77)	[0.80]
Business conditions	0.00 (0.01)	−0.91** (0.33)	[−0.22]
Group ambivalence × pre-election CE (or IP)	−0.25** (0.10)	17.82** (7.10)	[0.99, 0.34]
Candidate ambivalence × pre-election CE (or IP)	−0.17 (0.12)	0.37 (4.07)	[0.79, 0.65]
Party ambivalence × pre-election CE (or IP)	−0.06 (0.11)	−0.75 (4.77)	[0.82. 0.68]
Value conflict × pre-election CE (or IP)	0.09 (0.07)	0.07 (2.73)	[0.77, 0.76]
Information × pre-election CE (or IP)	−0.06 (0.07)	5.95* (2.58)	[0.44, 0.95]
Ideological extremity × pre-election CE (or IP)	−0.05 (0.07)	1.54 (2.79)	[0.69, 0.84]
Constant	−0.43** (0.02)	1.67** (0.53)	
Number of cases	1273	982	
R^2	0.74	n/a	
Percent correctly predicted	n/a	88.4	

Note: Data are from 2000 American National Election Study. Entries are unstandardized regression coefficients (column 1) and logit coefficients (column 2), with associated standard errors in parentheses. For first-order effects, the number in brackets indicates change in the probability of voting Republican by moving from minimum to maximum value on the listed variable, holding all other variables at their means. For interaction terms, the number in brackets indicates change in the probability of voting Republican by moving from minimum to maximum value on issue proximity (IP), first for the minimum value and then for the maximum value on the listed moderator variable (e.g., group ambivalence, information, and so on), holding all other variables at their means. Gender and education exerted nonsignificant effects and are not shown. All variables in the table are scored from 0 to 1 except those involved in interaction terms, which are mean-centered.

** $p \leq .01$; * $p \leq .05$.

in the right-hand column of table 1.4 indicate that both party ID and issue proximity (but not ideology) have a strong impact on vote choice. Also, among respondents with policy attitudes equidistant from the two candidates (issue proximity = 0), group ambivalence exerts a strong effect such that those with ideologically mixed group feelings were 57 percent more likely to vote for Gore than Bush than those with maximally bipolar group feelings. Only two of the interaction terms reach significance. First, the positively signed issue proximity × information interaction suggests that informed voters rely more on policy considerations than do the uninformed. Second, the negatively signed issue proximity × group ambivalence interaction indicates that voters with ideologically mixed feelings rely less on issues than do voters with maximally bipolar group feelings.

The pairs of numbers in brackets adjacent to the interaction coefficients in table 1.4 represent the change in probability in voting for Bush as issue proximity moves from its minimum to maximum value; the number on the left represents the change in probability when the moderator variable (e.g., group ambivalence) is at its minimum value, and the number on the right represents the probability change when the moderator reaches its maximum value. Looking first at the change in probability in voting for Bush at *minimum* group ambivalence (highly polarized group feelings), we see that the effect of issue proximity is exceedingly strong, altering the probability of voting for Bush by 99 percent as it moves from maximal policy agreement with Gore to maximal agreement with Bush. However, when group ambivalence reaches its *maximum* (ideologically inconsistent group feelings), movement on issue proximity from agreement with Gore to agreement with Bush alters the probability of voting for Bush by only 34 percent, a reduction in issue voting by two-thirds across levels of group ambivalence. As the other bracketed predicted probabilities show, group ambivalence exerts a stronger effect than any of the other variables in conditioning voters' reliance on issues in making their vote choices.

Finally, we consider the direct impact of group ambivalence on political behavior. So far, we have seen several pieces of evidence indicating that group-ambivalent voters experience electoral indecision: they tend to experience more instability and more error variance in their electoral preferences, and to arrive at their decisions later in the campaign than voters with bipolar group feelings. Is it also true that group-ambivalent voters are less likely to cast ballots, and more likely to support different parties for president and Congress when they do vote? The relevant analyses are shown in the second and third columns of table 1.3, which show that group ambivalence encourages ticket-splitting but does not inhibit turnout. From column 3, we see that turnout is largely a function of cognitive ability, political interest, and partisan extremity; none of the ambivalence terms are significant. In contrast, group ambivalence does significantly promote ticket-splitting; in fact, it is by far the strongest factor in the model, changing the probability of voting for different parties by 27 percentage points. Thus, group-ambivalent voters often attempt to heed the conflicting political implications of their group feelings by casting "two-sided" votes.

CONCLUSIONS

The last decade has seen a surge in research on ambivalence in both political science and psychology. Questions about its nature, prevalence, causes, and consequences have produced some important insights, such as providing an interpretation of inconsistency in public opinion that reaches beyond the old debate of uncrystallized attitudes versus deficient measurement. Because most citizens do not possess strong ideological commitments, the American public—or at least that part which decides presidential elections—is presumably open to messages from both sides of the partisan divide, creating the conditions for ambivalence (Greenberg 2004). In the research reported here, we pursued two basic questions. First, given the contrasting standards of evidence that have been used to attest to its existence (e.g., Alvarez and Brehm 2002; Hochschild 1981; Zaller and Feldman 1992), we attempted to sharpen the definition of ambivalence, and to provide a set of empirical criteria for determining when it is present. Second, we examined a generalized form of ambivalence, one with the potential to affect a wide range of political choices.

With regard to the first question, we argued that the experience of ambivalence is something more than the possession of inconsistent considerations. Although individuals may see merit in both sides of a political choice, they may themselves experience little indecision on the matter. At the outset of the chapter, we defined ambivalence as an *internalized conflict* about a specific political choice. The key, then, to any empirical realization of ambivalence, is specifying the conditions necessary and sufficient to produce such a conflict. We identified three empirical conditions. The first is that the competing considerations should be of equal relevance to the choice in question. For example, even if both egalitarianism and individualism are seen as relevant (with opposite implications) to racial policy, little ambivalence should result if one is viewed as more relevant or important to the choice than the other. Second, the competing considerations should instigate ambivalence only if they dominate the political choice. So, even if egalitarianism and individualism are seen as equally relevant to racial policy decisions, little ambivalence should ensue if the choice is determined largely by other considerations, such as racial animus or self-interest. And third, ambivalence should occur only when strong support for two competing considerations demonstrably inhibits reliable expression of the political choice.

Beyond deriving criteria that can be used to determine whether ambivalence is present, we also identified a generalized form of ambivalence rooted in feelings toward social groups. Noting that affect toward such groups as homosexuals, evangelicals, blacks, and big business is an important component of public opinion, we hypothesized that citizens who fail to organize their group feelings along ideological lines will experience ambivalence about a variety of political choices. This hypothesis was borne out in our empirical analysis. Controlling for a variety of other forms of attitudinal conflict, as well as for both political information and engagement, we found that ideologically inconsistent group feelings produced ambivalence toward choices involving policies, political predispositions, and candidates. In particular, the constituent elements of our group ambivalence measure (feelings toward liberal and conservative groups) amply satisfied the three conditions we set for inferring the existence of ambivalence.

We also found that group ambivalence has important electoral consequences. Group-ambivalent voters tend to make up their minds later, to hold more unstable candidate preferences throughout the campaign, and to exhibit higher levels of split-ticking voting, than do voters with bipolar group feelings. Moreover, in each case, group ambivalence exerts among the strongest effects in the model, outpacing even partisan strength; and only ambivalence toward social groups moderates voters' reliance on issues in determining vote choice. These findings suggest two things. First, they suggest that the structure of group feelings, at the individual level, matters greatly for a variety of aspects of electoral behavior. Those who like groups on the left or the right (but not both) make up their minds more easily, stick with a preferred candidate, vote consistently for the same party across elections, and rely strongly on issues in rendering their votes. By contrast, those with group affections across the political spectrum make up their minds much later, hold wobbly opinions, split their tickets, and rely much less on issues. Second, these results imply that inconsistency influences political behavior only when it produces demonstrable internalized conflict, or ambivalence. That is, when inconsistency fails to produce such a conflict, it tends to make little behavioral difference.

Given these results, we believe that future work on ambivalence should take steps to demonstrate its existence within the context of a specific political choice. As we have shown, the failure to find that ambivalence has consequences may result from the fact that it simply doesn't exist in the data. More generally, analysts should exercise caution before labeling the myriad inconsistencies that do exist in mass politics as ambivalence. While some of them are likely to reflect bona fide internal conflicts, others undoubtedly reflect uncertainty, indifference, neutrality, and confusion. These are quite different attitudinal states of mind, and researchers should refrain from assuming that they are uniformly caused by underlying conflict among political beliefs.

Notes

1. Scholars disagree about the prevalence of ambivalence. Studies of policy attitudes suggest that ambivalence is fairly uncommon (Alvarez and Brehm 2002; Jacoby 2002; Steenbergen and Brewer 2000; but see Craig, Martinez, and Kane 2002 and Craig *et al.* 2005b). In contrast, studies of candidates and parties suggest that it is quite widespread (Basinger and Lavine 2005; Lavine 2001; McGraw, Hasecke, and Conger 2003; Meffert, Guge, and Lodge 2000). The extent to which variation across studies in estimates of ambivalence can be explained by attitude object type (e.g., issues vs. candidates), measurement strategy, or something else is an important question that awaits future research.

2. Among the most notable findings in Alvarez and Brehm's book *Hard Choices, Easy Answers* (2002) is that ambivalence is actually quite rare and, contrary to much conventional argument (e.g., Katz and Hass 1988), does not appear to characterize opinion on racial issues. This conclusion was based on the authors' failure to find that support for both egalitarian and individualist values increased response error in racial policy attitudes. It is not surprising, though, in light of two aspects of Alvarez and Brehm's data: (1) egalitarianism exerted a much stronger effect on racial policy attitudes than did individualism (violating our equal influence requirement); and (2) racial policy attitudes were dominated by another consideration altogether, namely modern racism (violating our predictive dominance requirement).

3. Increased error variance can itself be seen as a consequence of ambivalence, rather than as a defining feature of its occurrence. In either case, error variance is evidence of decision difficulty, which we view as a prerequisite for ambivalence to influence political behavior (e.g., ticket-splitting, turnout).

4. Social groups also have figured prominently as symbols in research involving symbolic politics theory (e.g., Sears, Hensler, and Speer 1979).

5. These individual differences refer to variation in the way that respondents map the warmth of their feelings onto the 101-point feeling thermometer scale values. For example, some people may consider 75 degrees to reflect only "lukewarm" feelings, whereas others consider 75 degrees to reflect very positive (warm) feelings. Thus, relatively charitable respondents might rate groups they like at 90 and groups they dislike at 60, while those who are less charitable might rate liked groups at 60 and disliked groups at 30. As Green (1988) demonstrated, such differences distort aggregate-level estimates of the relationship between affect toward different groups.

6. In this chapter, we do not examine the ideological polarity of the political environment and will therefore not explicitly consider Weisberg, Haynes, and Krosnick's (1995) claim about the conditionality of group ambivalence.

7. Our approach here is similar to that used by Sniderman, Brody, and Tetlock (1991) to measure "ideological affect," and by Alvarez and Brehm (2002) to measure "coincident values."

8. To capture the intensity of group feelings, we employed an alternative formula, $[(|L - 50| + |C - 50|)/2] - |L - C|$, that incorporates the intensity of group feelings and more closely resembles the formula suggested by Thompson, Zanna, and Griffin (1995). The term within the brackets captures the deviation of respondents' feelings from the midpoint of the feeling thermometer scale. Results of the two formulas were very similar. We favor the similarity-only term

here for the reason that respondents' affective neutral points are likely to vary (see Winter and Berinsky 1999).

9. For candidates, the question asks, "Is there anything in particular about Al Gore [George Bush] that might make you want to vote for [against] him?" Four follow-up probes are provided ("Anything else?") in each instance. For parties, the question asks: "Is there anything in particular that you like [dislike] about the Democratic [Republican] Party?" Again, four follow-up probes ("Anything else?") are offered.

10. Intermediate ambivalence scores result when reactions are less intense. When reactions to the parties are univalent but weak (e.g., when P_R and N_D are 2, and N_R and P_D are 0), party/candidate ambivalence scores are less negative (e.g., -1); when reactions are ambivalent but weak (e.g., when all four components are 2), ambivalence scores are less positive (e.g., $+2$).

11. Because the same items were used to measure both abstract opposition to government and the value of individualism, we are unable to assess the relative effects of value conflict and inconsistent views about the government in the same analysis. Our strategy is to report the effects for value conflict in the tables, and to report in footnotes the results of separate analyses in which the role of government terms are substituted for the value terms.

12. A complete listing of the ANES questions employed in this analysis can be obtained from our website at http://www.sunysb.edu/polsci/hlavine/index.html

13. Although we cannot identify the score that divides positive from negative feelings, in practice only a very small percentage of respondents have mean scores below 50 degrees for both liberal and conservative groups on the feeling thermometers.

14. Projection and persuasion effects notwithstanding (see Krosnick 1988), it seemed theoretically unlikely that evaluative reactions toward parties or candidates would causally influence ideology or policy direction; the predominant causal effects here would seem to be in the other direction. Thus, reactions toward Bush, Gore, and the Democratic and Republican parties were excluded.

15. Conflicting attitudes about the role of government also fail both equal relevance and dominance of influence tests for all four political choices. Concrete attitudes about government spending do not reach statistical significance in either the party ID or vote choice models, and their effects on policy attitude direction ($-.09$) and ideology ($-.17$) are comparatively weak in any case. It does not appear, then, that conflict in abstract versus specific views about the role of government generates ambivalence about policy, ideological, party, or electoral choices.

16. In a separate set of analyses, we substituted the role of government terms for the value terms depicted here. Consistent with our observations in note 15, inconsistent beliefs about the role of government did not heighten error variance for any of the four political decisions in table 1.2. Based on its failure to survive any of the tests of ambivalence, we do not include this variable in subsequent analyses.

CHAPTER TWO

AMBIVALENCE AND ATTITUDE CHANGE IN VOTE CHOICE: DO CAMPAIGN SWITCHERS EXPERIENCE INTERNAL CONFLICT?

Patrick Fournier

Vote choice is arguably the most fundamental dependent variable in political science. First, the decision is quite momentous: in a representative democracy, voters are responsible for selecting the individuals who control government and drive the elaboration of public policy. Second, by the sheer volume, variety, and importance of work on the topic, vote choice is a dominant concern of political studies. From this large body of research, the discipline has achieved a rather impressive understanding of the determinants of vote choice. We essentially know why a person favors one party over another, and there is widespread agreement as to the list of key ingredients in the vote choice recipe (party identification, leader evaluations, values, issue positions, economic conditions, strategic preoccupations, and a handful of others). We may argue about the relative proportions of each main ingredient or the relevance of secondary seasonings, but the central dimensions of the recipe are evident.

It is a different story for movement in vote choice. Our comprehension of why people change their voting preferences, of why people switch sides, is relatively modest. In part, this flows from the nature of the available data. Panel or longitudinal studies are grossly outnumbered by cross-sectional studies, which hinder the examination of dynamics and change. A list of potential sources of campaign dynamics has emerged from prior research, including events (such as a candidates' debate), priming, advertising, learning, media effects, and so on. However, it is not yet clear under what conditions these factors do or do not lead to campaign movement, nor do we know which individuals are most likely to be influenced.

The present study seeks to fill some of this gap by identifying the types of citizens who tend to change their voting intentions during a campaign. Ambivalence, an important source of attitude change on political issue positions (Zaller and Feldman 1992), is perhaps the main contender for top determinant of attitude change on vote choice. This study's contributions are threefold. First, the impact of ambivalence on voting opinion change is ascertained in a variety of contexts. My analysis relies on panel surveys conducted by the last three American National Election Studies (ANES) (1992, 1996, 2000), the two latest British Election Studies (BES) (1997, 2001), the three most recent Canadian Election Studies (CES) (1993, 1997, 2000), and the 2003 Ontario Election Study (OES).[1] In all cases, attitude change is captured by comparing pre- and post-election vote choice. Second, ambivalence is tested against an extensive list of potential determinants of attitude change: indifference, opinion strength, issue importance, political sophistication, strength of party identification, education, gender, age, and income. Finally, a new measure of ambivalence is proposed and compared to the two most frequently used indicators of that concept.

CONTEXT

Social psychology has offered the most impressive and inspiring avenues to explain susceptibility to attitude change. The latter apparently can be a function of subject characteristics that include, for example, personality traits (Hovland and Janis 1959), ego-involvement (Sherif, Sherif, and Nebergall 1965), salience (Fishbein 1967), cognitive dissonance (Festinger 1957), adherence to social norms or self-representation of norms (Fishbein and Ajzen 1975), and the amount of cognitive involvement with a given issue (Petty and Cacioppo 1986). Persuasion may also be affected by source characteristics such as credibility (Hovland, Janis, and Kelly 1953) and attractiveness (Eagly and Chaiken 1975); by message characteristics such as structure and content (O'Keefe 1990); and by social context (Katz and Lazarsfeld 1955).

Although research has considerably improved our understanding of attitude change in general, a case can be assembled about the particularities of *political* attitude change (Mutz, Sniderman, and Brody 1996). However, comprehension of this specific form of change is not very advanced. Despite increased attention within political science (Cobb and Kuklinski 1997; Koch 1998), our understanding of the phenomenon remains sketchy. According to Diana Mutz and her colleagues (1996: 8), "there is precious little evidence specifying who can be talked out of what beliefs, and under what conditions." What are the individual correlates of openness to voting attitude change? Who can be induced to change their intended vote choice during a campaign? The present study focuses on this overly neglected topic, and it does so by giving center stage to an issue-specific concept (ambivalence) that has emerged as the most promising determinant of political attitude change.

Ambivalence, as the term is employed here, refers to the extent to which the elements people take into account when making a decision push toward opposing positions simultaneously (in contrast to elements entirely consistent with a single position). This notion has appeared under various incarnations over the years, including "memberships in groupings of different political allegiances which exert contradictory and opposing influences" (Lazarsfeld, Berelson, and Goudet 1944; Berelson, Lazarsfeld, and McPhee 1954), "attitude conflict and consistency" (Campbell *et al.* 1960), "opposing considerations that might lead [people] to decide the issue either way" (Zaller 1992; Zaller and Feldman 1992), "internalized conflict due to core beliefs in opposition to one another" (Alvarez and Brehm 1995, 1997), and various others. These definitions differ only with regard to the items identified as the source of internal conflict: social allegiances, attitudes, considerations, and values, respectively.

We know that ambivalence has significant consequences on political cognition and behavior. Ambivalent individuals tend to favor the status quo rather than important political change (Nadeau and Fleury 1994), to delay the formation of political preferences (Lavine 2001), to express more moderate and less certain political judgments (Guge and Meffert 1998), to exhibit greater variability in policy preferences (Alvarez and Brehm 1995), and to change their issue positions more frequently over time (Zaller 1992; Zaller and Feldman 1992; Craig, Martinez, and Kane 2005a) or in response to counterarguments (Fournier 2003). The studies presented in this volume and its companion (Craig and Martinez 2005) have provided new insights into these and other potential consequences of ambivalence.

In particular, the expectation is that ambivalence will be an important predictor of attitude change on vote choice, and that this will be true regardless of whether such change occurs as (1) a product of variation in the set of salient considerations people sample when they form their attitudinal responses (Zaller and Feldman 1992), or (2) a result of persuasion stemming from exposure to and acceptance of communicative messages (Zaller 1992). Because of their skewed prior information, non-ambivalent individuals are likely, on the one hand, to successively sample considerations that support the same position and, on the other hand, to reject the messages that are at odds with their initial position. Because of their mixed set of ideas and beliefs, however, ambivalent citizens are likely, on the one hand, to sample different considerations pushing different positions from one time to the next and, on the other hand, to be receptive and responsive to persuasive messages from various sides. Thus, people experiencing little ambivalence, since they are insulated within a comfortable state of cognitive consonance, should be relatively immune to movement in their voting preferences; in contrast, ambivalent individuals, who are torn between two or more positions and who have reasons to support different electoral competitors, should be more susceptible to change in vote choice.

It has been shown that the link between pre- and post-election presidential vote choice in the United States is mediated by ambivalence (Lavine 2001). I wish to explore this relationship more fully by examining direct measures of voting attitude change in a number of different electoral contexts, and by comparing the impact of ambivalence with that of other individual-level factors that might influence the likelihood of change. Let us briefly consider three of these factors, in order of their declining conceptual proximity to vote choice.

First, closely related to ambivalence, is the notion of *indifference*. Indifference exists when there are a large number of considerations that are neutral in nature, that is, considerations where the respondent is undecided or where s/he takes a moderate position, and that do not decisively push toward a certain preference. It is reasonable to expect that people who do not have many reasons to support either side of a campaign contest probably have electoral opinions that are vulnerable to persuasion. Therefore, the more numerous the neutral considerations a person holds, the higher the indifference and the greater the likelihood of attitude change should be.

A second factor is *strength of opinion*. Whenever you refer to the intensity of an opinion, to the confidence that an individual attaches to an opinion, or to the certainty that a person expresses about an opinion, you draw on the notion of opinion strength. It is logical to assume that opinions that are weak, uncertain, unconfident, or less intense are more susceptible to change (Petty and Krosnick 1995; Alvarez and Brehm 1997). Accordingly, I control here for the role of strength of opinion as a predictor of attitude change on vote choice. It should be noted that such a control imposes a difficult hurdle on ambivalence, since ambivalence may itself be a causal source of opinion strength. One can imagine that it is because people are ambivalent about the electoral options that they tend to have weak voting preferences.

Third, *issue importance* can be defined as "the degree to which a person is passionately concerned about and personally invested in an attitude" (Krosnick 1990: 60). Krosnick's research on the topic (1988, 1990) provides evidence that important issue positions are modified less frequently than unimportant ones. "Policy attitudes that citizens consider important are highly accessible in memory, are highly resistant to change, are highly stable over time, are extensively linked to and consistent with individuals' basic values, instigate polarized perceptions of competing presidential candidates' policy attitudes, and are powerful determinants of candidate preferences" (Krosnick 1990: 70). It is a reasonable extension to think that voting attitude change might occur more often among voters who do not deem a particular election to be of high importance.

These potential determinants of voting attitude change are at a very close conceptual proximity to citizens' electoral preferences, that is, they are specific to the decision being made in a given election. My analysis also takes into account a variety of factors that constitute more general predispositions toward political attitude change. Most notably, I examine the impact of *political sophistication*, which has been identified as determinant of susceptibility to agenda-setting, framing and priming effects (Iyengar, Peters, and Kinder 1982; Iyengar and Kinder 1987; Kinder and Sanders 1990; Krosnick and Kinder 1990; Krosnick and Brannon 1993; Miller and Krosnick 1996), ideologically guided attitude consistency (Judd and Krosnick 1989; Judd and Downing 1990; Jacoby 1991), information processing (Fiske, Lau, and Smith 1990; McGraw, Lodge, and Stroh 1990; McGraw and Pinney 1990; McGraw and Steenbergen 1995), issue-based voting (Luskin and Ten Barge 1995), interpersonal heterogeneity in decision-making (Stimson 1975; Sniderman, Brody, and Tetlock 1991; Fournier 2000), and attitude change (Zaller 1992, 1996).

Following Zaller (1992), the expectation here is that political sophistication is a non-monotonic mediator of political attitude change. Sophisticated people are more likely to be exposed to persuasive campaign communications. However, since they possess relatively large, wide-ranging, and interconnected belief systems, the most sophisticated should also be better equipped to withstand persuasive pressures. Conversely, individuals with a more limited understanding of politics ought to be more vulnerable to attempts at modifying their opinions, but they are less likely to encounter persuasive messages in the first place. Since the probabilities of reception to and acceptance of persuasive attempts are not combined at high levels among these two groups, attitude change should not be likely among the most and least sophisticated. As a result, people with moderate levels of sophistication should be the most susceptible since they are more likely to *both* receive *and* accept persuasive communications.

Citizens who do not feel a strong historical attachment to a political party also should exhibit greater variability in vote choice. We must consider the possibility, however, that *weak party identification*, like strength of opinion, stems in part from ambivalence, that is, mixed feelings for a party may prevent someone from developing strong ties to any party. Finally, it is anticipated that political attitude change will be more common among the *less educated, women*, the *young*, and the *poor*. Since these groups all experience some level of estrangement from politics (Luskin 1990; Delli Carpini and Keeter 1996; Fournier 2002), their commitment to electoral preferences might be more fleeting.

Does ambivalence surpass any or all these other factors as a source of voting opinion change? This is the question to be addressed by the analysis presented below.

DATA AND MEASURES

To identify who changes their vote intention (and who does not) during an election campaign, a number of panel surveys are used. Recent election studies in the United States (1992, 1996, 2000), Britain (1997, 2001), Canada (1993, 1997, 2000), and Ontario (2003) all contain a pre- and post-election panel component. Table 2.1 shows the proportion of respondents who report having voted identically and dissimilarly to the vote intentions they indicated during the campaign. On average, approximately one out of seven electors in Britain and Canada (14 percent), and one out of ten in Ontario, changed their mind between the pre- and post-election waves; the comparable figure is smaller in the United States (6 percent).[2] Despite the fact that relatively few people switch sides over the course of a short campaign (or, in America, over the two months of the campaign captured by these surveys), these unstable voters may nonetheless have a decisive impact on a closely contested race. It therefore should be interesting to uncover what kinds of people they are.

The analyses conducted here will be limited to reversals of opinion among individuals with spontaneous vote intentions in the pre-election

Table 2.1 Distribution of stable and unstable vote choice across panel waves

	Percent stable vote choice	Percent unstable vote choice	Number of cases
Britain 1997, pre1/pre2 (BES)	93	7	816
Britain 1997, pre1/post (BES)	86	14	1,017
Britain 1997, pre2/post (BES)	90	10	1,029
Britain 2001, pre/post (BES)	83	17	1,408
Canada 1993, pre/post (CES)	83	17	1,954
Canada 1997, pre/post (CES)	86	14	1,550
Canada 2000, pre/post (CES)	88	12	1,405
Ontario 2003, pre/post (OES)	90	10	608
United States 1992, pre/post (NES)	97	3	1,201
United States 1996, pre/post (NES)	92	8	1,009
United States 2000, pre/post (NES)	94	6	950

Note: See text and note 2 for description of datasets.

campaign wave; in other words, I excluded respondents who reported that they were inclined to vote a certain way but were not yet sure. It seems considerably more instructive to explain the instability of respondents who were confident enough about their electoral preferences to express a vote intention without prompting, yet who ultimately changed their mind, than to explain the instability of a tentative choice. Regardless, analyses pertaining to the entire sample of voters yielded results similar to those reported here.[3]

Traditionally, there are two principal approaches to the measurement of ambivalence. One relies on self-reports of attitudes, such as whether people say their views about an object are mostly one-sided or mixed (e.g., Tourangeau *et al.* 1989b). The other is based on the balance of positive and negative reactions to an object in response to open-ended questions, such as the National Election Study (NES) likes/dislikes items about presidential candidates (e.g., Zaller 1992).[4] Although these two approaches are sometimes said to yield "subjective" and "objective" measures of ambivalence, respectively (Priester and Petty 1996), they both actually depend a great deal on citizens' ability to gauge, and willingness to reveal, their internal conflict. Yet a person might not be the best judge of his or her own decision-making processes. Perceptual bias, rationalization, and social desirability can undermine the quality of both types of ambivalence measures (Nisbett and Wilson 1977; Lodge, McGraw, and Stroh 1989; Smith 1989; Rahn, Krosnick, and Breuning 1994; Bassili 1996).

This study employs a novel measurement strategy, labeled *actual ambivalence*, that avoids these potential problems and has the further advantage of being adaptable to almost all surveys, both past and present, without the need for asking any additional question(s). Both actual ambivalence and indifference are operationalized using the same series of questions. Like previous work (Zaller and Feldman 1992; Lavine 2001), I consider that internal conflict should stem from the various types of reasons that can motivate an individual to favor one political preference over another (values, beliefs, opinions, perceptions, and so on). But instead of relying on open-ended questions to capture considerations, I use correlates of the decision. All items measured at time t_1 that were found to be associated with vote intentions at time t_1 were considered candidates for relevant considerations; the six strongest correlates of each electoral decision were retained for scale construction. Relevant considerations differed from one voting preference to another, since the link between ambivalence and decision-making appears to be candidate-specific (Lavine 2001). To take one example: The 2000 NES list includes Clinton's job approval, comparative evaluations of Bush and Gore based on feeling thermometer ratings, party identification, ideological self-placement, assessments of the best party for handling the economy, and of the best party for avoiding war.[5] Responses to each of these six items were coded as being consistent with the respondent's initial position, neutral (discrete or moderate), or inconsistent with vote intention at t_1. Thus, if a person intended to vote for George W. Bush for president, party identification was coded as follows: Republican identification (consistent consideration), Democratic identification (inconsistent consideration), and Independent identification (neutral consideration).

Actual ambivalence is measured as the difference between the proportion of inconsistent considerations and the proportion of consistent considerations; this difference was then rescaled so that scores ranged from 0 to 1. The small number of individuals with more inconsistent than consistent considerations were assigned a score of 1, the same value as an ambivalent citizen having an equal number of consistent and inconsistent considerations. Thus, a high score denotes someone who is torn between two or more positions because s/he possesses reasons to support opposing sides. In the 2000 NES, for example, a person with a Bush vote intention would receive a score of 1 if he liked Bush more than Gore, identified as Republican and conservative, but also approved of Clinton and believed the Democrats were the best party to handle the economy and avoid war. In contrast, a low score on the ambivalence measure reveals an individual whose considerations are generally consistent, reinforcing his or her initial preference. In 2000, a score of 0 would be allocated to a Gore supporter who approved of Clinton, rated Gore higher than Bush, considered him/herself a Democrat and a liberal, and thought the Democrats would do a better job of handling the economy and staying out of war.

The indicator of indifference is simply the standardized sum of neutral considerations. A person with a high indifference score holds few reasons to support any electoral competitor, while a person with a low score holds many. For example, in the 2000 American survey, the greater the tendency to be neutral about Clinton's performance, to give similar ratings to Bush and Gore, to be an independent, to be ideologically moderate, and to state that neither party would be better with the economy and war avoidance, the greater the value on the indifference scale.

Let us next review the potential determinants of voting attitude change to be used as controls. First, when available, the two traditional measures of ambivalence (see above) are inserted into the analyses. In wave 1 of the Ontario 2003 survey, a question tapping subjective ambivalence was asked: "When you think about [the party the respondent intends to support], would you say your views of that party are almost all positive, mostly positive with some negative views, or an equal mix of both negative and positive views?" People with mixed views about their intended vote choice score high on subjective ambivalence, while those who only have positive views receive a low score. In addition, objective indicators of ambivalence can be constructed among the three NES studies, using indices based on respondents' answers to open-ended likes/dislikes questions about the presidential candidates (Lavine 2001). The calculation formula proposed by Thompson, Zanna, and Griffin (1995) is employed, that is,

$$\text{Objective Ambivalence} = [(P + N)/2] - |P - N|$$

where P is the positive reaction score and N is the negative reaction score.[6] Individuals exhibit ambivalence when they have a similar number of positive and negative reactions toward their preferred candidate; they do not when their reactions are completely positive.

The indicator for strength of opinion is drawn from a simple question asking respondents to rate the strength of their vote preference. This question, administered immediately after people expressed their voting opinion, should reflect the intensity, certainty, and/or confidence with which the vote intention is held. Someone with a stronger preference scores high on the opinion strength scale, while an individual with a weak attitude scores low. To capture issue importance pertinent for vote choice, I rely on interest in the election: citizens expressing great interest score high on issue importance, while those with little interest score low.

For political sophistication, following the lead of previous work, I employ measures of general factual knowledge about politics (Luskin 1987; Fiske, Lau, and Smith 1990; Zaller 1990; Delli Carpini and Keeter 1993).[7] Items include the respondent's ability to correctly identify party leaders (CES, Ontario), political figures (CES, NES, Ontario), party positions (BES, CES), and electoral regulations (BES). Numerous correct responses translate into a high value on the political information index, while many incorrect or "don't know" answers translate into a low score. Each index is then recoded into two dummy variables, representing the lowest third and highest third of the distribution, to allow for non-monotonic effects.

Finally, several dummy variables are employed. These take the value of 1 if the respondent possesses a strong party identification, is a woman, is under age 30, is aged 60 or older, has a total household income in the lowest third, has an income in the upper third, or has income information missing, respectively. Education is entered into the model linearly.

The analysis proceeds in three stages. First, the capacity of actual ambivalence to explain individual variation in susceptibility to attitude change in vote choice is tested against numerous controls and the conventional measures of ambivalence (subjective and objective ambivalence) in the American and Ontario data. Then, the key independent variable is examined as a predictor of instability in voting preferences in Canadian parliamentary elections. Lastly, issues regarding the timing of the measurement of actual ambivalence are explored with British data.

RESULTS

Stage One: United States (NES) and Ontario (OES)

Table 2.2 presents the results of binary logistic regressions, one for each of four surveys: NES 1992, 1996, 2000, and OES 2003. The dependent variable in each instance takes a value of 1 if the respondent switched sides

Table 2.2 Determinants of attitude change, three measures of ambivalence

Variable	NES 1992	NES 1996	NES 2000	OES 2003
Subjective ambivalence	n/a	n/a	n/a	0.50
				(0.54)
Objective ambivalence	0.27†	0.20*	0.33*	n/a
	(0.15)	(0.10)	(0.16)	
Actual ambivalence	2.50**	1.83**	3.88**	2.03**
	(0.77)	(0.47)	(0.74)	(0.56)
Indifference	1.89	0.58	−0.32	−1.15
	(1.24)	(0.83)	(0.90)	(1.17)
Strength of opinion	−0.23	−1.18**	−0.80*	−0.45
	(0.45)	(0.29)	(0.36)	(0.50)
Issue importance	−0.64	−0.53	0.28	−0.47
	(0.60)	(0.43)	(0.54)	(0.67)
Political information (low-tier)	0.33	−0.41	0.13	0.69†
	(0.43)	(0.44)	(0.37)	(0.40)
Political information (high-tier)	−1.34†	0.27	−0.98*	0.27
	(0.80)	(0.31)	(0.48)	(0.38)
Strong party identification	0.80†	−1.15**	−0.21	−0.51
	(0.47)	(0.43)	(0.47)	(0.35)
Education	−0.33	−0.79	−0.09	−0.29
	(0.83)	(0.57)	(0.72)	(0.50)
Woman	0.36	0.32	0.43	0.07
	(0.42)	(0.27)	(0.33)	(0.30)
Age (under 30)	−0.45	−0.03	0.20	0.27
	(0.59)	(0.45)	(0.41)	(0.39)
Age (60-plus)	−0.36	−0.12	−0.02	−0.61
	(0.52)	(0.34)	(0.47)	(0.44)
Income (low-tier)	0.18	0.59	0.19	−0.21
	(0.54)	(0.40)	(0.51)	(0.37)
Income (high-tier)	0.51	0.45	0.12	−0.47
	(0.51)	(0.36)	(0.48)	(0.39)
Income (missing)	1.03	1.06*	0.56	−0.67
	(0.75)	(0.46)	(0.51)	(0.67)
Constant	−5.22**	−2.52**	−4.54**	−2.75**
	(1.07)	(0.66)	(0.97)	(0.88)
Adjusted Pseudo R^2	0.14	0.32	0.33	0.19
Percent correctly predicted	97.3	92.5	94.0	90.2
Number of cases	1130	965	933	606

Note: Table entries are unstandardized logit coefficients with associated standard errors (in parentheses); see appendix for variable codings.

**$p \leq .01$; *$p \leq .05$; †$p \leq .10$.

(from one voting preference to another) between the two panel waves, and 0 if the initial vote choice remained unchanged. As can be seen in the table, actual ambivalence is a significant correlate of susceptibility to attitude change in all four models. In fact, it is the most important predictor of opinion movement in all cases: individuals whose considerations pull in opposite directions are much more likely to shift preferences during the campaign than individuals whose considerations converge toward a single position. Simulations show that moving from one end of the ambivalence scale (0, totally consistent considerations) to the other (1, an equal number of consistent and inconsistent considerations) raises the likelihood of instability in vote choice by 12 percentage points, on average, in the three American studies, and by 16 percentage points in the Ontario election.[8]

Actual ambivalence outperforms the two traditional measures of ambivalence. When actual and objective ambivalence are entered into different models (not shown), the parameter estimates and model fit statistics are significantly greater for the specification containing actual ambivalence.[9] When actual and objective ambivalence are simultaneously entered into a model (columns 1 through 3 of table 2.2), both effects are consistently positive and significant, but actual internal conflict has a more decisive impact on attitude change. Simulating a movement of one standard deviation on each measure yields objective effects less than half the size of those for actual ambivalence. It is interesting to note that the two sets of parameters in table 2.2 have roughly the same magnitude when each variable is examined separately. This suggests that the two types of indicators each captures a distinct dimension of ambivalence that does not overlap the other. Nevertheless, actual ambivalence remains steadily more effective in accounting for change in vote choice.

In the Ontario data, actual ambivalence is tested against the single-item subjective ambivalence. This second traditional operationalization of ambivalence does not reach standard levels of statistical significance, whether entered separately or concurrently with the new measure (column 4 in table 2.2). It is clearly outshined by actual ambivalence.

No control variable is systematically linked to variability in voting preferences, with only sporadic effects being evident. Strength of opinion has a significant negative impact on persuasion in two columns out of four; in those models, people having a strong vote choice are, as expected, less likely to reverse their opinion. The coefficients for strong party identification reveal two significant but conflicting relationships with attitude change, one positive and the other negative. Information is sometimes an important explanatory factor, but the results do not follow the anticipated non-monotonic pattern; instead, high knowledge is twice associated with a lower proportion of persuasion, while low knowledge is once positively correlated with opinion instability. The other potential determinants of attitude change are irrelevant.

Indifference, issue importance, and the sociodemographic variables are never significantly linked to instability of opinion in any of the four elections.

As indicated by the adjusted pseudo R-squared,[10] these specifications do a reasonably good job of explaining individual susceptibility to attitude change, especially in the American data. Considering the relatively low occurrence of vote change in the United States, the good model fit is perhaps not surprising.

Stage Two: Canada's Parliamentary Elections (CES)

Table 2.3 replicates the analysis reported in the previous table for movement in Canadian voting preferences during the last three federal election campaigns.

Table 2.3 Determinants of attitude change, Canada

Variable	CES 1993	CES 1997	CES 2000
Actual ambivalence	1.26**	1.54**	1.50**
	(0.22)	(0.27)	(0.32)
Indifference	0.05	0.59	−0.23
	(0.42)	(0.64)	(0.60)
Issue importance	−0.06	−0.33	−0.24
	(0.26)	(0.38)	(0.42)
Political information (low-tier)	0.20	−0.69**	0.23
	(0.17)	(0.27)	(0.25)
Political information (high-tier)	−0.06	−0.75**	0.00
	(0.16)	(0.21)	(0.22)
Strong party identification	−0.15	−0.51*	−0.82**
	(0.19)	(0.24)	(0.29)
Education	0.19	−0.28	−0.08
	(0.34)	(0.44)	(0.49)
Woman	−0.12	−0.08	0.46*
	(0.14)	(0.17)	(0.19)
Age (under 30)	0.19	0.09	0.27
	(0.16)	(0.21)	(0.24)
Age (60-plus)	−0.21	−0.25	−0.28
	(0.21)	(0.26)	(0.27)
Income (low-tier)	−0.35†	0.12	0.12
	(0.19)	(0.22)	(0.24)
Income (high-tier)	−0.28	−0.16	0.33
	(0.17)	(0.22)	(0.24)
Income (missing)	−0.30	−0.18	−0.13
	(0.20)	(0.37)	(0.43)
Constant	−2.11**	−1.99**	−3.00**
	(0.32)	(0.42)	(0.48)
Adjusted Pseudo R^2	0.07	0.13	0.11
Percent correctly predicted	82.3	86.4	89.1
Number of cases	1677	1282	1239

Note: Table entries are unstandardized logit coefficients with associated standard errors (in parentheses); see appendix for variable codings.

**$p \leq .01$; *$p \leq .05$; †$p \leq .10$.

The decision in these cases pertains to a choice between political parties rather than presidential candidates. Once again, we see that ambivalence provides the best explanation for attitude change in all models: people who experience conflicting pressures are much more likely to shift their vote preference over the course of the campaign than individuals who feel no such conflict. Simulations indicate that spanning the ambivalence scale increases the likelihood of switching sides by 17, 16, and 13 percentage points in 1993, 1997, and 2000, respectively.

As was the case in the United States, some of the other potential moderators of attitude change do contribute significantly to the account of volatility in vote choice, but they never do so consistently across surveys. In 1997, political information works as Zaller (1992) suggested, with the more and less knowledgeable being less unstable than the middle category, the moderately informed; but knowledge does not matter in the other two campaigns. Having a strong party identification is associated with a lower tendency of opinion reversal in just two elections out of three. Similarly, there are only two instances where one of the sociodemographic groups (the less privileged in 1993, women in 2000) behaves differently from other respondents, above and beyond their attitudinal profile. First differences reveal that the predicted impact of ambivalence on the likelihood of opinion change is always at least twice as large as the impact of these other significant effects. The contributions of indifference, issue importance, education, age, and income to the explanation of party switching are null across the board. Overall, the model fit in the Canadian models is less impressive than in table 2.2.

Stage Three: The Timing of Change in Britain (BES)

The British data allow us to explore the variability over time in ambivalence's capacity to predict voting attitude change. The 1997 BES contained a three-wave campaign panel, with respondents being interviewed two times during the campaign and once after the election. The relevant considerations were only captured at time t_1, so only one measurement of actual ambivalence can be obtained. However, we can compare the impacts of this particular level of ambivalence on different configurations of the dependent variable: movements between t_1 and t_2, between t_1 and t_3, and between t_2 and t_3. Table 2.4 reports the results of four binary logistic regressions, three for 1997 and one for 2001.

In each model, ambivalence emerges yet again as the dominant determinant of individual dynamics in vote choice. Being torn between two or more voting preferences is consistently associated with a higher likelihood of party switching. Simulations indicate that the probability of changing sides is 15 percentage points higher, on average, among respondents who

Table 2.4 Determinants of attitude change, Britain

Variable	BES 1997 $(t_1 - t_2)$	BES 1997 $(t_1 - t_3)$	BES 1997 $(t_2 - t_3)$	BES 2001
Actual ambivalence	3.53**	1.88**	1.09*	1.26**
	(0.62)	(0.37)	(0.46)	(0.29)
Indifference	−1.14	0.23	1.20	0.02
	(0.90)	(0.64)	(0.82)	(0.45)
Issue importance	−0.14	−0.82	−0.77	0.68*
	(0.68)	(0.51)	(0.65)	(0.31)
Political information (low tier)	−0.16	−0.43	−0.50	−0.20
	(0.40)	(0.27)	(0.35)	(0.28)
Political information (high tier)	0.16	0.00	0.28	−0.08
	(0.43)	(0.29)	(0.37)	(0.19)
Strong party identification	−0.32	−0.47	−0.38	−0.80**
	(0.62)	(0.47)	(0.59)	(0.31)
Education	−0.29	0.10	−0.25	0.07
	(0.58)	(0.40)	(0.52)	(0.24)
Woman	0.06	0.11	0.15	0.00
	(0.32)	(0.23)	(0.29)	(0.17)
Age (under 30)	−1.29*	0.12	0.40	0.05
	(0.63)	(0.30)	(0.36)	(0.27)
Age (60-plus)	0.06	−0.01	−0.00	−0.50*
	(0.39)	(0.28)	(0.36)	(0.22)
Income (low-tier)	0.11	0.16	0.09	0.06
	(0.44)	(0.30)	(0.37)	(0.25)
Income (high-tier)	0.18	−0.18	−0.30	0.09
	(0.47)	(0.33)	(0.44)	(0.22)
Income (missing)	−0.25	0.13	0.14	0.09
	(0.67)	(0.38)	(0.47)	(0.25)
Constant	−4.42**	−2.68**	−3.02**	−2.59**
	(0.77)	(0.50)	(0.62)	(0.33)
Adjusted Pseudo R^2	0.19	0.11	0.07	0.10
Percent correctly predicted	93.0	86.4	92.0	83.3
Number of cases	778	877	846	1173

Note: Table entries are unstandardized logit coefficients with associated standard errors (in parentheses); see appendix for variable codings.

**$p \le .01$; *$p \le .05$.

have an equal number of consistent and inconsistent considerations (1 on the ambivalence scale) than among those whose considerations are all compatible with the preference they initially expressed (0 on the ambivalence scale).

Ambivalence (measured at time t_1) is most effective at forecasting opinion change when t_1 is the reference point. First differences of 0.19 are uncovered for the impact of ambivalence on instability in vote choice between both $t_1 - t_2$ and $t_1 - t_3$; in contrast, early campaign ambivalence increases the likelihood of opinion movement between t_2 and t_3 by just 7 percentage points.

This suggests that the timing of ambivalence measurement is important, perhaps because ambivalence actually fluctuates over time. Under the circumstances, if multiple observations are not possible, it probably should be captured at t_1 rather than subsequently.

Matching the situation found in the two previous countries, no other factor is systematically linked to opinion change. Only two attitudes, issue importance and strong party identification, have a significant coefficient in either election, with those who are politically interested and who do not strongly identify with a political party displaying greater over-time variability in 2001. Indifference, political information, and all sociodemographic variables except age fail to achieve statistical significance in any of the two surveys. Overall performance of the model, as indicated by the adjusted pseudo R-squared, is fairly small, on par with the Canadian data.

CONCLUSIONS

This study examined the role of ambivalence as a source of interpersonal variation in voting attitude change. Indeed, ambivalence proved to be a very important predictor of vote choice instability across a variety of political contexts and election years. For eleven different decisions, measured in nine surveys conducted in three countries, the voting preferences of individuals who were ambivalent proved to be systematically much more volatile than those of the non-ambivalent. In fact, the magnitude of ambivalence's effects was fundamentally the same in each context. And for the first time, the relationship between ambivalence and political attitude change was assessed while controlling for numerous alternative determinants of opinion dynamics, most notably indifference, strength of opinion, issue importance, political information, and strength of party identification. Ambivalence came out on top in every case; moreover, no other factor was consistently a significant explanation of attitude change in all models.

To avoid the potential risks involved in relying on people's personal judgments to gauge their level of ambivalence, the balance of a decision's correlates was used. This approach clearly surpasses conventional measures of ambivalence in accounting for attitude change. The evidence presented here cannot, however, speak to the nature of, and the interconnections between, these indicators. Are actual, subjective, and objective ambivalence distinct dimensions that differently affect political cognitions and behaviors? Is actual ambivalence the best operationalization of ambivalence for all research agendas? More work is required, with actual ambivalence being tested on other topics.

Since it is clear that ambivalent voters are disproportionately likely to switch their voting preferences during the course of an electoral campaign, the next logical step is to ascertain how this process really works. Do the ambivalent fluctuate haphazardly, more or less oblivious to the events and context of the campaign? Or, conversely, are they responsive to comprehensible real-world campaign influences such as candidate (or party) discourses and debates, paid ads, and news coverage? More generally, do they react reasonably to campaign events? To the extent that ambivalent citizens constitute—as appears to be the case—the main ranks of swing voters, these are important questions to be addressed by future research.

A central practical implication also flows from the findings presented above, especially if it turns out that specific campaign effects are in fact stronger among the ambivalent. In order to be successful and efficient, campaign messages and persuasive attempts obviously do not need to be directed at the entire population. Campaign strategists already recognize the importance of concentrating their scarce communications resources on the most vulnerable targets; this study has shown that one type of individual (defined attitudinally rather than sociodemographically) tends to be consistently more susceptible to influence. Specifically, the opinions of persons who are torn between conflicting positions are relatively more malleable than those of their less ambivalent counterparts. As a result, for any given issue there seems to be a portion of the public that finds itself sitting on the proverbial fence, leaning toward one side perhaps, but open to counterarguments and ready to reverse their position in certain circumstances.

How does one go about reaching ambivalent citizens? Answering such a question exceeds this chapter's mandate, though it seems clear that the task is far from simple. Since they are not very distinctive sociodemographically, beyond a tendency to be younger and somewhat less educated, ambivalent individuals are seldom a highly visible target. The challenge, then, is for candidates and parties to use the fact that potential converts already share some but not all of their side's viewpoints to craft more effective persuasion messages—messages that are designed to influence the balance of consistent and inconsistent considerations in the minds of torn voters, without alienating the campaign's current base of support.

Let me close with a caveat. While ambivalence represents the best predictor of attitude change across a variety of contexts (in term of geography, institutions, and time), it has not proven to be entirely sufficient to account for all changes in vote intention. Both the predicted simulated impacts on the likelihood of persuasion and the model fit statistics indicate as much. Some ambivalent people simply are not swayed during a campaign. Experiencing ambivalence appears to be a necessary but insufficient condition for political persuasion to occur. It remains to be seen why some ambivalent citizens change their mind while others do not. Further research should seek to determine under what conditions the potential for attitude change actually manifests itself.

Appendix

The following datasets and variables were utilized in the analysis for this chapter (see note 2):

- BES 1997: British Election Study 1997, ICPSR #2619.
- BES 2001: British Election Study 2001, www.essex.ac.uk/bes.
- CES 1993: Canadian Election Study 1993, ICPSR #6571.
- CES 1997: Canadian Election Study 1997, ICPSR #2593.
- CES 2000: Canadian Election Study 2000, ICPSR #3969.
- NES 1992: American National Election Study 1992, ICPSR #6067.
- NES 1996: American National Election Study 1996, ICPSR #6896.
- NES 2000: American National Election Study 2000, ICPSR #3131.
- OES 2003: Ontario Election Study 2003.

Attitude Change. Stability of vote choice over panel waves, scores ranging from 0 to 1. BES 1997 (dcpartyb, dcpartyc, voted), BES 2001 (aq7b, bq8b), CES 1993 (cpsa3, pesa4), CES 1997 (cpsa4, pesa4), CES 2000 (cpsa4, pesa3a, pesa3b), NES 1992 (v923805, v925609), NES 1996 (v960548, v961082), NES 2000 (v000793, v001249), OES 2003 (b1, p2).

Subjective Ambivalence. Self-reported ambivalence, scores ranging from 0 to 1. OES 2003 (b4: "When you think about [the party the respondent intends to support], would you say your views of that party are almost all positive, mostly positive with some negative views, or an equal mix of both negative and positive views?").

Objective Ambivalence. Balance of favorable and unfavorable reactions in open-ended likes/dislikes questions concerning the respondent's preferred presidential candidate; formula is $((p + n)/2) - (abs(p - n))$, where p = positive reactions and n = negative reactions, scores ranging from -2.5 to 5.0. NES 1992 (v923109 through v923132), NES 1996 (v960205 through v960216), NES 2000 (v000305 through v000316).

Actual Ambivalence. Difference between proportion of inconsistent considerations (incompatible with initial vote choice) and proportion of consistent considerations (congruent with initial vote choice), rescaled (see formula in text), scores ranging from 0 (only consistent considerations) to 1 (equal number of consistent and inconsistent considerations).

List of Considerations:

BES 1997: best prime minister [bestpmb, bestpmc], national retrospective economy [econpstb, gecpstc], party identification [ptyallga], European currency [ecuviewb], government spending [taxspenb], cynicism [losetchb, votintrb, ptynmatb].

BES 2001: best party on most important issue [aq3], party identification [aq5a], leader evaluations [aq17a, aq17b, aq17c], government handling of education [aq4d], government handling of taxes [aq4i], government handling of transportation [aq4j], government handling of making life better [aq4l], left–right scale [aq25f].

CES 1993: leader evaluations [cpsd2a, cpsd2b, cpsd2c, cpsd2d], French language [cpsd3, cpsf1a], continentalism [cpsf2a, cpsl1, cpsl3], Quebec sovereignty [cpsg11], moral traditionalism [cpsg6b, cpsg6c, cpsg7a, cpsg7b, cpsg7e], national retrospective economy [cpsh1, cpsh1a, cpsh1b], power of trade unions [cpsk1a], do more for racial minorities [cpsk3a], welfare state [cpsl5a, cpsl5b, cpsl7b, cpsl7d, cpsl7e], macroeconomic policy [cpsl6a, cpsl9a], party identification [cpsm1].

CES 1997: taxes [cpsa1, cpsa2d, cpse1a], deficit [cpsa2b, cpsf5, cpsf8], cynicism [cpsb10a, cpsb10d, cpsb10e, cpsj13], evolution of unemployment [cpsc5], leader evaluations [cpsd1a, cpsd1b, cpsd1c, cpsd1d, cpsd1e], do more for Quebec [cpse3a, cpsj3], government performance on jobs [cpsf10c], government performance on election promises [cpsf10d], government performance on Quebec [cpsf10e], government performance on crime [cpsf10f], government performance on social programs [cpsf10g], regional alienation [cpsj12], young offenders [cpsj21], goods and services tax [cpsj2b], party identification [cpsk1], Quebec sovereignty [cpsk15, cpsk16].

CES 2000: cynicism [cpsb10d, cpsb11, cpspolit], death penalty [cpsc15], leader evaluations [cpschret, cpsclark, cpsstock, cpsducep, cpsmcdon], government performance on debt [cpsf10b], government performance on health care [cpsf10c], government performance on jobs [cpsf10d], government performance on getting along with provinces [cpsf10e], government performance on taxes [cpsf10f], government performance on social welfare [cpsf10h], government performance on Quebec [cpsf10j], moral traditionalism [cpsf3, cpsf18], regional alienation [cpsj12], party identification [cpsk1a, cpsk1b], religiosity [cpsm10b], do more for racial minorities [cpsc11], social programs spending [cpspla24], Quebec sovereignty [pesc6].

NES 1992: Bush job approval [v923320], leader evaluations [v923305, v923306], party identification [v923634], government services [v923701], best party to handle economy [v923545], best party to keep country out of war [v923602], ideology [v923513].

NES 1996: Clinton job approval [v960296], leader evaluations [v960272, v960273], ideology [v960368], party identification [v960420], government services [v960450], government health insurance [v960479], best party to keep country out of war [v960408], best party to handle economy [v960397].

NES 2000: Clinton job approval [v000341], leader evaluations [v000360, v000361], ideology [v000446], best party to handle economy [v000505], best party to keep country out of war [v000506], party identification [v000523], government services [v000550].

OES 2003: party identification [po1], leader evaluations [e1x, e2x, e3x], importance of education [j2], importance of economy [j6], importance of taxation [j9], government approval [j12], increase or decrease taxes [j20], government electricity policy [j21].

Indifference. Proportion of neutral considerations (moderate/don't know), scores ranging from 0 (no such answers) to 1 (only such answers); list of considerations same as for actual ambivalence.

Strength of Opinion. Strength of intended vote choice, scores ranging from 0 to 1. NES 1992 (V923806: "Would you say that your preference for this candidate is strong or not strong?"), NES 1996 (V960549), NES 2000 (v000794), OES 2003 (b3: "How strongly do you support that party?").

Issue Importance. Interest in the election, scores ranging from 0 to 1. BES 1997 (politica), BES 2001 (aq1), CES 1993 (cpsb1), CES 1997 (cpsb4), CES 2000 (cpsb4), NES 1992 (v923101), NES 1996 (v960201), NES 2000 (v000301), OES 2003 (d1).

Political Information. Low-tier (dummy variable, which takes the value, of 1 when respondent's score on an index of general factual knowledge about politics is in the lowest one-third of the distribution) and high-tier (dummy variable, which takes the value of 1 when score on knowledge index is in the highest one-third of the distribution). BES 1997 (knwprc, knwcttxc, knwoptoc, knwscotc, knwrailc, knwmnwgc), BES 2001 (bq68a, bq68b, bq68c, bq68d, bq68e, bq68f), CES 1993 (cps3a1, cpsg3b1, pese17a, pese18a, pese19a, pese20a), CES 1997 (cpsf13, cpsf14, cpsf15, cpsl6, cpsl11, cpsl12, cpsl13), CES 2000 (cpslead1 to cpslead5, cpsl11, cpsl12), NES 1992 (v925916, v925917, v925918, v925919), NES 1996 (v961189, v961190, v961191, v961192), NES 2000 (v001447, v001450, v001453, v001456), OES 2003 (c1, c2, c3, c4, c5, c6).

Strong Party Identification. Dummy variable, which takes the value of 1 when respondent's party identification is strong. BES 1997 (idstrnga), BES 2001 (aq5d), CES 1993 (cpsm1, cpsm2), CES 1997 (cpsk1, cpsk2), CES 2000 (cpsk1a, cpsk1b, cpsk2a, cpsk2b), NES 1992 (v923634), NES 1996 (v960420), NES 2000 (v000523), OES 2003 (po2a).

Education. Highest level of education completed, scores ranging from 0 to 1. BES 1997 (hedquala), BES 2001 (aq42), CES 1993 (cpso3, refn2), CES 1997 (cpsm3), CES 2000 (cpsm3), NES 1992 (v923908), NES 1996 (v960610), NES 2000 (v000913), OES 2003 (educ).

Age. Less than 30 (dummy variable, which takes the value of 1 when respondent is less than thirty years old), and 60-plus (dummy variable, which takes the value 1 when respondent is aged sixty or older). BES 1997 (ragea), BES 2001 (ageall), CES 1993 (cpsage), CES 1997 (cpsage), CES 2000 (cpsage), NES 1992 (v923903), NES 1996 (v960605), NES 2000 (v000908), OES 2003 (age).

Woman. Dummy variable, which takes the value of 1 when respondent is female. BES 1997 (rsexa), BES 2001 (genall), CES 1993 (cpsrgen), CES 1997 (cpsrgen), CES 2000 (cpsrgen), NES 1992 (v924201), NES 1996 (v960066), NES 2000 (v001029), OES 2003 (x11).

Income. Low-tier (dummy variable, which takes the value of 1 when total household income is in the lowest one-third of the distribution), high-tier (dummy variable, which takes the value of 1 when total household income is in the highest one-third of the distribution), and missing (dummy variable, which takes the value of 1 when respondent refused to reveal income). BES 1997 (hhincoma), BES 2001 (incomes), CES 1993 (cpso18), CES 1997 (cpsm16, cpsm16a), CES 2000 (cpsm16a), NES 1992 (v924104), NES 1996 (v960701), NES 2000 (v000994), OES 2003 (income).

Notes

I would like to acknowledge the financial support of the *Fonds Québécois de la Recherche sur la Société et la Culture* (FQRSC) and the *Social Sciences and Humanities Research Council of Canada* (SSHRC). I thank Angelo Elias, Simon McDougall, and the editors of this volume for their comments and assistance.

1. The principal investigators of the 2003 Ontario Election Study were Fred Cutler and Greg Lyle; data from that study are expected to become publicly available shortly. Other data used in this chapter are freely accessible through the Inter-University Consortium for Political and Social Research (www.icpsr.umich.edu), the British Election Study (www.essex.ac.uk/bes), the Canadian Election Study (www.ces-eec.umontreal.ca), or the National Election Study (www.umich. edu/~nes).

2. See the appendix for additional information about this and other variables employed in the analysis below.

3. Results are available from the author on request.

4. A related approach, derived from experimental work in social psychology, is proposed by Craig, Kane, and Martinez (2002; also see Craig, Martinez, and Kane 2005a and chapter four in this volume), who ask survey respondents to rate separately how positively and how negatively they feel toward various contingencies of the dependent variable (support for abortion rights and for gay rights). While capturing conflicted reactions for more than a single target is commendable, people's judgments also play an essential role in this approach to measuring ambivalence.

5. Each dataset's list of considerations is found in the appendix to this chapter.

6. For a discussion of different formulas, see Priester and Petty (1996).

7. Although political information is only one component of political sophistication, it often serves as a proxy indicator of sophistication because (a) it is much more easily measured than the other components, and (b) it seems to predict overall sophistication reasonably well (Luskin 1987).

8. Unless stated otherwise, all simulations presented in this study calculated first differences for a movement from 0 to 1 on a reference variable, while holding all other variables unchanged.

9. Results are available from the author on request.

10. This refers to Hagle and Mitchell's (1992) correction of the Aldrich and Nelson (1984) pseudo R-squared.

CHAPTER THREE

WHAT HAPPENS WHEN WE SIMULTANEOUSLY WANT OPPOSITE THINGS? AMBIVALENCE ABOUT SOCIAL WELFARE

Jason Gainous and Michael D. Martinez

Since the New Deal, issues relating to social welfare policy have created a divide in the United States. This divide has been a defining characteristic of party politics at both the elite (Sinclair 1978; Barrett and Cook 1991; Ansolabehere, Snyder, and Stewart 2001) and mass levels (Berelson, Lazarsfeld, and McPhee 1954; Campbell *et al.* 1960; more recently, see Green, Palmquist, and Schickler 2002; Stonecash 2000; Layman and Carsey 2002) for over seven decades. It has been suggested, however, that many Americans are internally torn between the contending sides of governmental activism versus governmental restraint, especially with regard to spending programs that provide benefits to individual citizens, disadvantaged or otherwise (Cantril and Cantril 1999; Feldman and Zaller 1992; Hodson, Maio, and Esses 2001). The present study takes a closer look at this *ambivalence*, which is said to exist whenever someone simultaneously possesses both positive and negative evaluations of an attitude object (Alvarez and Brehm 1995; Zaller 1992; Zaller and Feldman 1992; Eagly and Chaiken 1993).

Our focus is primarily on the question of why certain kinds of people tend to be more ambivalent than others about social welfare policy. Employing a measurement approach adapted from experimental work for use in large-sample surveys (Craig, Kane, and Martinez 2002; Craig *et al.* 2005b), we assess the level of ambivalence about social welfare issues that is present in the mass public and argue that variations across individuals are shaped, in part, by the conflict that exists among a person's *core values*, the *relative salience* of the values that are potentially in conflict, and the person's *underlying preferences* (liberal or conservative) in that policy area. In the remaining sections of this chapter, we (1) review the existing literature on ambivalence about social welfare policy; (2) discuss the roles of value conflict, the personal importance of values, and issue positions as potential sources of ambivalence; and (3) test an empirical model of these sources based on a statewide survey of registered voters in Florida.

POLITICAL ATTITUDES AND AMBIVALENCE ABOUT SOCIAL WELFARE

Although the simplest way to think about and measure people's attitudes is on a bipolar continuum that ranges from positive to negative, with a neutral point in between (Thurstone 1928; Thurstone and Chave 1929; Eagly and Chaiken 1993), there is growing evidence that many people are in fact ambivalent about a broad range of attitude objects, both political and otherwise. Social psychologists (e.g., Abelson *et al.* 1982; Thompson, Zanna, and Griffin 1995; Priester and Petty 1996; Armitage and Conner 2000; Newby-Clark, McGregor, and Zanna 2002; Conner *et al.* 2002), political scientists (Feldman and Zaller 1992; Zaller 1992; Alvarez and Brehm 1995; Lavine 2001; Steenbergen and Brewer 2000; Craig, Kane, and Martinez 2002; Craig *et al.* 2005b; Haddock 2003; McGraw, Hasecke, and Conger 2003; Craig and Martinez 2005), and scholars in other disciplines (Sparks *et al.* 2001; Jewell 2003; Cunningham *et al.* 2003; van der Maas, Kolstein, and van der Pligt 2003) have increasingly embraced the idea that attitudes are a product of a range of potentially conflicting considerations.

As for ambivalence relating to issues of social welfare policy, the evidence is mixed. Whereas some assert that many Americans are ambivalent (Feldman and Zaller 1992; Cantril and Cantril 1999; Hodson, Maio, and Esses 2001), others counter that conflicting attitudes about social welfare are not very prevalent among the general public (Steenbergen and Brewer 2000; Jacoby 2005). The data presented below are clearly at odds with the "not-so-ambivalent" position, suggesting instead that conflict within this important policy domain is fairly common. It is our contention that conclusions drawn on both sides of the argument have typically been based on data that have serious limitations and, as a result, further examination (and a fresh approach) is needed.

Let us begin with Cantril and Cantril (1999; also see Free and Cantril 1967), who concluded that there is a substantial amount of ambivalence within the American public on social welfare issues. Unfortunately, their empirical evidence is not entirely convincing. Lacking direct measures of ambivalence (in a 1996 *New York Times*/CBS News opinion survey), the authors simply *assumed* that ambivalence is present whenever an individual expresses inconsistent opinions about the size of government on the one hand, and spending for social programs on the other, that is, when s/he expresses support for both smaller government and higher spending, or vice versa. Ambivalence, though, is properly defined as the condition of simultaneously possessing both positive and negative evaluations of an attitude object (Alvarez and Brehm 1995; Zaller 1992; Zaller and Feldman 1992; Eagly and Chaiken 1993; Albertson, Brehm, and Alvarez 2005). That being the case, the patterns described by Cantril and Cantril may not signify ambivalence at all because having *inconsistent* positions about government size and government spending is not the same as having *conflicting* positive and negative evaluations regarding a *single object*. While the issues of size and spending are obviously related, there is evidence indicating that attitudes about the former tend to structure attitudes about the latter (Zaller and Feldman 1992; Goren 2001); the implication, then, is that the two are conceptually distinct from one another.

Jacoby (2005) also has questioned the work of Cantril and Cantril, but for different reasons. He argued that the seemingly contradictory (or inconsistent) attitudes identified in that study are not a product of ambivalence, but rather they represent distinctions made by citizens between different types of government spending. His analysis proceeded in three stages. First, using data from the 1992 American National Election Study (NES), Jacoby was initially able to replicate the Cantril–Cantril results reasonably closely. Second, however, he demonstrated that people tend to evaluate government spending based upon whether it involves traditional (and sometimes controversial) "welfare-based" assistance programs (e.g., helping the homeless or poor people, child care, food stamps, aid to big cities or to blacks) or other categories of spending that are very popular and therefore constitute something close to valence issues (e.g., helping college students, protecting the environment, social security, AIDS research). Finally, Jacoby created scales to represent these dimensions and regressed respondents' attitudes about the size and power of government[1] on each. He reasoned that ambivalence would be a plausible explanation if beliefs about government size were found to exert a weak impact on spending preferences; instead, he found a strong positive relationship, even when controlling for a number of other theoretically relevant variables. Thus, he concluded that ambivalence about social welfare policy is not widespread in the United States.

Other patterns of survey response offer support for Jacoby's argument. Most notably, research indicates that some people express opinions in favor of both decreasing government size and increasing government services when the questions are asked separately (Free and Cantril 1967; Sears and Citrin 1985); there is, however, a tendency for this contradiction to dissipate when respondents are made aware of the inherent trade-off (Welch 1985), which suggests that it may not be indicative of genuine ambivalence.

By the same token, the presence of consistencies between attitudes about government size and government spending preferences do not necessarily signify the *absence* of ambivalence. An individual may, for example, believe that government spending should be limited and that services should be reduced, and yet this tells us nothing about the ambivalence that s/he may feel regarding food stamps or any other specific government program. Omnibus surveys (such as the NES and the General Social Survey) simply do not include indicators of social welfare attitudes that gauge simultaneous positive and negative evaluations of the relevant attitude objects. As a result, scholars who use these data to examine ambivalence end up focusing more of their attention on some of the potential *sources* of ambivalence (e.g., value conflict, group affect) than on the actual phenomenon of interest.

The problem is evident again with Steenbergen and Brewer (2000), whose examination of the 1992 NES led them to conclude that the American public is "not-so" ambivalent about social welfare. As with Jacoby, however, a better description of their findings is that the potential sources of social welfare ambivalence (and perhaps ambivalence in other issue domains as well) are "not-so" prevalent. According to Steenbergen and Brewer, studies that assume ambivalence and value conflict to be synonymous are defining ambivalence too narrowly and, consequently, overlooking other types of conflict such as that which may involve a clash between cognition and affect. By including both cognitive-cognitive (value versus value) and cognitive-affective (value versus group affect) conflict in their analysis, these authors attempted to give ambivalence the benefit of the doubt; in the end, they found little evidence of conflict and assumed low levels of ambivalence. To repeat: conflict involving two separate attitude objects is *not* ambivalence; it is a potential (though not the only potential) source of ambivalence. As a result, showing that conflict is low is not the same thing as showing that ambivalence is low. People who experience conflict may or may not experience ambivalence.

Feldman and Zaller (1992) found not only that ambivalence about social welfare is fairly common, but also that there are certain patterns of ambivalence among the mass public. Specifically, liberals are more likely than conservatives to be ambivalent because, according to Feldman and Zaller, the former experience a greater degree of value conflict: whereas equality and individualism are of roughly equal importance for liberals, conservatives tend to place more emphasis on individualism; thus, individualism usually trumps egalitarianism for conservatives, while it is fair fight between the two values among liberals—a fight that supposedly leads to higher levels of ambivalence about social welfare. However, evidence from a number of studies raises questions about key aspects of the Feldman–Zaller argument. Women and blacks, for example, generally support social welfare programs in disproportionate numbers (Kaufmann and Petrocik 1999; Goren 2001; Gilens 1988, 1995; Bobo and Kluegel 1993; Tate 1994;

Kinder and Winter 2001), but the relative importance of equality and individualism do *not* appear to be roughly equivalent among women and blacks, as Zaller and Feldman might lead us to expect (Kinder and Sanders 1996; Feather 2004; also see Jacoby 2002).

It is possible that Feldman and Zaller's findings are to some extent a function of the indicators they employed. They measured ambivalence by counting the number of conflicting considerations (e.g., a mix of liberal and conservative comments), spontaneous statements of ambivalence (e.g., "I see merit in both sides"), and two-sided remarks (e.g., "People should try to get ahead on their own, but government should help when necessary") that were offered in response to open-ended probes in the 1987 NES Pilot Study.[2] The problem is that any or all of these comments might be offered without ambivalence necessarily being present. For example, research suggests that many African Americans would probably agree with the statement, "Although I think people are responsible for their financial conditions, I nevertheless support social welfare" (see Kinder and Sanders 1996). Under the coding scheme employed by Feldman and Zaller, black respondents who make such a statement would be categorized as ambivalent when in fact they may not be—especially if those respondents happen to place a higher priority on egalitarian values than on individualist values.

In sum, the existing literature does not provide a definitive answer either way regarding the prevalence of ambivalence about social welfare issues. Further, because of the limitations of the data used by those on both sides of the debate, it is unclear what kinds of people are likely to be ambivalent and what kinds of people are not. The remainder of this chapter provides a fresh approach to the measurement of social welfare ambivalence, and an exploration of its potential causes.

THE POTENTIAL SOURCES OF AMBIVALENCE: VALUE CONFLICT, VALUE IMPORTANCE, AND POLICY PREFERENCES

As is evident from our brief review, discussions about the prevalence of ambivalence and its sources are often conflated. Some observers presume that where they think they see ambivalence, there must be value conflict, while others suggest that where there is value conflict, there must be ambivalence. As we shall see, value conflict is an important part of the story of ambivalence, but it is hardly the whole story.

Core Values and Attitudes about Social Welfare

People possess a range of core values that help to structure their attitudes toward specific objects (Rokeach 1973; Schwartz and Bilsky 1987;

Schwartz 1992; see Feldman 2003 for a review). As in chapter four, core values are defined here as "overarching normative principles and belief assumptions about government, citizenship, and American society" (McCann 1997: 565), including, for example, egalitarianism, individualism, and moral traditionalism. These principles and assumptions facilitate position-taking in more concrete domains by serving as general focal points in an otherwise confusing political environment (Jacoby 2002). Accordingly, prior research has shown that values such as egalitarianism (Feldman 1988; Feldman and Zaller 1992; McCann 1997; Feldman and Steenbergen 2001; Goren 2001; also see Gilens 1995) and economic individualism (Feldman 1988; Feldman and Zaller 1992; McCann 1997; Goren 2001; also see Gilens 1995) are related to citizens' attitudes about social welfare.[3] Although different studies may conceptualize, operationalize, and label the values in different ways, there is broad agreement that greater individualism is associated with less support, and greater egalitarianism with higher support, for social welfare programs and spending.

Value Conflict and Value Importance

What happens when a person possesses both individualist *and* egalitarian values? One might assume that conflict such as this will result in ambivalence and, indeed, value conflict is the most often mentioned source of ambivalence in the literature (Katz and Hass 1988; Katz, Wackenhut, and Hass 1986; Eagly and Chaiken 1993; Alvarez and Brehm 1995; Craig, Martinez, and Kane 2002; Craig *et al.* 2005b, and chapter four in this volume; Newby-Clark, McGregor, and Zanna 2005). Yet even if the assumption here is correct, it is possible that *value hierarchies* (Rokeach 1973; Schwartz 1992; Jacoby 2002) exist and are structured in ways that sometimes serve to reduce the likelihood of ambivalence occurring. If an individual places more importance on one value than another, and if an issue arises that happens to pit these values against each other, the conflict won't necessarily matter; simply, the preferred value will prevail and determine the person's response to the issue in question. Jacoby (2002) presents evidence suggesting that most citizens can, in fact, rank their values in some order of importance, that is, they infrequently place equal importance on values of equality and liberty, among others. Thus, if conflict between egalitarianism and individualism is *potentially* a source of ambivalence about social welfare policy, we nevertheless should expect lower levels of ambivalence among people who consider one of those two values to be much more important than the other.

Policy Preferences

Previous research has suggested that the probability of an individual feeling ambivalent about a policy issue may be related to the person's position on that issue. As noted earlier, Feldman and Zaller (1992) concluded that social welfare liberals, who tend to place a high value on both egalitarianism and individualism, are more prone to ambivalence than conservatives. The doubts that we have raised about this finding notwithstanding, there are issues on which policy preferences are related to ambivalence. Pro-life voters, for example, tend to be more ambivalent about whether abortion should be legal under "traumatic" circumstances, while pro-choice voters are more ambivalent about the legality of "elective" abortions (Craig, Martinez, and Kane 2002). Also, people with more positive views about homosexuality in general are less ambivalent about gay rights on issues that do *not* directly involve children or marriage (Craig *et al.* 2005b).

Putting all of these various ideas together, the following analysis tests a model of social welfare ambivalence that examines the impact of *value conflict, value importance,* and *policy preferences.* The argument is fairly straightforward: first, we expect to find more ambivalence about social welfare policy among those who hold conflicting individualist and egalitarian values. Next, as one value becomes more important relative to the other, the level of ambivalence should decline. Finally, liberal social welfare policy preferences are predicted to be negatively (not positively, as in the Feldman–Zaller study) associated with ambivalence about social welfare.

DATA AND MEASUREMENT

The present study is based on a telephone poll conducted from May 10 to 22, 2004 by the *Florida Voter* survey organization. Six hundred and seven respondents were chosen randomly from a list of all registered voters in the state of Florida; only those whose names were drawn from the list were actually interviewed. Up to four callbacks were attempted on all working numbers and initial refusals. The margin of error is plus or minus 4 percentage points. The survey itself included measures of values, value importance, social group membership, attitudes about social welfare, ambivalence about social welfare, and a variety of control variables.[4]

The dependent variable, *ambivalence about social welfare,* is measured using a method that was adapted from the experimental literature by Craig and his colleagues (2002, 2005b; also see chapter four in this volume). Respondents were asked to indicate *both* how positively *and* how negatively they viewed several aspects of social welfare policy, using batteries of questions that were introduced as follows:

> I'm now going to read you a series of *statements* about the kinds of things some people think the government should be doing to address certain problems that are facing the country. After each, I'd like you to rate the statement

on a 4-point scale to indicate how *positively* you feel toward it. If you do not have any positive feelings, give it the lowest rating of 1; if you have some positive feelings, rate it a 2; if you have generally positive feelings, rate it a 3; and if you have extremely positive feelings, rate it a 4. Please rate each statement based solely on how positively you feel about it, *while ignoring or setting aside for the moment any negative feelings you may have.* The first statement is . . .

The statements were then read and respondents were asked to rate each one separately. Then, following a number of filler questions, the introduction was repeated except with the words "positive" and "positively" replaced by "negative" and "negatively." If a person seemed unsure or confused at any point, interviewers were told to repeat the instructions as many times as necessary.

The specific aspects of social welfare policy (based on questions from the NES as well as recent news stories) that respondents were asked to evaluate are as follows: "The government should . . ."

- ensure that every citizen has adequate medical insurance;
- provide programs to help homeless people find a place to live;
- ensure that every child has access to a good education;
- provide programs that improve the standard of living of poor Americans;
- see to it that everyone who wants a job has one;
- provide childcare programs to assist working parents;
- ensure that the retirement benefits that citizens have built up over the years are protected.

An index of *ambivalence about social welfare policy* was calculated using the algorithm developed by Thompson, Zanna, and Griffin (1995; also see Kaplan 1972).[5] Specifically,

$$\text{Ambivalence} = \frac{P+N}{2} - |P-N|$$

where P is the positive reaction score and N is the negative reaction score. The range of scores for each of the seven items described above is -0.5 through 4.0, with intervals of 0.5 (see Craig, Martinez, and Kane 2002). A principal components factor analysis confirmed that all seven load on a single factor, and the reliability of an additive index constructed from them is very good ($\alpha = .860$).

To measure core values, respondents were read a series of companion statements and asked to say which came closer to their own opinion. For *individualism*,[6] the item pairs were (1) the government should see to it that every person has a job and a good standard of living; or, the government should just let each person get ahead on their own; and (2) we need a strong government to handle today's complex economic problems; or, the free market can handle these problems without government being involved. For *egalitarianism*, the item pairs were (1) we have gone too far in pushing equal rights in this country; or, we should do more to make sure that everyone is treated equally; and (2) if people were treated more equally in this country, we would have many fewer problems; or, this country would be better off if we worried less about how equal people are. In all cases except the last, responses were coded from 1 (strong support for the first statement in the pair) to 5 (strong support for the second statement); for the second egalitarianism pair, this scoring was reversed to provide consistency in direction of wording. The two sets of items were then combined into indices with scores ranging from 2 to 10 (high values reflecting stronger support for individualist or egalitarian values).[7]

A measure of *value conflict*, which captures the magnitude of the difference between them, was calculated using the same algorithm as the one described earlier for measuring social welfare ambivalence; that is,

$$\text{Value Conflict} = \frac{[\text{individualism} + \text{egalitarianism}]}{2} - |\,\text{individualism} - \text{egalitarianism}\,|$$

with higher values representing more conflict. *Value importance* is based on responses to two separate items, introduced as follows: "As you know, not everyone agrees on the different goals or values that our nation ought to pursue. I'm going to list three different goals and have you tell me how important each of them is to you personally." The importance of egalitarianism and individualism was then determined based on answers to a pair of questions:

- The first goal is *equality*, by which we mean a narrowing of the gap in wealth and power between rich and poor. How important is equality to you—extremely important, important, only somewhat important, or not important at all? . . .
- And the third goal is *a free marketplace*, by which we mean all citizens having a chance to get ahead on their own without the government getting involved. How important is a free marketplace to you— extremely important, important, only somewhat important, or not important at all?[8]

Responses were recoded to range from 1 to 4, with higher values representing greater importance. In the aggregate, respondents regarded egalitarianism and individualism as being about equally salient; the mean score for egalitarianism is 3.00 (with a standard deviation of 0.90), and for individualism is 3.03

(with a standard deviation of 0.87). Thus, each value was seen as important, but neither was universally acclaimed. At the individual level, the absence of a relationship between the two measures ($r = -.02$, $p = .61$) confirms our suspicions that they are tapping separate constructs.

In addition, the *relative* importance of one value as opposed to the other was calculated as the absolute value of individualism importance subtracted from egalitarianism importance; higher numbers on a scale of one to three indicate that one of these values has priority over the other for the individual. There is a moderate negative correlation ($r = -.30$, $p < .01$) between relative importance and the absolute level of importance attached to egalitarianism, and a slight negative relationship ($r = -.07$, $p = .08$) between Relative and Absolute importance of individualism.

Two separate items are used to measure respondents' social welfare policy preferences. First, it has been suggested that attitudes about social welfare are shaped in part by one's perceptions of which groups gain most from the various programs; apart from the obvious (poor people), many citizens think of African Americans as being among the principal beneficiaries of governmental welfare policies (e.g., Sniderman, Brody, and Tetlock 1991; Cook and Barrett 1992; Bobo and Kluegel 1993; Gilens 1995; see also Jacoby 2005). Accordingly, *feelings about welfare beneficiaries* is measured by an additive index ($\alpha = .772$) based on answers to two questions tapping respondents' affect toward "poor people" and "blacks."[9] Next, *general preferences on social welfare* were measured by asking respondents the following question:

> Some people think the government should provide fewer services, even in areas such as health and education, in order to reduce spending. Others feel it is important for the government to provide more services to citizens even if it means an increase in spending. Which of these positions is closer to your own views? [Do you feel strongly or not so strongly about this?]

Answers were scored from 1 (strongly prefer fewer services and reduced spending) to 5 (strongly prefer more services even if it means higher taxes).[10]

We also include control variables for *race* (0 = non-black, 1 = black) and *gender* (0 = male, 1 = female). The particular importance of social welfare issues in defining both the gender gap (Gilens 1988; Kaufman and Petrocik 1999; Goren 2001) and the racial cleavage (Bobo and Kluegel 1993; Tate 1994; Gilens 1995; Kinder and Winter 2001) in American politics suggests the possibility that women and blacks might be, *ceteris paribus*, less ambivalent about social welfare policies than men and non-blacks, respectively.[11] In sum, the model we propose can be stated as follows:

Social welfare ambivalence $= a + \beta_1$ Value Conflict $+ \beta_2$ Egalitarianism Importance $+ \beta_3$ Individualism Importance $+ \beta_4$ Relative Importance of Values + β_5 Feelings about Beneficiaries + β_6 General Preferences on Services/Spending + β_7 Female + β_8 Black + e

RESULTS

The results shown in table 3.1 suggest that, while there is some degree of variability in the levels of ambivalence observed across seven program areas that form the basis for the social welfare ambivalence index, these levels are far from trivial. For the sample as a whole, mean scores are higher on policies that would assist the homeless, improve the standard of living of poor Americans, ensure full employment, and provide childcare programs to assist working parents; on each of these issues, more than half of the Florida sample have ambivalence scores greater than 0. Ambivalence is less common with regard to universal medical insurance, programs to ensure that all children receive a good education, and protecting retirement benefits. Overall, despite the variation that is evident here, a single seven-item social welfare ambivalence index scales well (see above) and will be used as the dependent variable for the remainder of this analysis.

Table 3.2 displays the bivariate correlations (Tau$_b$) between each of the independent variables and the social welfare ambivalence index. As expected, value conflict is positively correlated with ambivalence in this important policy area; in other words, to the degree that an individual simultaneously supports both egalitarianism and individualism, the more likely that person is to express ambivalence about social welfare. The effects

Table 3.1 Frequency and intensity of ambivalence about social welfare

Condition	Mean score	Standard deviation	Percent ambivalent (%)
Medical insurance	0.41	1.32	35.4
Homeless	0.95	1.27	61.4
Education	0.31	1.40	27.3
Standard of living	0.97	1.26	61.4
Job guarantee	0.89	1.36	56.5
Child care	0.76	1.29	52.6
Retirement benefits	0.36	1.46	28.0
Ambivalence index	4.65	6.90	48.3
Number of cases	607		

Note: Data are from a *Florida Voter* survey of registered voters conducted in May 2004. Table entries indicate the (a) mean ambivalence score for each item (scores ranging from -0.5 to $+4.0$), and for the combined scale (scores from -3.5 to $+28.0$); (b) associated standard deviation; and (c) percentage of respondents with scores greater than zero for a given item. The 48.3 percent listed at the bottom of column three is the mean percentage who are ambivalent across the seven items.

Table 3.2 Correlations between independent variables and social welfare ambivalence

Independent variable	Tau_b	Significance
Value conflict	0.15	0.00
Egalitarianism importance	−0.19	0.00
Individualism importance	−0.13	0.00
Relative importance	−0.02	0.72
Feelings about beneficiaries	−0.20	0.00
General preferences about social welfare: services/spending	−0.11	0.24
Gender (female)	−0.07	0.03
Race (black)	−0.15	0.00
Number of cases	607	

Note: Data are from a *Florida Voter* survey of registered voters conducted in May 2004. Social welfare ambivalence is measured using the seven-item index described in the text. The meaning of high scores on race and gender variables is shown in parentheses.

of value importance also are evident in table 3.2: as egalitarianism and individualism increase in importance for respondents, ambivalence tends to decrease. Relative importance of the two values has no significant zero–order relationship with ambivalence but, as we shall see, this result changes in the more fully specified model presented below. The correlations here also indicate that blacks are less ambivalent than non-blacks, women are less ambivalent than men, and ambivalence is lower among those respondents (1) who express more positive sentiments toward potential welfare beneficiaries, and (2) with more favorable general dispositions to support social welfare.

As the ambivalence index is best seen as an ordinal variable, we employed an ordered logit procedure to estimate the multivariate model. Table 3.3 shows that there are multiple sources of ambivalence about social welfare policy among respondents in our sample. Much of the existing literature focuses on the relevance of value conflict as a precursor to ambivalence, and that is borne out in these findings. The positive and significant coefficient on the value conflict variable indicates that people who expressed higher levels of both individualism *and* egalitarianism also exhibited higher levels of ambivalence, *ceteris paribus*. That is hardly surprising, of course, in light of previous research on ambivalence in other policy areas (including abortion, gay rights, and race).

We also see from table 3.3 that value importance accounts for a portion of the variation in social welfare ambivalence: respondents who regarded either egalitarianism or individualism (or both) as important were less likely to be ambivalent, which suggests that a person's core values can sometimes

Table 3.3 Multivariate model of social welfare ambivalence

Independent variable	Coefficient	Standard error	Confidence intervals (95%)	
Value conflict	0.13	0.02	0.08	0.17
Egalitarianism importance	−0.35	0.09	−0.52	−0.18
Individualism importance	−0.44	0.09	−0.61	−0.28
Relative importance	−0.25	0.09	−0.41	−0.08
Feelings about beneficiaries	−0.19	0.05	−0.28	−0.09
General preferences about social welfare: services/spending	−0.15	0.05	−0.25	−0.05
Gender (female)	−0.18	0.15	−0.46	0.11
Race (black)	−0.95	0.26	−1.47	−0.43
−2 log likelihood	4,290.997			
Nagelkerke pseudo R^2	0.191			
Number of cases	607			

Note: Data are from a *Florida Voter* survey of registered voters conducted in May 2004. Table entries are ordered logit coefficients, associated standard errors, and 95% confidence intervals; threshold levels are not shown. The meaning of high scores on race and gender variables is shown in parentheses.

block out conflicting feelings about social welfare. This is especially so among those who score high in relative importance (rating one of the values above the other); that is, a larger *difference* between the importance attached to individualism and egalitarianism is negatively and significantly associated with ambivalence, even when controlling for the levels of importance accorded to the values themselves. Thus, while value conflict normally tends to heighten ambivalence, ambivalence becomes less likely to occur when one value is held more dearly than the other.

Ambivalence also is asymmetric with respect to policy preferences. The significant and negative coefficients in rows 5 and 6 of the table indicate that respondents who are more supportive of higher levels of government services and spending, as well as those who feel more warmly about the likely beneficiaries of welfare programs, tend to be less ambivalent about social welfare policy as a whole. Since ambivalence is related to attitudinal pliability (e.g., Craig, Martinez, and Kane 2005a), this finding has the important political implication that conservatives may be more likely than liberals to be "talked out of" their general opposition to social welfare in specific circumstances and conditions. Whereas Feldman and Zaller (1992) maintained that social welfare liberals are more conflicted than conservatives, hence more ambivalent, these results suggest that (controlling for value importance and value conflict), liberals actually are *less* torn between the pros and cons of social welfare policy.

Finally, gender is not significant but the coefficient for race indicates that black respondents tend to be significantly less ambivalent than non-blacks, *ceteris paribus.* Preliminary analyses showed that women were less ambivalent about social welfare than men (4.11 and 5.44, respectively, on the index, $p(t) = .02$), but the trivial logit coefficient in the multivariate model demonstrates that this difference is accounted for by value conflict, value importance, feelings toward beneficiaries, and attitudes about government services and spending. The same is not true for race, as the black coefficient remains negative and significant in the multivariate model. This result may reflect the impact of cultural factors, with the longstanding support of blacks, in the aggregate, for social welfare programs having perhaps become a part of their political identity. While the data employed here do not permit a test of that argument, the pattern for blacks raises further questions about the assertion that liberals are more ambivalent about social welfare than conservatives.

Conclusion

Questions about the appropriate breadth of the social safety net that has helped to define political cleavages in the United States since at least the New Deal realignment remain difficult ones even today. The American creed respects the worth and liberty of the individual, as well as beliefs in equality of opportunity and compassion for people who have been deprived of opportunities by fates not under their own control. In the polity and society as a whole, the clash of those values is played out again and again through political battles in campaigns, the media, legislatures, bureaucracies, and the courts. Individual citizens, as well, often struggle to reconcile how (and whether) their underlying values relate to current manifestations of the policy debates about the social safety net.

In this chapter, we began by arguing that a fresh approach is needed to measuring ambivalence about social welfare. Some scholars, including those who have wrongly inferred the existence of ambivalence from observations of value conflict, maintain that it is fairly common; others, using indicators that are equally indirect, disagree. An accurate assessment requires some approach to capturing ambivalence that is separate from its hypothesized antecedents and consequences. The measure employed here, adapted from previous work in social psychology and political science (Craig, Kane, and Martinez 2002; Craig *et al.* 2005b), suggests that a sizable chunk of the American public is, in fact, ambivalent to some degree about social welfare.

The findings also indicate that ambivalence about social welfare is multifaceted. Previous literature has focused on value conflict as a precursor of ambivalence, and that conclusion is supported in the analysis presented here. Other attributes of values and attitudes, however, also underlay ambivalence for some individuals. Specifically, the felt importance of values (both absolute and relative), as well as a person's policy preferences, shape ambivalence in ways that have interesting theoretical and political implications. It may therefore be fruitful to consider whether and how various aspects of value hierarchies or attitude structure affect ambivalence on public policy issues.

Finally, while the evidence indicates that liberals are less ambivalent about social welfare than conservatives, and blacks are less ambivalent than non-blacks, the reason(s) for these differences are not entirely clear. Further exploration into value differences across groups is needed in order to more fully understand why some kinds of people are more ambivalent than others. For now, though, we have clear evidence that many citizens have conflicting views about one of the central cleavages in contemporary American politics.

Notes

1. This measure was a three-item index tapping people's beliefs about whether (a) government should be more or less active; (b) today's complex economic problems should be left to the free market or handled by a strong government; and (c) government has grown because our problems are bigger or because it has become involved in things that people should do for themselves. See Jacoby (2005).
2. The probes ("what ideas come to mind . . . ?") were asked in conjunction with standard forced-choice questions relating to job guarantees, aid to blacks, and government services and spending.
3. Feldman and Steenbergen (2001) contend that "humanitarianism" also is important as a predictor of citizens' attitudes about social welfare.
4. Additional information can be obtained from the authors, or from *Florida Voter* directly (954–584–0204). In order to avoid an unacceptable loss of cases in our analysis, we employed the MICE ("multiple imputation using chained equations"; see Horton and Lipsitz 2001) routine in the R statistical package to impute missing data. MICE does this by replacing each missing value with a random draw from a distribution estimated from a maximum likelihood function based on other variables in the dataset. The imputed dataset was based on the mean values from five replicate datasets created by MICE.
5. This model is derived from a version of the semantic differential (Osgood, Suci, and Tannenbaum 1957), as modified by Kaplan (1972) in an effort to show that people's overall attitudes are made up of both positive and negative elements. Thompson and her colleagues (1995) adjusted the model to better account for the presence of polarized beliefs. See Craig, Kane, and Martinez (2002) for a more complete discussion of this measure as employed in a large-sample survey.
6. These questions were designed to tap support for *economic* individualism, or a belief in the freedom to accumulate wealth. Scholars with a different substantive focus might prefer to measure individualism differently, for example, conceptualizing it in terms of a belief in freedom of expression.

7. Correlations (Pearson's r) are .180, $p < .001$ for the two individualism pairs and .244, $p < .001$ for the two egalitarianism pairs. The stronger relationships that are typically found when similar items are presented individually to respondents rather than as pairwise comparisons (e.g., see Goren 2001) may be, to some degree, a product of the response set problem that often plagues agree–disagree questions.

8. The survey included a measure of the salience of traditional moral values, which was asked in between these two questions.

9. These particular items were drawn from a battery of questions (using the same format as that employed for measuring ambivalence) asking respondents to state how positively (and how negatively, though the latter is not examined here) they felt about a number of social and political groups; as before, scores range from 1 (no positive feelings) to 4 (extremely positive feelings). While poor people and blacks are obviously not the same thing, empirical results both here and elsewhere (e.g., Goren 2001) reveal a strong pattern of covariation in how people feel about the two groups.

10. This item was part of an experiment in which half the sample was asked the question with one additional option ("or are you torn between the two?") added at the end. People were naturally more likely to select a "mixed" response that was presented to them (24.0 percent said they were torn) than to volunteer one on their own (12.5 percent). Both groups are combined for purposes of the analysis here. In addition, we added a dummy variable for question form, as well as an interaction between that dummy and scores on the services/spending item, to the multivariate analysis presented below. The coefficients for both the form dummy and the interaction term were trivial, and their inclusion had no substantive effects on the interpretation of the remaining coefficients. For the sake of parsimony, those variables are therefore omitted from the model as reported in table 3.3.

11. Since Latinos in the aggregate are more liberal, at least on certain issues, than whites (Welch and Sigelman 1993; DeSipio 1996; Uhlaner, Gray, and Garcia 2000; Alvarez and Bedolla 2003; also see de la Garza, Falcon, and Garcia 1996), we might normally expect their level of social welfare ambivalence to be similar to that found among blacks and women. Unfortunately, this proposition cannot be tested because the race indicator used here does not make distinctions among different groups of Latino citizens. In particular, we know that Cubans tend to be more conservative than other Latinos (especially Puerto Ricans, but also Mexicans; see de la Garza *et al.* 1992) and there is a large Cuban population in Florida. As a result, it is not surprising to learn that the Latinos in the *Florida Voter* survey do not, on average, differ significantly from whites in terms of the variables that are most critical to our analysis.

CHAPTER FOUR

AMBIVALENCE AND VALUE CONFLICT:
A TEST OF TWO ISSUES

Michael D. Martinez, Stephen C. Craig,
James G. Kane, and Jason Gainous

The essays in this volume and its companion, *Ambivalence and the Structure of Political Opinion* (Craig and Martinez 2005), add to a growing literature on the frequency, nature, and consequences of ambivalence in public opinion. It now seems clear, for example, that considerable proportions of the population do not necessarily possess a single "true" attitude on many political issues, but rather a store of multiple and sometimes conflicting attitudes that they might draw upon at any given time (Zaller and Feldman 1992; also see Tesser 1978; Hochschild 1981; Tourangeau and Rasinski 1988; Zaller 1992; Schwartz and Bless 1992; Wilson and Hodges 1992; Hill and Kriesi 2001). While scholars have collectively explored the existence of ambivalence across a number of policy domains (e.g., Alvarez and Brehm 1995, 1997; Craig, Kane, and Martinez 2002; Craig *et al.* 2005b; Jacoby 2005), its source has yet to be conclusively identified. Theory contends that the principal underlying source of attitudinal ambivalence is value conflict (Alvarez and Brehm 1995; Eagly and Chaiken 1993; Zaller 1992; Katz and Hass 1988), but that conclusion is more often assumed or inferred than empirically demonstrated at the individual level. In this chapter, we focus on the issues of abortion and gay rights, offering evidence in support of the argument that ambivalence is indeed rooted in the clash of core values.

Why abortion and gay rights? Both seem to be quintessentially "easy" issues, as defined by Carmines and Stimson (1980; also see Leege *et al.* 2002): they are highly symbolic, have been on the public agenda for decades, and are frequently discussed in terms of "policy ends" rather than as means toward achieving a policy objective. In the years since the 1973 Supreme Court ruling in *Roe v. Wade*, abortion has polarized a sizable portion of the voting public (Abramowitz 1995) and appeared at times to turn elections, from school board to Congress, into referendums on abortion alone. For activists, the stakes are especially high. On one side, there is talk of genocide being waged against unborn children; on the other, the issue is framed in terms of maintaining personal freedoms that it took women decades (and considerable effort) to achieve.

Much the same thing can be said about gay rights, especially in the years since the 1969 Stonewall Riots in New York City prompted many gays and lesbians to come out of the closet politically. This development, in turn, encouraged the Christian Right to mobilize against what they perceived as an emerging "gay agenda." Whereas gays and lesbians have portrayed their cause as a quest for equality, linked to similar struggles by other underrepresented groups, much of the opposition is rooted in traditionalism and the defense of social institutions that once supported the traditional family (D'Emilio 2000; Green 2000).

Activists on both sides of these issues are generally portrayed as having strong, consistent, and relatively extreme opinions. In contrast, surveys indicate that at least a plurality of Americans hold centrist or "situationalist" views on abortion (Bardes and Oldendick 2003: 190–192), and that public attitudes toward gay rights have grown noticeably more tolerant in recent years (Wilcox and Wolpert 2000).[1] In the analysis presented here, we show that many citizens are ambivalent about each of these controversial issues and, further, that such ambivalence is rooted in value conflict. Based on these findings, it is our contention that neither the nature nor the political relevance of public opinion regarding abortion and gay rights can be fully understood without taking ambivalence into account.

THE CONCEPT OF AMBIVALENCE

Researchers traditionally have assumed that attitudes can be measured as if they lie somewhere along a bipolar continuum that ranges from positive (or favorable) to negative (or unfavorable), with a neutral point in between (Thurstone 1928; Thurstone and Chave 1929; see Eagly and Chaiken 1993 for a review). This unidimensional view conforms to our intuitive sense that people tend to think in bipolar terms about most things. When they watch a movie or eat a meal, they usually classify it as either "good" or "bad" (or, representing the continuum and its neutral point, as "so-so"); and in the political realm, candidates and elected officials are often described ideologically as being either "liberal," "conservative," or "middle-of-the-road."

On the surface, describing something as both good *and* bad, or a candidate as both liberal *and* conservative, seems counterintuitive. Yet in real life we can, and do, evaluate objects as if they contained separate components. Politicians, for example, are seen as being liberal on some issues but conservative on others (Abelson *et al.* 1982), with the summation of these perceptions presumably telling us whether they fall, overall, into one category or the other. Feldman (1995: 266) described this process as the "distributions of considerations" and argued that an opinion expressed in response to a survey question provides only an estimate of the central tendency of an individual's attitudes or beliefs on that subject.

When someone's evaluations or beliefs about an attitude object are in conflict, we describe that person as being *ambivalent*. The concept of ambivalence is not new (e.g., Kaplan 1972; Scott 1969), especially to social psychologists who on numerous occasions have used experimental data to demonstrate empirically the existence of an ambivalence dimension based on the assumption that attitudes can indeed contain separate positive and negative components (see Newby-Clark, McGregor, and Zanna 2002; Hodson, Maio, and Esses 2001; Armitage and Connor 2000; Jonas, Diehl, and Brömer 1997; Priester and Petty 1996; Thompson, Zanna, and Griffin 1995; Cacioppo and Berntson 1994; Katz, Wackenhut, and Hass 1986; Klopfer and Madden 1980). The essays in this volume highlight the greater attention that political scientists and survey researchers have paid to ambivalence in recent years (see Craig and Martinez 2005; McGraw, Hasecke, and Conger 2003; Craig, Kane, and Martinez 2002; Frankovic and McDermott 2001; Lavine 2001; Meffert, Guge, and Lodge 2000; Cantril and Cantril 1999; Alvarez and Brehm 1995; Feldman and Zaller 1992). Nevertheless, neither social psychologists nor political scientists have offered clear empirical evidence of the origins of attitudinal ambivalence.

THE ORIGINS OF AMBIVALENCE

Why are some people ambivalent and others are not? In recent years, researchers have increasingly become aware of the central role played by core values in structuring citizens' behavior and their views on specific issues. Values are "overarching normative principles and belief assumptions about government, citizenship, and American society. . . . Individualism, faith in the free enterprise system, a sense of equality or fair play, and views on public morality are all examples of core values that Americans might call upon" (McCann 1997: 565; also see Jacoby 2002; Feldman and Zaller 1992; Feldman 1988). Although it is generally believed that ambivalence occurs when there is a *conflict* involving a person's core values (Alvarez and Brehm 1995; Eagly and Chaiken 1993; Katz and Hass 1988), the evidence showing this to be the case is limited. In their study of political tolerance, Peffley and his colleagues (2001) assumed that value conflict and ambivalence are interchangeable terms yet failed to demonstrate an actual link between the two using either objective or subjective measures of ambivalence. Using a very different approach, Alvarez and Brehm (1995; also see Albertson, Brehm, and Alvarez 2005) inferred the presence of ambivalence in citizens' attitudes about abortion from patterns of error variance in heteroskedastic probit models of binary choice. However, their interpretation rests on an inference about an individual level attribute (ambivalence) from aggregate-level data (error variance), and they *define* the existence of ambivalence as error variance that is correlated with the coincidence of conflicting values. Thus, although Alvarez and Brehm can compare the level of ambivalence in the general public across issues, the relationship between ambivalence on any given issue and value conflict is assumed rather than tested directly at the individual level.

Several studies have reported a relationship between such core values as authoritarianism, moral traditionalism, and individualism on the one hand, and citizens' attitudes on either abortion or gay rights on the other (Brewer 2003; Wilcox and Wolpert 2000; Whitley and Lee 2000; Lewis and Rogers 1999; Luker 1984; Schnell 1993; Domke, Shah, and Wackman 1998; Zucker 1999). It is widely assumed, for example, that the current mix of supportive (civil rights and liberties) and nonsupportive (morality) beliefs shared by popular majorities are due in part to the fact that many Americans "hold clashing values in the debate over gay rights—traditional morality versus individual freedom and equality" (Wilcox and Norrander 2002: 138). In other words, evidence that the mass public as a whole is of two minds on these issues may reflect a considerable amount of ambivalence at the individual level, and that ambivalence may be a product of the conflicting core values shared by many citizens. These are the central hypotheses regarding the origins of ambivalence that are tested in the following analysis.

DATA AND METHODOLOGY

The present study is based on three telephone polls of Florida residents conducted by the *Florida Voter* survey organization. All three designs were cross-sectional statewide surveys. Two of these (March 1998, $N = 608$; January/February 1999, $N = 708$) focused on abortion attitudes, while the third (June 2002, $N = 601$) examined attitudes toward homosexuality and gay rights. Both sampling frame (registered voters in 1998–1999, adult residents aged 18 and above in 2002) and selection procedure (random-digit dialing in 1998 and 2002, random selection from voter registration rolls in 1999) varied somewhat across the three surveys.[2] Despite this, however, the overall similarity of our results for 1998 and 1999, and of the social and political composition of the samples in all years, gives us confidence that we are dealing with three essentially equivalent groups.

We employ a measure of ambivalence that is modeled on experimental work by social psychologists and adapted for use in large-sample surveys (see Craig, Kane, and Martinez 2002; Craig *et al.* 2005b).[3] Respondents were asked to indicate *both* how positively *and* how negatively they viewed several aspects of the abortion and gay rights issues, using batteries of questions that were introduced as follows:

> I'm now going to read a series of statements about [abortion/issues involving homosexuals, that is, gay men and lesbians]. After each, I'd like you to rate each statement on a 4-point scale to indicate how *positively* you feel toward the statement. If you do not have any positive feelings toward the statement, give the statement the lowest rating of 1; if you have some positive feelings, rate it a 2; if you have generally positive feelings, rate it a 3; and if you have extremely positive feelings, rate it a 4. Please rate each statement based solely on how positively you feel about it, *while ignoring or setting aside for the moment any negative feelings you may have for the statement.* The first statement is . . .

The various statements were then read and respondents were asked to rate each one separately. Subsequently, the same introduction was repeated except with the words "positive" and "positively" changed to "negative" and "negatively." If a person seemed unsure or confused at any point, interviewers were told to repeat the instructions as many times as necessary.

For the 1998 and 1999 abortion surveys, respondents were asked to evaluate either six or seven statements based on questions that have been a more-or-less regular feature of the General Social Surveys since the early 1970s: "A woman should be able to obtain a legal abortion if . . ."

- there is a strong chance of serious defect in the baby;
- she is married and does not want any more children;
- the woman's own health is seriously endangered by the pregnancy;
- the family has a very low income and cannot afford any more children;
- she became pregnant as a result of rape;
- she is not married and does not want to marry the man;
- she wants it for any reason.[4]

In the 2002 survey, respondents evaluated a series of eight statements derived from various opinion polls, published scholarly research, and recent news stories:

- Homosexuals should be allowed to teach in schools.
- Marriages between homosexuals should be recognized as legal.
- Homosexuals should be allowed to serve in the United States military.
- Homosexuals should be legally permitted to adopt children.
- What homosexuals do in the privacy of their own homes is nobody else's business.
- There should be laws to protect homosexuals against discrimination in their jobs.

- Homosexuals should be allowed to join the Boy Scouts and other youth organizations.
- Homosexual couples should be able to obtain family health insurance coverage, the same way other people do.

For both abortion and gay rights, we calculate a measure of ambivalence using the algorithm developed by Thompson, Zanna, and Griffin (1995); that is,

$$\text{Ambivalence} = \left[\frac{P + N}{2}\right] - |P - N|$$

where P is the positive reaction score and N is the negative reaction score.[5] The resultant scores range from -0.5 ("extremely" positive and no negative feelings, or "extremely" negative and no positive) to $+4.0$ ("extremely" positive *and* negative feelings for the same statement).

AMBIVALENCE ABOUT ABORTION AND GAY RIGHTS

Our data indicate that many Floridians have ambivalent feelings about both abortion and gay rights (see table 4.1). In the 1998 survey, 67.8 percent exhibited at least a minimal level of ambivalence (defined as scores of 0.5 or greater) on at least one of the GSS abortion statements, 49.1 percent on at least two of them, and 28.9 percent on three or more; the corresponding totals for 1999 are 73.6, 58.8, and 41.5 percent, respectively. The "average" respondent[6] was ambivalent on 1.66 of the six statements presented in 1998, and 2.24 of the seven in 1999.[7] There was no significant difference between self-described pro-choice and pro-life voters in either survey, that is, a similar proportion of citizens on both sides of this issue seemed to be experiencing some degree of internal conflict.

Although the level of ambivalence observed on any single abortion item is less than overwhelming, it is far from negligible. Floridians were least ambivalent about a rape victim's right to obtain a legal abortion (21.4 percent in 1998, 24.5 percent in 1999), and most ambivalent about the "family too poor" condition in 1998 (33.7 percent) and "no more children" in 1999 (36.3 percent). Cook and her colleagues (1992: 33) found that Americans were considerably more supportive of a woman's right to choose what they called a *traumatic abortion* (under circumstances involving "woman's health," "rape," or "birth defect") as opposed to an *elective abortion* ("too poor," "no more children," "not married," "any reason").[8] Our results mimic that finding for self-identified pro-life and pro-choice voters alike.

In addition to sanctioning elective abortion less often, we can see from table 4.1 that Floridians were slightly more ambivalent about abortions

Table 4.1 Frequency and intensity of ambivalence on abortion and gay rights

Condition	1998 (Abortion)		1999 (Abortion)	
	Percent	Mean	Percent	Mean
Woman's health	27.1	0.15	27.6	0.23
Rape	21.4	0.03	24.5	0.14
Birth defect	25.5	0.11	26.5	0.19
Family too poor	33.7	0.25	36.0	0.31
No more children	28.6	0.10	36.3	0.31
Not married	29.0	0.15	36.2	0.30
Any reason	n/a	n/a	34.9	0.26
Number of cases	552 to 557 (weighted)		642 to 650	

Condition	2002 (Gay rights)	
	Percent	Mean
Teach school	33.3	0.23
Legal marriage	32.0	0.18
Serve in military	32.8	0.23
Adopt children	32.7	0.21
Privacy of own homes	22.6	0.06
Job discrimination	31.2	0.25
Boy scouts	35.1	0.27
Health insurance	32.0	0.26
Number of cases	534 to 556	

Note: Data are from *Florida Voter* surveys conducted in March 1998 (weighted by party registration), January/February 1999, and June 2002 (heterosexual respondents only). Table entries indicate (a) the percentage of respondents (excluding those with missing values) who have ambivalence scores greater than zero for a particular condition; and (b) the mean ambivalence score for each item (ranging from -0.5 to $+4.0$).

obtained in elective than in traumatic circumstances. Further, principal components factor analyses indicate that people who were ambivalent with regard to one traumatic condition ("woman's health," "rape," "birth defect") also tended to be more ambivalent about the other two conditions; likewise, those who expressed ambivalence about one elective circumstance ("too poor," "no more children," "not married," "any reason") were more likely to experience conflict with regard to the others as well. Based on these results, we constructed separate indices for ambivalence about traumatic ($\alpha = .721$ in 1998, .777 in 1999) and elective abortion ($\alpha = .765$ in 1998, .792 in 1999). Perhaps surprisingly, ambivalence in one domain was only modestly related to ambivalence in the other ($r = .11$, $p < .05$ in 1998; $r = .26$, $p < .001$ in 1999)—a pattern that indicates that many people are ambivalent about only some rather than all aspects of the abortion issue. Even if this is true, however, and even if the increased levels of ambivalence observed from 1998 to 1999 are largely an artifact of differences between the two surveys (see note 7), there can be little doubt that a substantial number of Florida voters have conflicting views about abortion.

Table 4.1 also reveals a fair amount of aggregate-level ambivalence on issues relating to gay rights. Among these items, ambivalence was most common (35.1 percent) on the question of whether homosexuals should be permitted to join the Boy Scouts and other youth organizations, and least common (22.6 percent) when respondents indicated whether it was anyone else's business what gays and lesbians do within the privacy of their own homes.[9] On seven of the eight measures (all except "privacy of own homes"), more than three in ten Floridians expressed at least a minimal degree of ambivalence (scores of 0.5 or higher); this is roughly equal to the proportions that were ambivalent about a woman's right to obtain an elective abortion, and more than indicated ambivalence about abortions obtained under traumatic circumstances. Looking at the data another way (not shown), we see, first, that nearly three-fourths of respondents in the present study were ambivalent (again using the 0.5 threshold) on at least one of the eight statements; and, second, nearly one-third were ambivalent about three or more. Like abortion, it appears that ambivalence is a fairly prominent feature of public opinion on gay and lesbian rights.

Just as ambivalence on abortion proved to be multidimensional, a factor analysis revealed that responses to the eight gay rights questions fell into two separate domains. One of these captured attitudes toward children and family relationships ("teach school," "legal marriage," "adopt children," "Boy Scouts"), while the other involved ambivalence primarily on issues involving basic civil rights and liberties ("serve in military," "privacy of own homes," "job discrimination," "health insurance"). Accordingly, we constructed indices for ambivalence on gay rights with regard to *children and families* ($\alpha = .664$), and what we have termed *adult roles* ($\alpha = .705$; see Craig *et al.* 2005b for a more complete discussion). There is a stronger correlation ($r = .50, p < .001$) between ambivalence in the two dimensions relating to gay rights than there was between elective and traumatic abortion.

VALUE CONFLICT

Any fair test of the hypothesis that value conflict is a source of ambivalence requires independent measures of these two concepts, but one of the difficulties in constructing such a test is specifying *which* conflicting values might lead to ambivalence. The Florida surveys used here included measures of values that we expected, based on theory as well as our own political intuition, to be related to attitudes about abortion and gay rights. Specifically, the 1999 survey contained a series of questions that tapped two values (*traditional lifestyles* and *traditional marriage roles*) relevant to the abortion issue, while in 2002 we measured the same two values plus two others (*egalitarianism* and *individualism*) that seemed likely to shape citizens' attitudes on gay rights.[10]

Prior research has shown that support for gay rights is stronger among individuals who are committed to the norms of general social equality, and weaker among those who hold traditional views about what constitutes proper moral behavior (Brewer 2003; Wilcox and Wolpert 2000). It is not clear, though, how or even whether such value orientations should be related to gay rights ambivalence (or to abortion ambivalence for that matter), and we make no predictions about what our data will show in this regard. Instead, our central hypothesis is that ambivalence will be greater when the values of traditional morality (which should predispose someone to oppose gay rights) *clash* with those of either egalitarianism or individual freedom (which should have the opposite effect; see Wilcox and Norrander 2002). Similarly, for abortion, we anticipate that ambivalence will be higher among those whose beliefs about lifestyle and marriage roles are in conflict.[11]

Our measure of *traditional lifestyles* in the 1999 survey was based on strong or weak agreement/disagreement[12] with the following statements:

- This country would have many fewer problems if there were more emphasis on traditional family ties (TL_1).
- The newer lifestyles are contributing to the breakdown of our society (TL_2).
- We should be more tolerant of people who choose to live according to their own moral standards even if they are very different from our own (TL_3).

In 2002, TL_3 was replaced with

- The world is always changing and we should adjust our view of moral behavior to those changes (TL_4).

Respondents' support for *traditional marriage roles* was measured in the 1999 survey as follows:

- All in all, family life suffers when the woman has a full-time job (TM_1).
- It is more important for a wife to help her husband's career than to have one herself (TM_2).
- A husband's job is to earn money; a wife's job is to look after the home and family (TM_3).[13]

On both of these indices, higher scores represent a more traditional outlook (strong agreement with TL_1, TL_2, plus all marriage role statements, strong disagreement with TL_3 and TL_4). Factor analyses on both datasets suggest that these items capture distinct value dimensions, though they are positively correlated ($r = .39$, $p < .001$ in 1999; $r = .37$, $p < .001$ in 2002).

The 2002 survey tapped two additional core values. Our measure of *egalitarianism* ($\alpha =$ a weak .483) was derived from respondents' strong or weak agreement/disagreement with the following statements:

- We have gone too far in pushing equal rights in this country (E_1)
- This country would be better off if we worried less about how equal people are (E_2).
- If people were treated more equally in this country, we would have many fewer problems (E_3).

Higher scores (strong disagreement with E_1 and E_2, strong agreement with E_3) represent a positive commitment to egalitarian values. Finally, *individualism* was captured with a single item (strong disagreement indicating an individualistic outlook): "Having your own ideas is important, but there are times when people need to set those ideas aside and go along with what the majority wants."[14]

We measured value conflict using the same algorithm that was used in assessing ambivalence (see Steenbergen and Brewer 2000), as in

$$\text{Value Conflict (E, TL)} = \left[\frac{E + TL}{2} \right] - |E - TL|$$

In this example, value conflict is highest when an individual scores either high or low on *both* egalitarianism *and* traditional lifestyles. In 2002, we constructed comparable measures to capture conflict between egalitarianism and traditional marriage roles, individualism and traditional marriage roles, and individualism and traditional lifestyles. For the 1999 abortion rights study, we reversed the *traditional* marriage role index to create an *egalitarian* marriage role variable, and used our algorithm to construct a measure of value conflict between traditional lifestyles and egalitarian marriage roles.

VALUES, VALUE CONFLICT, AND AMBIVALENCE

Although a developing literature stresses the importance of core values as underpinnings of political attitudes, our data suggest that core values (or at least the ones measured in our study) are not themselves strongly associated with ambivalence. In 1999, traditionalists were *more* ambivalent than others about whether a woman should be able to obtain a legal abortion under traumatic conditions, but the relationships are rather weak ($r = .12$, $p < .01$ for lifestyles; $r = .14$, $p < .01$ for marriage roles). Along the same lines, while respondents with a traditional lifestyles orientation were slightly *less* ambivalent about abortion rights under elective conditions, the relationship is again rather faint ($r = -.09$, $p < .02$). In our 2002 gay rights survey, ambivalence on the adult roles dimension is negatively associated with egalitarianism ($r = -.13$, $p < .01$), and positively associated with lifestyle traditionalism ($r = .13$, $p < .01$), but these coefficients are also weak. In addition, none of the relationships between core values and ambivalence regarding children and families achieve conventional levels of statistical significance ($p \leq .05$).

At first glance, ambivalence also appears to be largely unrelated to the *value conflicts* that we are able to explore with our survey data. In 1999, conflict between traditional lifestyles and egalitarian marriage roles is uncorrelated with ambivalence regarding abortion rights in both traumatic ($r = .01$, $p = .73$) and elective conditions ($r = .04$, $p = .36$). Similarly, in 2002, we see only faint signs of a relationship between ambivalence on adult roles and conflicting views about egalitarianism and traditional marriage roles ($r = .06$, $p = .20$), and between ambivalence and conflicting views about individualism and traditional marriage roles ($r = .07$, $p = .11$). For children and family issues, the correlation between ambivalence and value conflict on egalitarianism and traditional lifestyles is also weak ($r = .05$, $p = .21$).

These zero–order results provide virtually no support for the hypothesis that ambivalence in general, and ambivalence about gay rights and abortion in particular, is a product of value conflict. However, we cannot rule out the possibility that conflict between other unknown values might produce ambivalence, or that the effects of value conflict on ambivalence can only be seen in a more fully specified model. In essence, core values and the conflict between those core values may be partially concealing one another's effects on ambivalence in bivariate relationships. To consider that argument, we tested multivariate models of ambivalence using core values, value conflict, and a number of different control variables. For the 1999 abortion rights data, we estimated

Ambivalence (traumatic) $= \alpha + \beta_1$ egalitarian marriage roles values $+$ β_2 traditional lifestyles $+ \beta_3$ value conflict (egalitarian marriage roles, traditional lifestyles) $+ \beta_4$ age $+ \beta_5$ education $+ \beta_6$ gender (female) $+$ β_7 religious attendance $+ \beta_8$ religious guidance $+ \beta_9$ abortion position (pro-life) $+ \beta_{10}$ abortion importance $+ e$

where "religious attendance" refers to the frequency of attending services; "religious guidance" is a measure of the extent to which religion guides one's day-to-day living; "abortion position" is 1 for people who identify themselves as pro-choice, 3 for those who identify themselves as pro-life, and 2 for those who volunteer that neither label describes their views on the issue; and "abortion importance" is the respondent's self-assessment of "how important the abortion issue is to you personally." Separate models were estimated for traumatic and elective ambivalence.

Results are presented in table 4.2.[15] Model 1 in the table shows that ambivalence about abortion under traumatic conditions was significantly higher among women, among those who attended church more frequently, and among the pro-life respondents (the latter finding confirming the bivariate observations we reported in Craig *et al.* 2002). Religious guidance, age, education, and the subjective personal importance of the abortion issue were not significantly related to traumatic ambivalence, *ceteris paribus.* Controlling for all these factors, core values remain faintly related to ambivalence; that is, respondents committed to egalitarian marriage roles were slightly less ambivalent about abortion rights in traumatic circumstances ($b = -.074$, $p < .02$), as were those who preferred traditional lifestyles ($b = -.067$, $p = .07$). More central to our main theoretical concern, people who experienced conflict between those two values also tended to have

Table 4.2 A multivariate model of ambivalence about abortion: traumatic and elective dimensions

Variable	Model 1: traumatic		Model 2: elective	
	Coefficient	S.E.	Coefficient	S.E.
Values:				
Egalitarianism (marriage roles)	−0.074*	0.031	−0.013	0.028
Moral traditionalism	−0.067†	0.037	−0.049	0.035
Value conflict	0.065*	0.026	0.024	0.024
Controls:				
Age (older)	−0.000	0.005	0.004	0.005
Education (better educated)	−0.003	0.028	−0.018	0.027
Gender (female)	0.418**	0.148	0.217	0.139
Religious attendance (frequent)	0.145**	0.051	0.056	0.048
Religious guidance (strong)	0.081	0.103	−0.181†	0.096
Abortion (pro-life)	0.634***	0.089	−0.325***	0.084
Abortion importance (very)	0.047	0.100	−0.350***	0.094
−2 log likelihood	3227.39		4056.02	
Nagelkerke pseudo R²	0.17		0.09	
Number of cases	708		708	

Note: Data are from a *Florida Voter* survey conducted in January/February 1999. Table entries are ordered logit coefficients and associated standard errors; threshold levels are not shown. The meaning of high scores on control variables is indicated in parentheses.

***$p \leq .001$; **$p \leq .01$; *$p \leq .05$; †$p \leq .10$.

higher levels of ambivalence with regard to traumatic abortion issues ($b = .065$, $p < .02$). The relationship is weak, but it is evident in our multivariate model.

This finding is not generalizable to the elective abortion condition, however. Model 2 in table 4.2 shows quite a different set of relationships, as those who regard the abortion issue as personally important and prefer to call themselves pro-life rather than pro-choice are significantly less ambivalent than others about abortion in elective circumstances. Moreover, neither core values nor the conflict between them are significantly related to ambivalence in this model.

The 2002 dataset contains measures of other values (egalitarianism and individualism) that allow us to explore different conflicts that might be associated with ambivalence on gay rights issues. Because the several value conflict measures are based on various combinations of the same four core values, including all of them in a single model risked introducing excessive multicollinearity.[16] Instead, we tested two models with different sets of variables. The first of these (Model 3) is

Ambivalence = α + β_1 egalitarian values + β_2 traditional lifestyles values + β_3 traditional marriage role values + β_4 individualism values + β_5 value conflict (egalitarianism, traditional lifestyles) + β_6 value conflict (individualism, traditional marriage roles) + β_7 age + β_8 education + β_9 gender (female) + β_{10} religious attendance + β_{11} religious guidance + β_{12} attitudes about homosexuality + β_{13} know someone gay + β_{14} born that way + e

where "attitudes toward homosexuality" is a 6-item index tapping respondents' feelings about homosexuality *per se* rather than about gay rights;[17] "know someone gay" indicates whether the individual personally knows any gay men or lesbians; and "born that way" reflects beliefs about whether or not homosexuality is a matter of personal choice.[18]

In our next model (Model 4), we substituted variables representing conflicts between egalitarianism and traditional marriage roles, and between individualism and traditional lifestyles, for the value conflict measures in Model 3. This is stated as

Ambivalence = α + β_1 egalitarian values + β_2 traditional lifestyles values + β_3 traditional marriage role values + β_4 individualism values + β_5 value conflict (egalitarianism, traditional marriage roles) + β_6 value conflict (individualism, traditional lifestyles) + β_7 age + β_8 education + β_9 gender (female) + β_{10} religious attendance + β_{11} religious guidance + β_{12} attitudes about homosexuality + β_{13} know someone gay + β_{14} born that way + e.

Table 4.3 A multivariate model of ambivalence about gay rights: adult roles dimension

Variable	Model 3		Model 4	
	Coefficient	S.E.	Coefficient	S.E.
Values:				
Egalitarianism	−0.230*	0.092	−0.141†	0.076
Traditional marriage roles	−0.186*	0.076	−0.217*	0.086
Traditional lifestyles	0.005	0.094	0.078	0.087
Individualism	−0.105*	0.053	−0.127†	0.074
Value conflict:				
Egalitarianism/lifestyles	0.170*	0.078	n/a	n/a
Individualism/marriage roles	0.124†	0.067	n/a	n/a
Egalitarianism/marriage roles	n/a	n/a	0.124†	0.073
Individualism/lifestyles	n/a	n/a	0.078	0.073
Controls:				
Age (older)	0.002	0.005	0.002	0.005
Education (better educated)	0.011	0.030	0.007	0.029
Gender (female)	−0.214	0.158	−0.235	0.158
Religious attendance (frequent)	0.058	0.087	0.049	0.087
Religious guidance (strong)	−0.029	0.081	−0.014	0.080
Attitudes about homosexuality (positive)	−0.339***	0.076	−0.340***	0.076
Know someone gay (yes)	0.183	0.203	0.158	0.203
Born that way (yes)	−0.001	0.095	0.025	0.095
−2 log likelihood	3044.24		3048.28	
Nagelkerke pseudo R^2	0.11		0.10	
Number of cases	568		568	

Note: Data are from a *Florida Voter* survey conducted in June 2002. Table entries are ordered logit coefficients and associated standard errors (heterosexual respondents only); threshold levels are not shown. The meaning of high scores on control variables is indicated in parentheses.

***$p \leq .001$; *$p \leq .05$; †$p \leq .10$.

We did not test for conflict between egalitarianism and individualism, since there is no reason to expect that people who are high (or low) on both of these values will experience conflict that might affect their views on gay rights issues.

Let us turn first to the model predicting ambivalence about gay rights with regard to adult roles, shown in table 4.3. In both versions of the model portrayed here, we see that attitudes about homosexuality are strongly and negatively related to ambivalence, that is, more positive (or less negative) views tend to depress the level of ambivalence that people feel about gay rights issues relating to military service, privacy, job discrimination, and health insurance. Also in both Model 3 and Model 4, commitments to three of the four core values measured in our study (egalitarianism, traditional marriage roles, and individualism) are associated with lower levels of ambivalence. Most critically, there is at least modest support for the value conflict hypothesis: first, those who express a strong (or, less often, weak) simultaneous commitment to egalitarianism and traditional lifestyles tend to be more ambivalent ($p = .030$) on these particular aspects of the gay rights issue. Second, if conventional standards of statistical significance are relaxed just a bit, it appears that ambivalence also is associated with conflict between the values of individualism and traditional marriage roles ($p = .064$). Finally, in Model 4, conflict between egalitarianism and traditional marriage roles increases ambivalence ($p = .090$), though conflict between individualism and traditional lifestyles does not.

Results for the children/family dimension (teach school, legal marriage, adopt children, Boy Scouts; see table 4.4) provide further evidence that ambivalence is to some extent a function of value conflict. In Model 3,

Table 4.4 A multivariate model of ambivalence about gay rights: children/families dimension

Variable	Model 3		Model 4	
	Coefficient	S.E.	Coefficient	S.E.
Values:				
Egalitarianism	−0.287**	0.089	−0.140†	0.075
Traditional marriage roles	−0.240**	0.076	−0.255**	0.086
Traditional lifestyles	−0.128	0.094	0.023	0.086
Individualism	−0.161**	0.052	−0.160*	0.071
Value conflict:				
Egalitarianism/lifestyles	0.291***	0.078	n/a	n/a
Individualism/marriage roles	0.227***	0.067	n/a	n/a
Egalitarianism/marriage roles	n/a	n/a	0.185*	0.073
Individualism/lifestyles	n/a	n/a	0.094	0.071
Controls:				
Age (older)	−0.009*	0.005	−0.010*	0.005
Education (better educated)	−0.003	0.029	−0.009	0.029
Gender (female)	−0.180	0.157	−0.180	0.156
Religious attendance (frequent)	0.023	0.086	0.003	0.086
Religious guidance (strong)	−0.143†	0.080	−0.114	0.079
Attitudes about homosexuality (positive)	−0.047	0.075	−0.044	0.074
Know someone gay (yes)	0.236	0.203	0.191	0.202
Born that way (yes)	0.148	0.095	0.185†	0.095
−2 log likelihood	3111.20		3128.02	
Nagelkerke pseudo R²	0.08		0.05	
Number of cases	568		568	

Note: Data are from a *Florida Voter* survey conducted in June 2002. Table entries are ordered logit coefficients and associated standard errors (heterosexual respondents only); threshold levels are not shown. The meaning of high scores on control variables is indicated in parentheses.

***$p \leq .001$; **$p \leq .01$; *$p \leq .05$; †$p \leq .10$.

strong adherence to the values of egalitarianism, traditional marriage roles, and individualism lessen ambivalence, but the conflict between individualism and traditional marriage roles, and between egalitarianism and traditional lifestyles, are both associated with higher levels of ambivalence ($p \le .001$). In Model 4, traditional marriage roles and individualism weaken ambivalence, while the conflict between egalitarianism and traditional marriage roles increases it ($p = .012$); the effect of conflict between individualism and traditional lifestyles is not significant. In contrast to what we saw for adult roles, attitudes about homosexuality are unimportant here; high scores on this index are associated, as we would expect, with greater positivity ($r = .50$ to $.58$) and lesser negativity ($-.47$ to $-.55$) on the component items used to construct our children/family ambivalence index[19]—but not with greater (or lesser) ambivalence itself.

Although other factors not yet identified clearly play a role, these results offer some support for the assumption so often made by scholars that conflict among citizens' core values promotes ambivalence.[20] In fact, our analysis reveals that *multiple* conflicts are important in explaining ambivalence in mass opinion on abortion and gay rights.

DISCUSSION

The levels of ambivalence observed on two of the hottest of contemporary hot-button political issues suggest that neither is as "easy" for voters as some might have thought (cf. Carmines and Stimson 1980; Alvarez and Brehm 2002). Public opinion with regard to each of these issues has multiple dimensions, suggesting that citizens often make distinctions when faced with questions about when a legal abortion should be attainable and under what situations equal opportunity rights should be extended to gays and lesbians. Moreover, although many people undoubtedly have attitudes that are firmly entrenched on one side or the other, there are more than a few whose attitudes have roots stretching to *both* sides of the abortion and gay rights controversies. What are the origins of such ambivalence? Our analyses confirm the speculation and assumptions made by scholars in the past, specifically, that ambivalence is related to the conflict among core values— a relationship that can best be seen in multidimensional models that control for the effects of the underlying values themselves on ambivalence. Indeed, we have seen that, at least for gay rights (and perhaps for other issues not yet examined), there are multiple value conflicts that can promote ambivalence among the general public.

Our findings also remind us, of course, that value conflict is only part of the story; the multivariate models tested here leave little doubt that there is much more to understand about the sources of attitudinal ambivalence.

For example, we found that policy views and social beliefs are strongly related to ambivalence for some individuals; that is, (1) pro-choice voters were more ambivalent about abortions in elective circumstances; (2) pro-life voters were more ambivalent about abortions in traumatic circumstances; and (3) ambivalence on the adult roles dimension of gay rights (but not on the children/families dimension) was significantly less among those who expressed more positive attitudes about homosexuality in general. Ambivalence is neither randomly nor normally distributed across issue preferences, which may help to explain how seemingly large, but perhaps conflicted, majorities can be thwarted by issue-specific minorities with firmly held and harmonious values. In other words, by definition, people with ambivalent opinions can see both (or multiple) sides of an issue—and, as a result, they may understand and partially sympathize with intense, single-minded groups even though the latter do not fully accept or appreciate the complexity of the former's opinions.

Indeed, the outcome of an election campaign or issue controversy frequently depends on the ability of the non-ambivalent to frame the debate in such a way that a majority of those who are on the fence will decide to side with them rather than the opposition (see chapter six for a concrete example). While this is not a particularly novel observation, we believe that students of politics should define more carefully what it means to be "on the fence" (ambivalence is not necessarily a synonym for middle-of-the-road); identify the kinds of individuals who are most likely to be located there (and tell us why); and determine how cues (including framing) from political leaders, activists, the news media, and others help citizens to resolve the conflicts that signal the existence of ambivalence in the first place. Answers to questions such as these will provide us with a better understanding of the importance of attitudinal ambivalence, both in fact and potentially, in shaping the direction of contemporary American politics.

Notes

1. These changes have occurred mainly among Democrats, Independents, and ideological liberals (Sherrill and Yang 2000; also Haeberle 1999; Lewis and Rogers 1999), which suggests that voters' opinions on gay and lesbian issues, like those on abortion (Adams 1997), may be evolving along partisan lines. For a contrary view, however, see Lindaman and Haider-Markel (2002; also Brewer 2003, who found growing support for antidiscrimination laws and gays serving in the military among all partisan groups in the electorate).
2. Up to three (1998) or four (1999, 2002) callbacks were made to each working number in an effort to obtain a completed interview. Additional information about these polls can be obtained from *Florida Voter* directly (954–584–0204), or from the Graduate Program in Political Campaigning in the Political Science Department at the University of Florida (352–392–0262).

3. The technique is a version of the semantic differential (Osgood, Suci, and Tannenbaum 1957), as modified by Kaplan (1972) in an effort to show that people's overall attitudes are made up of both positive and negative elements.

4. The "any reason" item was asked only in the 1999 survey (Craig, Kane, and Martinez 2002). The two abortion surveys also differed in terms of question order: in 1998, the negative evaluation series was asked immediately following the positive evaluation series, whereas in 1999 (as in the 2002 gay rights survey), the positive and negative batteries were separated by a number of filler questions (Thompson, Zanna, and Griffin 1995).

5. Conceptually, the first part of the equation, $[(P + N)/2]$, states that with similarity held constant, greater intensity leads to greater ambivalence; that is, as the average value of positive and negative scores increases, so do feelings of ambivalence. The second part, $|P - N|$, indicates that when similarity increases (e.g., an equal number of positive and negative reactions), a lesser amount is subtracted from the ambivalence total than if similarity were reduced; consequently, greater similarity translates into higher scores on ambivalence.

6. One should exercise caution when interpreting the means in table 4.1 since these have been calculated based on the full range of ambivalence scores (-0.5 to 4.0) reported earlier.

7. To some degree, the observed increase is likely a function of differences between the surveys. In 1999, for example, we added the "any reason" condition (though greater ambivalence also is observed for each of the six original items; see table 4.1), placed a larger number of filler questions between the positive and negative reaction statements (Thompson, Zanna, and Griffin 1995), and asked the abortion preference questions after rather than before the reaction statements. Even if order effects are nonetheless present, they appear to affect mainly our estimates concerning the *frequency* of ambivalent responses and the *amount* of ambivalence exhibited by voters—and not the basic patterns and relationships described in the remainder of this chapter.

8. Pro-choicers approved, on average, 2.90 (1998) and 2.92 (1999) of the three conditions that constitute traumatic abortion, compared with 1.85 of the three (1998) and 2.53 of the four (1999) that constitute elective abortion. The comparable figures for pro-lifers were 1.76 (1998 traumatic) and 1.95 (1999 traumatic) versus 0.26 (1998 elective) and 0.35 (1999 elective). For the relatively small group falling into neither category it was 2.79 (1998 traumatic) and 2.82 (1999 traumatic) versus 1.15 (1998 elective) and 0.87 (1999 elective).

9. All analyses from 2002 are based on the 94.5 percent of our sample who claimed to be heterosexual. Although this figure almost certainly underestimates the number of gays, lesbians, and bisexuals in the larger population, it is similar to the results reported in other surveys (Wald 2000: 13).

10. Because values were not measured in the 1998 survey, the multivariate analysis that follows will be limited to 1999 (abortion) and 2002 (gay rights) only.

11. As a practical matter, this refers almost exclusively to people who were traditionalist on moral questions and egalitarian in their views about whether wives should be able to pursue their own careers; very few respondents were conflicted in the opposite direction.

12. Respondents also were offered the opportunity to "neither agree nor disagree" with these questions (1999), or to indicate that they "don't have an opinion either way" (2002).

13. The internal reliability of this index (α = .715 in 1999, .647 in 2002) was better than for our measures of traditional lifestyles (α = .465 and .489, respectively).

14. Individualism does not significantly correlate with any of the other core values in our study, though respondents who are egalitarian are less likely to express traditional views on both the lifestyles (r = −.22, p < .001) and marriage roles (r = −.31, p < .001) dimensions.

15. In order to avoid an unacceptable loss of cases in the estimation of these models (also see tables 4.3 and 4.4), we employed the MICE ("multiple imputation using chained equations"; see Horton and Lipsitz 2001) routine in the R statistical package to impute missing data. MICE does this by replacing each missing value with a random draw from a distribution estimated from a maximum likelihood function based on other variables in the dataset. Our imputed dataset was based on the mean values from five replicate datasets created by MICE.

16. The bivariate correlation between the two value conflict variables representing egalitarianism versus traditional marriage roles on the one hand, and egalitarianism versus traditional lifestyles on the other, is .39. The correlation between the value conflict variables representing individualism versus traditional marriage roles on the one hand, and individualism versus traditional lifestyles on the other, is .52.

17. The index (α = .901) was based on agreement or disagreement with the following statements: (a) Sex between two men is just plain wrong. (b) Sex between two women is just plain wrong. (c) I think male homosexuals are disgusting. (d) I think female homosexuals, or lesbians, are disgusting. (e) It is natural for some men to be sexually attracted to other men. (f) It is natural for some women to be sexually attracted to other women (cf. Herek 2002). Scores on the last two items were reversed to correct for direction of wording. High scores reflect a more positive attitude.

18. Our sample was evenly divided between "born gay" (38.9 percent said this statement came closer to their own opinion) and the contrasting view that "homosexuals are that way because they choose to be" (43.0 percent); 8.3 percent volunteered a mixed view, and 9.9 percent weren't sure.

19. Correlations with attitudes about homosexuality are similar, but slightly weaker, for the positivity (.35 to .53) and negativity (−.34 to −.47) items comprising adult roles ambivalence.

20. Each of our surveys also included a single agree–disagree question tapping *subjective* ambivalence: "I sometimes find myself being torn between two sides of the abortion issue" in 1999 (7-point scale indicating how close this statement was to the respondent's own feelings); and "I sometimes find myself being torn between two sides of issues involving gay and lesbian rights" in 2002 (5-point strongly agree to strongly disagree). Subjective ambivalence on abortion was correlated only weakly with objective ambivalence on the elective dimension, and not at all with objective ambivalence with regard to traumatic abortion. Similarly, subjective ambivalence on gay rights was weakly correlated with

objective children/families ambivalence but unrelated to objective adult roles ambivalence. Nevertheless, in line with the results reported above, subjective ambivalence was more likely to occur in the presence of value conflict than in its absence. In multivariate models, conflict between egalitarianism and traditional lifestyles was associated with greater ambivalence on gay rights, while conflict between moral traditionalism and egalitarian marriage roles tended to increase ambivalence on abortion.

CHAPTER FIVE

EDUCATION, IDEOLOGY, AND RACIAL AMBIVALENCE: CONFLICT AMPLIFICATION OR CONFLICT RESOLUTION?

Christopher M. Federico

Traditionally, social and political psychologists have assumed that most evaluatively laden beliefs and perceptions are structured in terms of a single bipolar affective dimension, with positive evaluations at one end and negative evaluations at the other (Schuman *et al.* 1997; also see Cacioppo and Berntson 1994; Cacioppo, Gardner, and Berntson 1999; Green and Citrin 1994; Levine, Carmines, and Sniderman 1999). This assumption implies that positive and negative evaluations should be reciprocally related, with the acceptance of positive evaluations necessarily leading to the rejection of negative ones. However, theory and research on affect increasingly point toward the existence of distinguishable positive and negative affective systems (Cacioppo and Berntson 1994; Cacioppo, Gardner, and Berntson 1999). In general, this *bivariate* model of the evaluative process suggests that separate "channels" may be responsible for positive and negative responses to various objects, and that these two channels may not always work in a reciprocal fashion. One of the more interesting phenomena highlighted by the bivariate model is *ambivalence*. Individuals who are ambivalent toward a particular object have both positive and negative perceptions of that object, rather than perceiving it in wholly positive or negative terms (Cacioppo and Berntson 1994; Cacioppo, Gardner, and Berntson 1999; Thompson, Zanna, and Griffin 1995). Research suggests that attitudes and perceptions in a number of social and political domains may be characterized by ambivalence (Alvarez and Brehm 2002; Craig, Kane, and Martinez 2002; Craig *et al.* 2005b; Lavine 2001; also see Cacioppo, Gardner, and Berntson 1999).

Ambivalence has received perhaps the greatest attention in regards to white Americans' attitudes toward African Americans. In this vein, there is a great deal of prior research indicating that whites' positive and negative responses to blacks are empirically distinct and largely orthogonal to one another. Using data from high school students in desegregated settings, for example, factor-analytic work by Patchen, Hofmann, and Davidson (1976) revealed that positive and negative attitudes toward blacks and whites fell on two separate and basically unrelated dimensions. Similarly, Katz and Hass (1988; also see Katz, Wackenhut, and Hass 1986) found that separate questionnaire measures of "pro-black" and "anti-black" attitudes loaded on different factors, with the correlation between the measures again being relatively small. Consequently, among a large number of whites, the relative orthogonality of these two dimensions would seem to reflect racial *ambivalence*, that is, a tendency to perceive and evaluate African Americans both positively and negatively at the same time (see Katz and Hass 1988; Katz, Wackenhut, and Hass 1986; Monteith 1996).

IDEOLOGY AND INDIVIDUAL DIFFERENCES IN RACIAL AMBIVALENCE

Despite evidence that whites' perceptions of blacks may be characterized by a considerable amount of ambivalence, researchers have devoted less attention to the question of precisely *whose* racial perceptions are likely to be ambivalent, and *why*. Studies have repeatedly shown that reliable individual differences exist in the degree to which whites simultaneously endorse both positive and negative perceptions of blacks (e.g., Hass *et al.* 1992). How, then, can we explain these individual differences? One factor that may be relevant is *ideology*. While this variable has received little attention from scholars who are interested in racial ambivalence, the broader race-and-politics literature reveals that it is related to whites' racial attitudes in a number of important ways (Sidanius *et al.* 2000; Sniderman and Carmines 1997). While many of these studies focus on the relationship between conservatism and *negative* perceptions of blacks (Federico and Sidanius 2002a, 2002b; Sidanius, Pratto, and Bobo 1996; Sidanius *et al.* 2000), my own recent work (Federico 2004) suggests that an emphasis on the relationship between conservatism and *negative* racial perceptions among whites may have caused researchers to miss a more subtle relationship between conservatism and deviations from affective bipolarity that result in *ambivalent* perceptions of blacks.

Why would white conservatives exhibit higher levels of racial ambivalence? Among other things, it may be because the distinct antecedents of positive and negative perceptions of blacks are more likely to come into conflict with one another among those whose politics fall further to the right. For example, both Lipset and Schneider (1978) and Katz, Wackenhut, and Hass (1986) have argued that positive and negative evaluations of blacks may be rooted in different value-related concerns. According to this account, humanitarian concerns about the fate of disadvantaged groups in society lead to positive racial affect, while individualistic concerns associated with the Protestant ethic lead to negative racial affect (Hass *et al.* 1992; Katz and Hass 1988). By extension, the argument here implies that whites who put a premium on *both* value concerns will be more conflicted about blacks themselves, that is, with humanitarian concerns causing them to perceive blacks positively, and individualistic concerns encouraging them to perceive blacks negatively at the same time (Katz and Hass 1988).

For a variety of reasons, white conservatives may be more likely than others to bring such a "conflicted" combination of humanitarian and individualistic concerns to bear on judgments about racial matters. On the one hand, basic humanitarian concern for blacks (chiefly in the form of support for equal treatment before the law) is now a consensual political norm: liberals and conservatives alike reject unequal treatment as a violation of basic liberal-democratic values (McClosky and Zaller 1984; Schuman *et al.* 1997; Sniderman and Carmines 1997; Sniderman and Piazza 1993). On the other hand, conservatives appear to be more troubled than either liberals or moderates by the belief that blacks fail to "help themselves" and by black demands for what are seen as "special favors" (Sears 1988; Sniderman and Carmines 1997). In short, individualistic concerns *do* seem to be of greater importance to individuals on the right.

Taken together, these arguments suggest that the chronic coactivation of humanitarian and individualistic concerns associated with deviations from affective bipolarity in the racial domain should increase as one moves toward the political right, leading to greater ambivalence among conservatives. Consistent with this hypothesis, I have reported elsewhere (Federico 2004) that conservatives' perceptions of blacks are disproportionately likely to display patterns consistent with the presence of ambivalence. A heteroskedastic regression analysis of data from the 2000 American National Election Study, for example, showed that conservatism was associated with greater error variability in whites' endorsement of black stereotypes—a relationship that suggests greater conflict in white conservatives' perceptions of blacks (cf. Alvarez and Brehm 2002; Harvey 1976). More directly, regression analyses of data from the 1991 National Race and Politics Study (NRAP) indicated that, among whites, conservatism was associated with higher scores on an ambivalence index constructed from separate measures of positive and negative perceptions of blacks (see below).

Importantly, further analysis showed that the relationship between conservatism and ambivalence was mediated by the degree to which respondents experienced conflict between humanitarian and individualistic concerns. At the same time, this analysis also revealed that conflict between the two sets of concerns may be more germane to the relationship between conservatism and ambivalence when the conflict occurs at a specifically *racial* level, that is, when the humanitarian and individualistic concerns in question refer directly to matters of racial politics. While prior work intimates that humanitarianism and individualism need only to come into conflict at the level of general values in order to produce higher levels of ambivalence (Katz and Hass 1988; Katz, Wackenhut, and Hass 1986), my results (in Federico 2004) suggest that the relationship between conservatism and ambivalence is mediated by conflict between humanitarianism and individualism at the level of racial politics, but *not* by conflict at the level of general values. Though somewhat anomalous from the perspective of past scholarship on racial ambivalence, this finding is consistent with a broader line of research showing that values intersect with racial perceptions at the level of beliefs about how those values relate to the experiences and life circumstances of different racial groups (Kinder and Mendelberg 2000; Sears and Henry 2003).

COGNITIVE SOPHISTICATION AS A MODERATOR: THE ROLE OF HIGHER EDUCATION

While instructive, these results do not provide a complete picture of the interface between ideology and racial ambivalence. As noted above, my earlier model indicates that the conservative belief system organizes humanitarian and individualistic concerns in a seemingly contradictory manner, thereby producing greater racial ambivalence. There is, however, cause to believe that the relationship between ideology and other race-related attitudes, beliefs, and perceptions is far from homogenous within the white population as a whole. In particular, a large and sometimes controversial body of research suggests that ideology relates very differently to racial attitudes, beliefs, and perceptions among whites at different levels of cognitive ability and cognitive engagement in politics. Given the relationship that is known to exist between higher education and the acquisition of cognitive sophistication, the literature in question typically focuses most closely on differences between whites who have completed a college degree and those who have not (Federico and Sidanius 2002a; Sidanius, Pratto, and Bobo 1996; Sidanius *et al.* 2000; Sniderman and Carmines 1997; Sniderman, and Piazza 1993; Sniderman, Brody, and Tetlock 1991; Sniderman, Crosby, and Howell 2000). In general, this line of inquiry demonstrates that college-educated whites tend to have a better understanding of (1) abstract political concepts such as liberalism and conservatism; (2) the relationships between these concepts and other sociopolitical values; and (3) their implications for what one "should" believe about various racial groups and racial policy issues.

In the present context, then, it is anticipated that the relationship between conservatism and racial ambivalence highlighted in Federico (2004) will be not be the same for whites who have completed college and those who have not. Unfortunately, prior research provides mixed signals as to whether the relationship between conservatism and racial ambivalence should be stronger or weaker among college-educated whites compared to others. A careful reading of the literature, in combination with my work on ideological differences, generates two competing hypotheses about how the relationships between conservatism, value conflict, and ambivalence might vary across educational levels.

First, my model implies that the relationship between conservatism and value-related conflicts—and by extension, the relationship between conservatism and racial ambivalence—will be *stronger* among cognitively sophisticated whites, and specifically among those with a college degree. As previously noted, this perspective suggests that conflict between humanitarian and individualistic concerns is an inherent feature of the conservative belief system, especially in the context of race. While conservative whites may be as likely as anyone else to have humanitarian concerns regarding blacks, they also are more likely than others to endorse individualism, resulting in a higher level of conflict between these two concerns as one moves to the right.

If this is indeed the "normative" pattern of belief-system structure for conservatives, then numerous studies on the acquisition of political attitudes, beliefs, and perceptions lead us to expect that the views of college-educated white conservatives will be characterized more strongly than those of liberals and moderates by conflict between humanitarianism and individualism. In this vein, a long line of work indicates that both education and other ability-related variables increase the likelihood that a given individual will adopt belief patterns normatively consistent with his/her ideological predispositions (as defined by the beliefs of political elites who share these predispositions; see Campbell *et al.* 1960; Converse 1964; McClosky and Zaller 1984; Zaller 1992; also see Sniderman, Brody, and Tetlock 1991; Sniderman, Crosby, and Howell 2000). In other words, if conflict between humanitarianism and individualism is truly normative on the right, then the improvement in cognitive sophistication associated with higher education should merely increase the likelihood that white conservatives will eventually endorse some combination of humanitarianism and individualism, particularly in the racial domain. In turn, this should result in more conflict between humanitarian and individualistic concerns and, hence, more racial ambivalence.

There is, however, an alternative hypothesis about the probable role of education-related gains in cognitive sophistication that can be derived from the race and politics literature. Certain aspects of this literature suggest that the relationships between conservatism and both value conflict and racial ambivalence may actually be *weaker* among college-educated whites. The argument here is that conservatism may serve as a motive for the establishment and maintenance of unequal relations between social groups, including racial ones (Sidanius and Pratto 1999; Sidanius, Pratto, and Bobo 1996). Among whites, then, conservatism should be strongly related to *negative* racial attitudes, beliefs, and perceptions, since all of the latter justify the continued existence of racial inequality. But more importantly, this line of thought proposes that the relationship should be especially strong among cognitively sophisticated whites, namely, those having a college education (Federico and Sidanius 2002a; Sidanius *et al.* 2000). More precisely, the increases in cognitive ability and engagement associated with education are thought to make it easier for college-educated whites to connect their attitudes toward various social groups with the overall orientation toward inequality represented by one's level of conservatism.

In the present context, humanitarianism and individualism (whether generalized or race-related) can be thought of as having *opposite* implications vis-à-vis the tolerance for inequality represented by conservatism. Whereas humanitarianism implies sympathy for the hardships faced by blacks, individualism asserts that those disadvantages are deserved and justified. If cognitively sophisticated whites are generally more likely to adopt attitudes, beliefs, and perceptions that are consistent with the orientation toward inequality implied by their level of conservatism, then college-educated conservatives should be less inclined to adopt *both* humanitarian and individualistic beliefs simultaneously. Instead, they should adopt the pattern of beliefs that is most likely to justify racial inequality, that is, a low level of humanitarianism and a high level of individualism—a combination that should produce a lesser amount of conflict between humanitarian and individualistic concerns and, consequently, less racial ambivalence.[1] In short, the alternative account I am considering states that the apparent relationship between conservatism and value conflicts, especially race-related value conflicts, may result from an ability-related failure to "correctly" reject humanitarianism while endorsing individualism, rather than from inherent features of the conservative belief system.

Unfortunately, the moderating role of education—and by extension, the role of cognitive sophistication—has yet to be examined in the context of the relationship between ideology and racial ambivalence. The present study attempts to fill this gap by addressing two key questions related to the competing sets of hypotheses described above:

(1) Does the relationship between conservatism and racial ambivalence differ among whites with different levels of cognitive sophistication, that is, those with a college education versus those without one? More precisely, is this relationship *stronger* or *weaker* among college-educated whites?

(2) Is the moderating effect of education, whatever its form, mediated by conflict between humanitarianism and individualism? That is, if the relationship between conservatism and ambivalence is *stronger* among college-educated whites, is this because conservatism is more strongly associated with higher levels of race-related value conflict among those with a college degree? Conversely, if the relationship between conservatism and ambivalence is *weaker* among college-educated whites, is this because conservatism is less strongly associated with higher levels of race-related value conflict among those with a college degree?

In addition to addressing these questions, the analyses reported below also return to the issue of whether conflict between humanitarianism and individualism plays a stronger mediating role at the general level or at a specifically racial level.

DATA AND METHODS

The relationship between ideology and racial ambivalence is examined using data from the 1991 NRAP. This study was conducted in two stages: a computer-assisted telephone survey, which reached a full sample of 2,223 individuals,[2] plus a second-wave mailback questionnaire completed by 1,198 of the original respondents. Because some items needed for the analyses were not included in the original survey, only respondents who completed both waves are examined here. Moreover, for obvious reasons, attention is limited to white respondents (final $N = 1,061$). Except for age and income, all variables were recoded to run from 0 to 1. Question wordings can be found in the appendix to this chapter.

The key independent variable, *conservatism*, was measured using a seven-point scale built from answers to a set of four branching items; scores range from strongly liberal to strongly conservative, with higher values indicating greater conservatism (after recoding, mean $= .56$ and s.d. $= .29$). The key dependent variable, *racial ambivalence*, was constructed from respondents' ratings of blacks on a series of unipolar trait items. Fourteen of these items asked respondents to indicate how well various traits describe blacks on a 0–10 scale, with 0 indicating that the trait in question describes blacks very inaccurately and 10 indicating that it describes them very well; nine of the traits were positive, five were negative (see appendix). Three additional items asked respondents to evaluate trait statements about blacks on a scale ranging from 1 ("definitely true") to 4 ("definitely false"); two of the statements were positive, one was negative. Since these last three items were originally worded such that higher scores indicated disagreement with the trait descriptor, all were reversed prior to construction of the ambivalence measure. Ambivalence was computed using a formula developed by Thompson, Zanna, and Griffin (1995), which takes into account both the similarity and intensity of individuals' positive and negative responses to an attitude object.[3] The scores produced by this formula were recoded to run from 0 to 1 (mean = .63, s.d. = .16).

Two measures of *conflict between humanitarian and individualistic concerns* also were constructed (Federico 2004). At the general value-orientation level, (1) humanitarian concerns were captured with a single question asking how much one should be concerned about the well-being of others (mean = .87, s.d. = .19), while (2) individualistic concerns were measured using a two-item scale that asked whether hard work paid off for people in the end (α = .83, mean = .78, s.d. = .21). In the specific context of racial politics, (3) humanitarian concerns were measured by a single item asking respondents how much they were angered by people being treated unfairly because of their race (mean = .88, s.d. = .20), and (4) individualistic concerns were assessed using a series of questions that tapped beliefs about whether blacks (rather than whites) are primarily to blame for black disadvantage, whether the government puts too much effort into fighting racism and helping minorities, and whether respondents are angered by the "special advantages" provided to minorities and by "minority spokesmen complaining about racism" (α = .67, mean = .57, s.d. = .20). Prior to creation of each humanitarianism and individualism scale, all items were put on a common 0–1 scale and recoded so that higher scores indicate higher levels of the construct in question. Then, each of the two conflict scores was computed using the Thompson–Zanna–Griffin (1995) formula described above (see note 3), with the corresponding humanitarian and individualistic concerns scores substituted, respectively, for the positive and negative perceptions values used to construct the racial-ambivalence measure. The scores produced by these two calculations were subsequently recoded to run from 0 to 1 (mean = .74, s.d. = .20 for general conflict; mean = .57, s.d. = .20 for conflict in the racial context).[4]

Following the precedent established by earlier studies (e.g., Federico and Sidanius 2002a, 2002b), cognitive sophistication was measured in terms of *education.* This variable was assessed using the survey's six-category measure of educational attainment. Since prior work on the role of education suggests that the completion of a college degree is a critical experience in the development of cognitive ability and the structuring of racial attitudes (Federico and Sidanius 2002a; Sidanius, Pratto, and Bobo 1996; Sidanius *et al.* 2000; also see Sniderman and Piazza 1993), and in the development of complex attitude structures more broadly (Judd and Milburn 1980; Sniderman, Brody, and Tetlock 1991), a dummy variable consisting of two categories was created: those who had completed a bachelor's degree ($N = 560$, coded as 1) and those who had not ($N = 1,281$, coded as -1). However, since the effects of education may be conflated with the effects of other variables related to cognitive ability and engagement, two additional controls were included as well. First, a measure of *political expertise* was constructed from two factual-knowledge questions regarding the maximum number of presidential terms and the number of justices on the Supreme Court. Correct responses to these items were given a score of 1, and all other responses a score of 0; each respondent's scores were then summed and divided by 2 to generate an expertise index (mean = .57, s.d. = .30). Second, a single item reflecting interviewer assessment of *respondent cooperativeness* was used to tap cognitive engagement in the survey itself (mean = .79, s.d. = .17). Finally, five demographic variables were employed as controls: *age* (years), *income* (thousands of dollars per year), *region* (-1 = non-South, 1 = South), *homeownership* (-1 = no, 1 = yes), and *gender* (-1 = female, 1 = male).

RESULTS

Ideology, Education, and Racial Ambivalence

The first and most basic question addressed in this chapter has to do with whether the relationship between conservatism and racial ambivalence reported in Federico (2004) differs as a function of education. To answer this question, a series of hierarchical ordinary least-squares regression models were estimated. In each of these models, the racial-ambivalence index discussed above was used as the dependent variable. Two models were estimated. In the first, ambivalence was regressed on age, income, region, gender, homeownership, political expertise, cooperativeness, the college-degree indicator, and the main effect term for conservatism. In the second model, the critical two-way interaction between conservatism and college degree was added to this initial set of predictors. For each of the models, and in all of the regressions that follow, HC3 robust standard errors are used as recommended by Long and Ervin (2000) for analyses with at least 250 cases. The HC3 method generates corrected standard errors for regression coefficients by adjusting the squared error for each case by that case's influence on the regression estimates. Studies suggest that this method yields standard errors that are less likely to be inflated by undetected heteroskedasticity, without lowering the power of the significance tests on individual coefficients.

Table 5.1 presents the unstandardized estimated coefficients for these models. Model 1, which looks simply at the main effects of conservatism and various controls, reveals a pattern identical to that discussed in Federico (2004): conservatism is significantly associated with higher levels of racial ambivalence ($b = 0.06$, $p \leq .001$), even after the statistical effects of the control variables are taken into account. In addition, cooperativeness, political expertise, and the college-degree indicator are associated with decreased ambivalence ($p \leq .01$ in all cases) as well. From the standpoint of the present study, however, Model 2 provides a more interesting result. The conservatism × college degree interaction added in this model addresses the critical question of whether the relationship between conservatism and racial ambivalence is different among whites with different levels of cognitive sophistication, that is, those with and without college degrees. As table 5.1 shows, this interaction is significant and positive ($b = 0.05$, $p \leq .01$),

Table 5.1 Explaining racial ambivalence: conservatism, education, and their interaction

Variable	Model 1		Model 2	
	Coefficient	S.E.	Coefficient	S.E.
Age	0.001**	0.000	0.001**	0.000
Income	−0.00	0.00	−0.00	0.00
Region	0.00	0.01	0.00	0.01
Gender	0.00	0.01	0.00	0.01
Homeownership	0.00	0.01	0.00	0.01
Political expertise	−0.06***	0.02	−0.06***	0.02
Cooperativeness	−0.08**	0.03	−0.08**	0.03
College degree	−0.014*	0.006	−0.014*	0.006
Conservatism	0.06***	0.02	0.07***	0.02
Conservatism × college degree	n/a	n/a	0.05**	0.02
Constant	0.60***	0.02	0.60***	0.02
F (degrees of freedom)	7.61 (9,931)***		7.24 (10,930)***	
R²	0.068		0.075	
Number of cases	941		941	

Note: Data are from the 1991 National Race and Politics Study. Table entries are unstandardized OLS regression coefficients, with associated HC3 robust standard errors. The dependent variable is racial ambivalence.

***$p \leq .001$; **$p \leq .01$; *$p \leq .05$.

suggesting that the relationship between conservatism and ambivalence is stronger among college-educated whites.

To further probe this interaction, simple slopes for the relationship between conservatism and ambivalence were calculated for respondents in each educational category. This was done by recoding the college-degree variable on a 0/1 basis; the category for which the simple slope was to be calculated was given a code of 0 in each analysis (Aiken and West 1991). Results indicate that conservatism is significantly and positively related to racial ambivalence among college-educated whites ($b = .11, p \leq .001$), but not among those without college degrees ($b = .02, p > .35$).

Conflict between Humanitarianism and Individualism as a Mediator

The results thus far are generally consistent with my hypothesis (see Federico 2004) regarding the interface between ideology, education, and racial ambivalence. Specifically, the relationship between conservatism and ambivalence is stronger among college-educated whites, suggesting that the gains in cognitive sophistication associated with education merely intensify a pattern of mixed feelings about blacks that is "normative" for white conservatives in the present era. However, the logic of the argument here raises the possibility that the interactive effect of conservatism and education on ambivalence may be mediated by increased conflict between humanitarian and individualistic concerns. This part of the hypothesis describes a pattern of "mediated moderation," that is, one in which conservatism and education interact to generate higher levels of conflict between humanitarianism and individualism, which in turn leads to increased racial ambivalence (for methodological details, see Baron and Kenny 1986; Wegener and Fabrigar 2000).

To determine whether conflict between humanitarianism and individualism plays a stronger mediating role at the general level or at a specifically racial level, the effects of both mediators were considered simultaneously (see Federico 2004). In the present context, three conditions must be met to demonstrate the aforementioned pattern of mediated moderation: (1) conservatism and the college-degree variable must interact to predict racial ambivalence; (2) conservatism and the college-degree variable must interact to predict the hypothesized mediators, conflict between humanitarianism and individualism at both general and racial levels; and (3) the interaction between conservatism and the college-degree variable must be reduced to nonsignificance, or at least significantly reduced in magnitude, in a regression containing both this interaction and the two conflict mediators, with the mediators remaining significant (see Baron and Kenny 1986).

The first of these conditions is satisfied by the key result presented in table 5.1, that is, the significant interaction between conservatism and the college-degree variable shown in Model 2. In turn, the second condition was tested by regressing general-conflict and racial-conflict indices on the same set of predictors from before; a separate two-step hierarchical analysis was done for each mediator. The results of these analyses are summarized in table 5.2. For conflict between humanitarianism and individualism at the general level, we can see that both the main effect of conservatism ($b = .05$, $p \leq .05$) and the impact of its interaction with the college-degree variable ($b = .05$, $p \leq .10$) are fairly modest. However, for conflict between humanitarianism and individualism in the racial context, the main effect of conservatism ($b = .17$, $p \leq .001$) and the effect of its interaction with college degree ($b = .12$, $p \leq .001$) are stronger. Consistent with this, the proportions of variance accounted for in the racial-level conflict models (11.4 and 14.3 percent for Model 1 and Model 2, respectively) are larger than those in the general-level conflict models (1.8 and 2.2 percent, respectively). Simple slope analyses in the college and no-college groups suggest a similar pattern: while the relationship between conservatism and general-level conflict is somewhat larger in the college group than the no-college group ($b = .10$, $p \leq .001$, versus $b = .02$, $p > .50$), the relationship between

Table 5.2 Explaining the two types of value conflict: conservatism, education, and their interaction

Variable	General conflict				Racial-level conflict			
	Model 1		Model 2		Model 1		Model 2	
	Coeff.	S.E.	Coeff.	S.E.	Coeff.	S.E.	Coeff.	S.E.
Age	−0.00	0.00	−0.00	0.00	−0.00	0.00	−0.00	0.00
Income	0.00	0.00	0.00	0.00	0.00	0.00	0.003†	0.002
Region	0.00	0.01	0.00	0.01	0.01	0.01	0.01	0.01
Gender	0.01	0.01	0.01	0.01	0.01	0.01	0.00	0.01
Homeownership	0.01	0.01	0.01	0.01	0.01	0.01	0.01	0.01
Political expertise	−0.04†	0.02	−0.04†	0.02	−0.07***	0.02	−0.07**	0.02
Cooperativeness	−0.03	0.04	−0.02	0.04	−0.02	0.04	−0.02	0.04
College degree	−0.01	0.01	−0.01	0.01	−0.03***	0.01	−0.03***	0.01
Conservatism	0.06*	0.02	0.06**	0.02	0.17***	0.02	0.19***	0.02
Conservatism × college degree	n/a	n/a	0.05†	0.02	n/a	n/a	0.12***	0.02
Constant	0.75***	0.03	0.75***	0.03	0.56***	0.02	0.55***	0.03
F (degrees of freedom)	1.82 (9,972)†		1.99 (10,971)*		12.24 (9,982)***		14.70 (10,981)***	
R²	0.018		0.022		0.114		0.143	
Number of cases	982		982		992		992	

Note: Data are from the 1991 National Race and Politics Study. Table entries are unstandardized OLS regression coefficients, with associated HC3 robust standard errors. The dependent variable is value conflict.
***$p \leq .001$; **$p \leq .01$; *$p \leq .05$; †$p \leq .10$.

conservatism and racial-level conflict is *much* larger in the college group than the no-college group (b = .31, $p \leq$ .001 versus b = .07, $p \leq$ .05). Thus, even at this stage, the results indicate that value conflict in the racial context plays a stronger mediating role than conflict at the general level.

Finally, the third condition was tested by adding the two mediators to a model in which ambivalence was regressed on conservatism, the college-degree variable, the conservatism × college degree interaction, and all controls (in other words, Model 2 from table 5.1). This stage of the analysis is summarized in table 5.3. As the estimates in this table show, conflict between humanitarianism and individualism in the racial context predicts racial ambivalence (b = .18, $p \leq$ .001), while general conflict does not (b = .04, $p >$ .15); further, the interaction term is reduced to nonsignificance (b = .02, $p >$ .15).[5] In turn, the actual indirect effect via each mediator is given by the product of the interactive effect of conservatism and education on each mediator and the effect of that mediator on ambivalence. For conflict in the racial context, the indirect effect is .022, while the corresponding effect via general conflict is just .002. A pair of Sobel tests (see Baron and Kenny 1986) indicate that the mediated effect via racial-level conflict is highly significant (z = 4.24, $p \leq$ .001), while the mediated effect via general conflict is nonsignificant (z = 1.10, $p >$ .25).[6] Thus,

Table 5.3 Explaining racial ambivalence: mediators of the interaction between conservatism and education

Variable	Coefficient	Standard error
Age	0.001**	0.000
Income	−0.00	0.00
Region	−0.00	0.01
Gender	0.00	0.01
Homeownership	−0.00	0.01
Political expertise	−0.05**	0.02
Cooperativeness	−0.07*	0.03
College degree	−0.01	0.01
Conservatism	0.03†	0.02
Conservatism × college degree	0.02	0.02
General-level conflict	0.04	0.03
Racial-level conflict	0.18***	0.03
Constant	0.60***	0.02
F (degrees of freedom)	10.87 (12,919)***	
R^2	0.123	
Number of cases	932	

Note: Data are from the 1991 National Race and Politics Study. Table entries are unstandardized OLS regression coefficients, with associated HC3 robust standard errors. The dependent variable is racial ambivalence.

***$p \leq$ .001; **$p \leq$ .01; *$p \leq$ .05; †$p \leq$ .10.

consistent with the hypothesis suggested by my prior work on the relationship between conservatism and racial ambivalence, the tendency for this relationship to be stronger among college-educated whites appears due to the fact that education strengthens the relationship between conservatism and conflict between humanitarian and individualistic concerns. Moreover, the interactive effect of conservatism and education vis-à-vis ambivalence is found to be mediated more strongly by value conflict in the racial context than by value conflict in the abstract.

CONCLUSIONS

Typically, research on racial attitudes, beliefs, and perceptions has assumed that whites will reject negative perceptions of blacks to the extent that they accept positive ones, and vice versa. However, a large body of research suggests that this is not always the case. In fact, many studies suggest that a significant number of whites are racially ambivalent, that is, they have both positive and negative perceptions of blacks at the same time. Although there appear to be individual differences in the degree to which whites' racial attitudes deviate from bipolarity in this fashion, researchers have not devoted a great deal of attention to identifying and explaining these differences. Nevertheless, recent work indicates that ideology may play a role, specifically, that (1) conservatism is associated with higher levels of racial ambivalence among white Americans, and (2) this relationship is mediated by increased conflict between humanitarian and individualistic concerns, particularly in the racial domain.

My purpose in the present chapter has been to examine the possibility that this pattern of relationships is different among whites who possess varying levels of cognitive sophistication, namely, college-educated whites versus those without a college education. As noted earlier, prior research offers two different sets of hypotheses about how increases in cognitive sophistication associated with higher education can moderate the relationship between conservatism and value conflict—and, by extension, the relationship between conservatism and racial ambivalence. On the one hand, my original analysis raised the possibility that conflict between humanitarianism and individualism is an inherent feature of ideological conservatism among whites, particularly in the context of racial attitudes. As such, education (traditionally thought of as an indicator of the ability to learn and apply "normative" patterns of political belief) may strengthen the relationship between conservatism and value conflict, ultimately producing a stronger relationship between conservatism and ambivalence.

On the other hand, research on the linkage between conservatism and group-based anti-egalitarianism (Sidanius, Pratto, and Bobo 1996;

Sidanius *et al.* 2000) suggests that the apparent relationship between conservatism and value conflict may result from an ability-related failure to adopt a pattern of beliefs that consistently justifies racial inequality, that is, by endorsing individualism and rejecting humanitarianism, rather than endorsing both. This account suggests that higher education makes it easier for white conservatives to adopt the "correct" system-justifying pattern of beliefs, thereby attenuating the relationship between conservatism and value conflict and the relationship between conservatism and ambivalence.

Based on several analyses using data from the 1991 NRAP study, the former set of hypotheses appears to provide a more accurate account of the connections among ideology, education, and racial ambivalence. To begin with, a series of regressions demonstrated that the relationship between conservatism and racial ambivalence is stronger among whites who are more cognitively sophisticated, that is, those having a college education. Further examination indicated that the interactive effect of conservatism and education vis-à-vis racial ambivalence is mediated by conflict between humanitarian and individualistic concerns; that is, conservatism and educa-tion interact to produce higher levels of value conflict, which in turn is asso-ciated with higher levels of racial ambivalence. Lastly, echoing my earlier findings, it once again appears to be conflict between humanitarianism and individualism in the racial context, rather than conflict between these two concerns at a general level, that plays a stronger mediating role.

On the whole, then, these findings clearly are consistent with the propo-sition that conflict between racial humanitarianism and racial individualism, and the ambivalence it gives rise to, is a "normative" feature of contempo-rary political conservatism among white Americans. Instead of producing a consistently system-justifying pattern of race-related value concerns (i.e., a low level of humanitarianism paired with a high level of individualism), the cognitive sophistication afforded by completion of a college degree appears to intensify conflict between humanitarianism and individualism among white conservatives, ultimately leading to greater ambivalence. In other words, value conflict and racial ambivalence are more pronounced among those white conservatives who are *most* likely to understand the "normative" beliefs central to conservatism in the present era. Thus, to use the terminology featured in the title of this chapter, the role of education appears to be one of *conflict amplification* rather than *conflict resolution*: instead of resolving the value conflicts that mediate the relationship between conservatism and ambivalence, higher education amplifies them.

From a somewhat different angle, these results also reinforce the conclu-sion that conflict between humanitarianism and individualism is more relevant to white racial ambivalence, and to the relationship between conservatism and ambivalence among whites, when such conflict occurs at a specifically racial level. While previous research implies that humanitarian and individualistic concerns need only come into conflict at a very general level in order to generate racial ambivalence (Katz and Hass 1988; Katz, Wackenhut, and Hass 1986), the results discussed here are consistent with my conclusion (Federico 2004) that conflict between these two concerns is more germane to racial ambivalence when it occurs specifically within the context of racial politics. More precisely, the interactive effect of conservatism and education is mediated by conflict between humanitarianism and individualism at the level of racial politics, but not by conflict between the two at the level of general value orientations. Like my previous results, this finding is consistent with a growing body of work indicating that value-related concerns intersect with race-related attitudes, beliefs, and perceptions not at a general level, but at the level of beliefs about how those values relate to or help to explain the circumstances faced by specific groups.

This appears to be especially true with regard to individualism. For example, the "symbolic racism" approach to white racial attitudes has long argued that racial resentment stems from a blend of antiblack affect and individualistic values (Sears 1988). Recent studies purport to show, however, that "racialized individualism"—that is, the belief that blacks are *particularly* lacking in individualistic values—is more relevant to hostility toward blacks than is generalized individualism (Kinder and Mendelberg 2000; Sears and Henry 2003). Thus, the results reported here add further weight to the notion that researchers interested in the relationship between value conflicts and racial perceptions need to pay closer attention to the different levels at which these conflicts might occur (see Federico 2004).

The results reviewed here have other implications as well. Like my earlier work on the relationship between conservatism and the affective structure of whites' racial perceptions, the present study's focus on racial ambivalence draws attention to relatively novel aspects of the relationship between ideology and racial perceptions. As noted above, most research on the interface between ideology and racial attitudes, beliefs, and perceptions has focused on the well-established relationship between conservatism and negative evaluations of blacks (Federico and Sidanius 2002a, 2002b; Sidanius, Pratto, and Bobo 1996; Sidanius *et al.* 2000). Yet the findings discussed here paint a more nuanced picture of white conservatives' evaluations of blacks. Rather than being wholly negative, white conservatives' perceptions of blacks appear to be more conflicted, *especially* among those with higher levels of cognitive sophistication, that is, the college-educated. In other words, the racial negativity typically attributed to white conservatives may be ambivalently intertwined with a certain amount of positivity.

Among other things, this implies that white conservatives' perceptions of blacks—while generally negative—may nevertheless be subject to a certain amount of situational variability. As several contemporary theories of the survey response suggest, the expressed opinions of individuals with conflicted or ambivalent attitudes are more likely to vary in response to features of the situation (question wording, order effects, media attention, etc.) that make certain attitude-related "considerations" more salient than others (Zaller 1992; Zaller and Feldman 1992; see also Alvarez and Brehm 2002). As such, situational cues that "prime" the positive component of conservatives' ambivalent perceptions of blacks, or the humanitarianism that lies behind those positive considerations, may attenuate the overall negativity of their expressed attitudes toward blacks and the policies designed to assist them. This tendency may be especially evident among educated white conservatives, since their racial perceptions and value concerns appear to be even more mixed in nature than those of nonconservatives. Future research should explore these possibilities.

More broadly, the findings discussed here attest to the importance of moving beyond the assumption that racial perceptions have an affectively bipolar structure. At both the conceptual and operational levels, most studies of whites' racial attitudes, beliefs, and perceptions have made this assumption and relied heavily on bipolar, positive-versus-negative survey items (for notable exceptions, see Katz and Hass 1988; Katz, Wackenhut, and Hass 1986; Patchen, Hofmann, and Davidson 1976). Consequently, these studies may not have been in a position to detect the full complexity of whites' racial perceptions. Researchers who wish to study racial perceptions, and the relationship between racial perceptions and other critical variables, may therefore want to include separate measures of respondents' positive and negative attitudes and cognitions. Doing so would undoubtedly add new dimensions to the understanding of white racial opinion currently offered by the broader race-and-politics literature.

Finally, the results of this study fit into a broader and rapidly growing literature on ambivalence (in addition to the essays in this volume, for example, see Craig and Martinez 2005; Alvarez and Brehm 2002; Lavine 2001; Cacioppo, Gardner, and Berntson 1999; Thompson, Zanna, and Griffin 1995; Zaller 1992). Among other things, the findings reported here provide further support for the "value-conflict" hypothesis, which holds that ambivalence is likely to result when core values relevant to the evaluation of particular political object—such as a social group or a public policy—come into conflict for a particular individual (Alvarez and Brehm 2002; Eagly and Chaiken 1993; Katz and Hass 1988). Although many ambivalence scholars assume this hypothesis to be true, few studies have actually examined it (but see Craig *et al.* 2005b; Katz and Hass 1988). Along with the analyses reported by Federico (2004), the present study takes a step in that direction. It also adds two new twists to the overall value-conflict story: first, in addition to demonstrating that value conflict may be directly associated with ambivalence in the racial domain, the findings reported here reinforce the idea that such conflict partially explains why ambivalence is more often found among individuals with certain political predispositions (e.g., ideological conservatism); simply put, value conflict may be "normative" in the context of some predispositions, leading to ambivalence about relevant attitude objects. Second, this study suggests that cognitive sophistication (such as that provided by higher education) may not encourage individuals with particular predispositions to "work out" the value conflicts central to their belief systems; instead, they may simply amplify these conflicts, as discussed earlier. Taken together, these results encourage the belief that further research on the relationship between predispositions, value conflict, and attitude ambivalence—as well as the moderating role of various sophistication-related dimensions—may go a long way toward helping both political scientists and psychologists understand the complexity of citizens' attitudes.

APPENDIX

The following are variable names and question wordings for items drawn from the 1991 NRAP Study:

Conservatism. Seven-point scale constructed from answers to IDEO ("Generally speaking, would you consider yourself to be a liberal, a conservative, a moderate, or haven't you thought much about this?"), plus IDE2 (If moderate: "Do you think of yourself as more like a liberal or more like a conservative?"), LIB (If liberal: "Do you think of yourself as a strong liberal or a not very strong liberal?"), and CONS (If conservative: "Do you think of yourself as a strong conservative or a not very strong conservative?").

Perceptions of Blacks. [*Introduction to trait items S1 to S14*] "Now I'll read a few words that people sometimes use to describe blacks. Of course, no word fits absolutely everybody, but, as I read each one, please tell me using a number from 0 to 10 how well you think it describes blacks as a group. If you think it's a *very good* description of most blacks, give it a 10. If you feel a word is a *very inaccurate* description of most blacks, give it a 0." *Positive traits*: S1 ("dependable"), S2 ("intelligent in school"), S5 ("smart with everyday things"), S6 ("lawabiding"), S8 ("determined to succeed"), S9 ("hardworking"), S10 ("friendly"), S12 ("keep up property"), and S14 ("are good neighbors"). *Negative traits*: S3 ("violent"), S4 ("lazy"), S7 ("boastful"), S11 ("irresponsible"), and S13 ("complaining"). [*Introduction to additional trait items M7A to M7C*] "Now here are comments some people have made about how black people live and how blacks and whites relate. Based on your own observations, please check one box for each, showing whether you think the statement is definitely or probably true or false." *Positive items*: M7A ("The average black child in America does as well in school as the average white child") and M7C ("When they have the chance to improve their economic position, most blacks make good use of such opportunities"). *Negative item*: M7B ("Poor black children are more likely to carry knives and other dangerous weapons to school than poor white children are").

Humanitarian concerns. General: M4H ("Everyone should be concerned about the well-being of other people"); response options ranged from 1 ("agree strongly") to 4 (disagree strongly"). *In the racial context*: ANG2 ("How about when people are treated unfairly because of their race? On a scale from zero to ten, how much does this anger you?").

Individualistic concerns. General: M4D ("Anyone who is willing to work hard has a good chance of succeeding") and M4E ("If people work hard enough, they can make a good life for themselves"); both of these items were scored using the same response format as M4H above. *In the racial context*: OVBD ("This country sometimes goes overboard in its efforts to fight racism these days," also using the same format as M4H), ATTN ("Taking everything into consideration, do you think the government has been paying too much attention to the problems of minorities, about the right amount of attention, or do you think they haven't been paying enough attention to these groups?"), ANG4 ("How about giving blacks and other minorities special advantages in jobs and schools? On a scale from zero to ten, how much does this anger you?"), ANG8 ("How about spokesmen for minorities who are always complaining that blacks are being discriminated against? On a scale from zero to ten, how much does this anger you?"), and a "blame index" based on BLAM ("To sum up, whose fault would you say it is that blacks are worse off than whites— would you say that white people are mostly to blame, that blacks themselves are mostly to blame, or would you say that they both share the blame equally?"), BB (If whites are to blame: "Even though you feel it's mostly the fault of whites, would you say blacks are partly to blame, or that blacks should bear none of the blame?"), and BW (If blacks are to blame: "Even though you feel it's mostly the fault of black people, would you say that whites are partly to blame, or that whites should bear none of the blame?").

Political expertise. PRES ("How many terms can the President of the United States serve?") and CORT ("Please tell me how many members of the U.S. Supreme Court there are?").

Respondent cooperativeness. IN10 (Interviewer's assessment of whether the word "cooperative" described the respondent "very well," "fairly well," "not too well," or "does not describe respondent").

Education. Based on EDUC.

Demographics. These include age (AGE), gender (SEX), income (ISUM), region (REGION), and homeownership (DWEL).

NOTES

The author would like to thank the Survey Research Center at the University of California, Berkeley for permission to use data from the 1991 National Race and Politics Study, and Damla Ergun, Paul Goren, and Brad Lippman for their comments and suggestions.

1. The reasoning described here is consistent with a long line of work to the effect that ability-related variables (such as education) make it easier for citizens to see implicational relations between different attitudes, beliefs, and perceptions (e.g., Judd and Krosnick 1989; Judd and Downing 1990; Lavine, Thomsen, and

Gonzales 1997; also see Converse 1964; Stimson 1975) and to "overcome" ambivalence and other forms of attitudinal conflict (Alvarez and Brehm 2002; Zaller 1992; Zaller and Feldman 1992).

2. The sampling frame for the 1991 NRAP was all English-speaking adults aged 18 and above, from households with telephones, living within the 48 contiguous states.

3. For this purpose, positive and negative trait items were averaged to form composite measures of white respondents' positive and negative perceptions of blacks ($\alpha = .88$, mean $= .59$, s.d. $= .14$ for positive; $\alpha = .80$, mean $= .50$, s.d. $= .17$, for negative). The Thompson formula was then used to compute ambivalence scores:

$$\text{Ambivalence} = \left[\frac{P + N}{2}\right] - |P - N|$$

where P is the respondent's score on the positive-perceptions scale and N is the respondent's score on the negative-perceptions scale (also see chapter four in this volume).

4. Scores on the two conflict measures were only moderately correlated (Pearson's $r = .13, p \leq .001$).

5. Notice also that addition of the two mediators yields a significant increase in R^2 over and above that for the model containing only ideology, college degree, the interaction between these variables, and controls ($p \leq .001$).

6. Identical results were obtained when the mediating role of each conflict variable was tested separately: conflict in the racial context had a significant indirect effect ($p \leq .001$), while general conflict did not ($p > .10$).

CHAPTER SIX

MANAGING VOTER AMBIVALENCE IN GROWTH AND CONSERVATION CAMPAIGNS

Dennis Chong and Yael Wolinsky-Nahmias

As cities and suburbs in the United States continue to sprawl and consume neighboring farmlands and open space, citizens are seeking methods to preserve their environments by controlling the rate of growth and development in their communities (The Trust for Public Land and Land Trust Alliance 2002; Fulton *et al.* 2001; Hollis and Fulton 2002; Myers 1999; Myers and Puentes 2001). Community purchase of open space and passage of regulations at the ballot box to manage the pace and location of development are driven in part by the same goals as the broader environmental movement. For over two decades, Americans have registered their worries about such environmental problems as air and water pollution and the loss of natural lands (Dunlap 1995; Dunlap and Scarce 1991). These concerns have spread more recently to the environmental consequences of unchecked development in urban communities, such as smog and pollution from automobile usage and the destruction of wildlife habitat for new housing construction. Current debates over urban growth, however, are not exclusively about the environment. They also revolve around worries that individuals have about the fiscal and social problems that often accompany commercial and residential development. As cities grow in size and population, residents must deal with overcrowding of schools, high costs of infrastructure, traffic congestion, and increased demands for public services (Downs 1994, 2000; Fulton *et al.* 2000; Hollis, Porter, and Tischler 2000; Katz and Bradley 1999; Orfield 1997, 2002).

Voters display considerable uncertainty and ambivalence about the best course of action to address growth and conservation issues. They generally favor protection of the environment and the public purchase of open space, but are also concerned about sustaining economic growth and are reluctant to pay higher taxes for conservation programs. Voters often endorse controls on development, while simultaneously believing in the right of individuals to use their property as they wish.

In this chapter, we show how public ambivalence on these issues shapes the campaign strategies of interest groups in referendums and initiatives dealing with growth and conservation. Many ballot measures are designed to pass without controversy but, when they are contested, the campaigns are usually led by local land trusts and environmental organizations against the opposition of the home building industry and business interests more generally. Each side tries to mobilize public support by educating voters to evaluate the consequences of the proposed policy in ways that are advantageous to its own ends. But whereas the success of environmental interest groups depends on *reducing* voter ambivalence by reconciling the competing priorities of voters within a single program, the aim of the building industry is to *heighten* voter ambivalence by showing that conservation programs cannot attain their goals without compromising other values. The concept of voter ambivalence is therefore not a constant in these campaigns, but a variable that is subject to manipulation by interested parties.

We illustrate the competing strategies in our analysis of a 2000 Arizona statewide citizen's initiative on growth management. This measure highlights the public's ambivalence toward more comprehensive solutions to urban sprawl, such as growth boundaries. Because the consequences of urban growth boundaries are difficult to judge, popular support for boundaries depends on whether the scenarios that people imagine for them are reassuring or threatening. Campaign debates can inform and influence public perceptions, because citizens are relatively untutored about the consequences of alternative solutions despite having strong intuitions about the need to confront the problems associated with rapid growth. Early polling in Arizona showed overwhelming public support for the citizens' initiative, but the measure was eventually routed at the polls following an intensely waged campaign led by developers and homebuilders in which doubts were raised about the social, legal, and economic effects of the initiative on local communities.

OPEN SPACE AND ENVIRONMENTALISM

Concern for the preservation of open space and containment of urban sprawl is a natural step in the long-term evolution of the environmental agenda in this country. Wilderness protection and land conservation have preoccupied mainstream environmental organizations like the Sierra Club and The Nature Conservancy since their founding. These "first-generation" environmental issues remained important throughout the last century, but the environmental movement broadened its agenda significantly during that time as new scientific evidence revealed the severity of water and air pollution, loss of biodiversity, and global climate change, among many other environmental issues.

Urban growth brings environmental concerns close to home. The debate is no longer about hunting African elephants or drilling in national parks, but rather slowing down residential and commercial construction, and improving water and air quality, by limiting development and automobile usage. The environment that residents are protecting may be state trust land on the outskirts of their cities, or neighborhood parks and trails within walking distance of their homes. In short, the environment that is being preserved is no longer remote (Diamond and Noonan 1996).

In general, the same groups of voters who favor preservation of open space and policies to combat urban sprawl also tend to support other forms of environmental protection. Our analysis of national data collected for the Trust for Public Land (TPL) in 1999 shows that support for urban growth controls is generally greater among those who are college educated, younger, politically liberal, who have contributed to environmental organizations in the past year, and who believe that local and state governments should place air and water quality highest on their list of priorities (also see Albrecht, Bultena, and Hoiberg 1986; Baldassare 1985, 1990; Connerly and Frank 1986; Gottdiener and Nieman 1981; Press 1999, 2002; Protash and Baldassare 1983).[1]

However, what makes urban growth an attractive political issue for politicians in both parties is that there are dimensions of the issue that appeal to both Democrats and Republicans, liberals and conservatives (American Institute of Architects 1999). Even though support tends to be higher among the same constituencies that support other environmental causes, the correlations between attitudes toward regulating growth and socioeconomic status, partisanship, and ideology are often modest. Moreover, while support for controls on growth is lower among conservative groups relative to liberal groups, it is fairly high in absolute terms (Chong and Wolinsky-Nahmias 2001). This reflects not only the general appeal of environmental goals to the American public, but the ideological diversity of benefits often promised by policies to manage growth. Voters can support these policies for a number of motivations, from saving wildlife habitat and conserving natural areas to reducing traffic congestion, providing parks and recreation areas for children and families, and boosting the values of their own homes.

FRAMING THE CONSERVATION DEBATE

While national polls indicate majority public support for environmental protection and limitations on growth, voters remain uncertain about the best policies to achieve these goals. This uncertainty is due both to the novelty of the growth issue and to the public's ambivalence over the right balance to strike between conservation and development. Ambivalence is defined by the simultaneous possession of two values or goals that are in conflict with respect to a particular choice (Alvarez and Brehm 2002; Craig, Kane, and Martinez 2002; Feldman and Zaller 1992). Because most voters have conflicting goals and do not hold firm positions on these issues, framing can have significant effects on their expressed preferences. By contrast, voters who possess strong opinions have clear frames of reference on growth issues and are more likely to resist attempts to change their views (Druckman and Nelson 2003; also see Nelson, Clawson, and Oxley 1997; Miller and Krosnick 2000; Kinder and Sanders 1990).

Framing is the strategic selection and representation of information to influence people's policy preferences (Chong 1996; Druckman 2001; Gamson 1992; Kinder and Sanders 1990; Nelson, Clawson, and Oxley 1997). Whereas persuasion involves changing beliefs about a policy, the goal of framing is to make certain assessments about a policy more salient than others (Mutz, Sniderman, and Brody 1996). The conceptual distinction between persuasion and framing is often cleaner in theory than in practice, however, as many messages are intended to persuade as well as frame. For example, when conservationists link sprawl to a host of quality-of-life problems within communities, they want to convince people to blame these problems on unchecked growth and, at the same time, to increase the salience of these concerns when people evaluate proposals to slow growth.

Organizations on both sides of the growth debate make the case that their policies improve community quality of life while also being true to widely accepted values. We reviewed a confidential report by a consulting firm advising a preservation organization on a number of strategies for linking policies to both values and solutions for community problems. The report urged the organization to root its proposals in values such as choice, freedom, privacy, sense of community, and responsibility to family: "Communications should make it clear that sprawl is about choice—We do have a choice between over-development and a better quality of life for individuals and communities. Smart-growth advocates must not be viewed on the wrong side of choice, as the values of choice and freedom are particularly powerful arguments against control, if left unanswered." In particular, the report warned that opponents of growth controls will emphasize other forms of freedom and choice, especially housing choice and the freedom to develop private property.

The public has inchoate views about different regulatory policies, but stronger opinions on issues that can be connected to sprawl, such as protecting the environment, saving open space, providing affordable housing, and reducing traffic congestion. Yet the connection between sprawl and these quality-of-life issues in the public's mind is often uncertain and susceptible to influence and manipulation by interest groups and opinion leaders. Some people, for example, think traffic problems *result* from sprawl while others regard sprawl development as a *solution* to urban traffic problems. The most readily accepted implication of sprawl among voters is damage to the environment. People see a direct relationship between urban sprawl and the destruction of open space, forests, and wildlife habitats. In conservation campaigns, voters have been persuaded that environmental protection is a valid reason for regulating growth and saving open space from development. The advantage of framing ballot measures in environmental terms is evident in the frequency with which ballot measure titles refer to "clean water," "streams," "parks," "trails," and "open space."

The building industry has tried to reduce public support for regulation by deflecting attention away from environmental protection toward the effects of these policies on community living conditions and the local economy. In particular, support for growth control tends to be undercut by concern over housing choice and affordable housing. Growth controls also have other potential vulnerabilities that can be brought to voters' attention: threats to private property, relocation of new development in residential neighborhoods, higher taxes, slowing of the economy, increased governmental regulation, and incompetent management of programs.

For example, when respondents in the TPL national survey were asked simply if they favored or opposed public programs to buy open space, almost 70 percent expressed support; this level diminished substantially when they were presented with arguments *against* as well as *in favor* of purchasing open space. Many of those who originally supported open space were persuaded that open space protection is better left in the hands of the marketplace, on the grounds that government programs create bureaucracy and inefficiency and threaten the property rights of landowners (see table 6.1). Further evidence of how the property rights argument undercuts support for regulation is found in a January 1999 CNN/*Time* national poll, which found strong support for drawing urban growth boundaries around the respondent's community: almost 60 percent favored "the establishment of a zone or greenbelt around your community where new homes, businesses, or stores could not be built on land that is currently undeveloped." In the same survey, however, a higher percentage of individuals, when asked to rank their priorities, felt that it was more important that "individuals do what they want with land that they own" than that government be able "to regulate residential and commercial development for the common good."[2]

Table 6.1   Evaluation of alternative arguments for and against the public purchase of land

Question: Which of the following comes closest to your own view about the purchase of public land?	(%)
Having the public purchase land is the fairest way to manage growth and development. It allows local communities to decide for themselves which areas they want to protect, without imposing unfair regulations on landowners and businesses.	38
Public purchase of land leads to increased government bureaucracy and inefficiency. Companies and private citizens know how to manage land better than the government does. Further, the public purchase of land will result in the government violating the private property rights of some citizens.	34
Not sure	28

Source: 1999 Trust for Public Land national survey (*N* = 800).

Whether citizens support growth controls depends greatly on how they imagine the local consequences of such policies. Land trusts, environmental organizations, and builders and developers regularly gather opinion data on growth and conservation issues to discover the best way to craft their messages and frame their case to voters (cf. Jacobs and Shapiro 2000). Polling is used to identify the themes that sway voters, as well as the people and organizations that are the most effective carriers of those messages. Specific information may be gleaned about acceptable levels and forms of taxation, and about particular lands that the public most wants preserved. However, the best themes may not refer to details of the policy but to evocative symbols, appealing phrases, and bucolic scenes.

MANAGING GROWTH AT THE BALLOT BOX

In the real world of local politics, open-space programs that require popular approval in a referendum vote have been promoted through a combination of environmental and economic arguments calculated to reduce voter ambivalence. Protection of streams and wilderness, and creation of parks and trails are attractive environmental goals for most citizens. If voters can be persuaded that achieving these goals *also* reduces traffic congestion, protects the community against flooding, improves air and water quality, and avoids the expense of building new infrastructure, then residents of all political persuasions can find reasons to vote in favor of conserving land.

Accordingly, hundreds of cities, towns, and counties around the country have succeeded in passing open-space ballot measures, thus confirming what many polls have reported about the willingness of citizens to pay higher taxes to restrict development in their communities (The Trust for Public Land and Land Trust Alliance 2002; Fulton *et al.* 2000; Hollis and Fulton 2002; Myers 1999; Myers and Puentes 2001). Between 1998 and 2001, there were over six hundred open-space measures across the country in which communities voted on programs designed to buy and protect land that might otherwise be used for commercial purposes. The vast majority of measures are financed either by increases in property tax rates, or by issuing bonds that are to be repaid over a fixed term through property tax increases, general revenues, or a specific revenue source; a smaller number of measures are funded through sales taxes, property transfer taxes, income taxes, or impact fees. These referendums have passed at a spectacular rate of roughly 80 percent and secured more than $19 billion for the preservation of land, expansion of parks and greenways, and protection of wildlife and water supplies. If votes on economic development, land use authority, infrastructure, and regulations such as urban growth boundaries are added to the open-space measures, there were 553 state and local ballot measures addressing growth (broadly defined) in November 2000 alone, of which 72.2 percent passed.[3] Almost half (45 percent) of the ballot measures dealt with open space, parks, and recreation issues (Myers 1999; Myers and Puentes 2001).

A key factor in the success of open-space referendums is that proponents of these programs have managed to tap into popular support for environmental causes without antagonizing the development community into forming an opposition. Without an opposition to contend with, conservationists have been able to run essentially one-sided campaigns that reconcile environmental and economic goals and accentuate those features of the program that the public finds most appealing. A lack of controversy over open-space programs leads to less voter ambivalence, which explains their high rate of success at the ballot box. The typical winning campaign has promised (1) a menu of immediate local benefits to be derived from protecting open space, such as trails, greenspaces, and parks, flood protection, less traffic congestion, and higher home values; (2) modest tax increases to pay for these programs; and (3) assurances to voters that their tax money will be competently administered by local government agencies (Kelly and Zieper 2000).

To the extent that open-space programs emphasize protecting the environment, are priced correctly, and do not threaten development and real estate interests, they can garner widespread community support from groups driven by a mixture of different motives, including a desire to save open space and recreational areas, leave a legacy to future generations, preserve home values, and limit overcrowding and traffic. There are enough self-interested and altruistic reasons for people of all partisan and ideological perspectives to get on board these programs, making open-space preservation the kind of consensus issue that politicians like to champion.

However, the smooth passage of many open-space referendums contrasts sharply with our case study of a November 2000 statewide citizen's initiative in Arizona, led by the Arizona chapter of the Sierra Club, which called for all communities to draw urban growth boundaries and develop comprehensive land use plans that would be submitted for local voter approval. As in other parts of the country, proponents of the initiative tried to mobilize voter frustration with the problems created by growth and development. They had tested the measure in public opinion polling and found widespread support for its central tenets. Yet unlike many open-space referendums, the Arizona campaign ran into concerted opposition from the building and real estate industries as well as the state legislature. A well-funded opposition turned public opinion against the measure by raising doubts about its fairness and the social and economic consequences of growth boundaries. Although early polling on the Arizona initiative suggested that it would pass handily, public support collapsed over the course of an intensely fought campaign, and the initiative ultimately was defeated by a 70–30 percent margin. Our case study focuses on how voter ambivalence about the costs and benefits of growth boundaries was amplified by the building industry's intense opposition campaign to realign public opinion.

THE CITIZEN'S GROWTH MANAGEMENT INITIATIVE

Phoenix is one of the fastest growing cities in the country and a poster city for urban sprawl. Its population is doubling every 20 years, and the expansion of the city consumes an acre every hour (Morrison Institute for Public Policy 2001). The Sierra Club has been a vocal proponent of urban growth boundaries and increased public involvement in planning neighborhoods and cities (Sierra Club 1998). In the mid-1990s, the Sierra Club began discussing a comprehensive ballot initiative to address growth issues in Arizona. The Arizona initiative focused on urban growth boundaries that would promote fill-in development within the city rather than on the urban fringe.

Following a false start in 1998 when not enough signatures were gathered by the deadline to qualify the initiative, a coalition of citizen groups led by the Sierra Club placed the Citizen's Growth Management Initiative (CGMI), also known as Proposition 202, on the 2000 state ballot. CGMI was a multipart initiative that would require cities, towns, and counties with more than 2,500 people to develop growth management plans that included urban growth boundaries drawn to accommodate ten years of future growth. The measure would also obligate builders to pay the full cost of infrastructure in their developments, including sewers, schools, roads, and parks. In addition, local citizens would vote on general development plans and would have the right to sue government for noncompliance.

The Republican-controlled state legislature had taken steps during this period to address growth issues and to forestall a citizen's initiative with two pieces of legislation, Growing Smarter and Growing Smarter Plus, passed in 1998 and 2000, respectively. One element of Growing Smarter Plus was a proposed amendment of the state constitution to allow preservation of up to 3 percent of state trust land having environmental and historical value. Because constitutional amendments require voter approval before taking effect, the state trust land proposal, known as the Arizona Conservation Reserve, was placed on the 2000 ballot as Proposition 100 (Morrison Institute for Public Policy 2001).

Opponents of CGMI argued that the legislature's program was more carefully conceived than CGMI and deserved an opportunity to work. Supporters of CGMI countered that the legislature's efforts were mainly symbolic and intended to undercut voter support for their initiative. Recent history showed that each time the Sierra Club wanted to move ahead with a comprehensive planning measure, the state legislature countered with a state trust lands proposal—a divide-and-conquer strategy that peeled away moderate elements from the environmental coalition. The Sierra Club maintained that conserving state trust lands was not a sufficient solution to growth problems. Efforts to negotiate a compromise with the governor and legislature over CGMI faltered.

Public opinion data gathered in the summer of 2000 by KAET public television showed overwhelming support (close to 70 percent) for both the Sierra Club's and the legislature's propositions. All components of CGMI had been tested in polling and focus groups. The Sierra Club had been prepared to leave out any elements of the initiative that were unpopular, but it found strong support for the imposition of growth boundaries, development impact fees, and voter approval of comprehensive community plans. Both proponents and opponents of CGMI had learned from their own internal polling that state residents were worried about rapid growth in the state and the problems this created for the affordability of housing, traffic and transportation, environmental pollution, and the loss of open space. It was common knowledge that residents were frustrated with the fast pace of growth and its consequences.

The Opposition to CGMI

Much of the responsibility for the demise of CGMI can be attributed to the campaign waged by Arizonans for Responsible Planning (ARP), a group organized in 1997 by the Homebuilders Association of Arizona. ARP was created to communicate with opinion leaders and legislators about growth management in the state, but in May 2000 it was transformed into a campaign committee to coordinate opposition to CGMI.

Opponents of CGMI recognized that residents were worried about rapid growth and traffic congestion in their communities. Their own polls showed that people wanted government to slow the pace of development and to impose developer impact fees to cover the full costs of public services and infrastructure. Despite having positive overall evaluations of the state legislature, Arizonans were critical of the government's performance in a number of areas related to growth and development. Most people believed that growth boundaries were the best method for stopping urban sprawl and protecting the environment. A slight majority accepted the idea that future development would be channeled inside the growth boundary into existing neighborhoods and vacant lots. Similarly, slight majorities were comfortable with the prospect of tougher citizen and city and county controls on re-zoning and developments over 20 acres.

However, ARP was doubtful that CGMI would pass because public opinion polling also showed that voters could be made to feel ambivalent about the concept of urban growth boundaries. Arizonans were susceptible to many negative suggestions about the potential implications of CGMI. They found the idea that the initiative would infringe on private property rights plausible. They agreed that obstructionists would probably exploit the initiative's lawsuit provision to tie up development in the courts. They expected that CGMI would slow economic growth in the state and reduce the number of jobs and tax revenues.

Thus, while citizens accepted the idea that boundaries would channel development to areas within the boundary, they worried that growth boundaries would make housing less affordable, increase traffic congestion and housing densities, and promote the construction of apartment buildings in their neighborhoods. They also were troubled by the possibility that those who resided outside of the growth boundary would not be able to get basic services, and that this might reduce the value of their property. ARP concluded from its polling that it could defeat CGMI by bringing these latent voter concerns to the surface in a well-orchestrated campaign designed to maximize voter ambivalence and doubt about the concept of growth boundaries.

Connecting Policies to Values

In political campaigns, the strategy of the competing sides is to maintain their core constituency while making a concerted effort to win over swing

Table 6.2 Priorities in managing growth

Question: If you were to determine the right priority on managing growth and development in your community, which one of the following issues would be your top concern? [rotated]

Conserving land and protecting the environment	(%)
Protecting the environment and open space	17.5
Stopping the spread of development in outlying areas	9.8
Preventing farm and ranch land from being developed	6.6
Maintaining homes and public goods	
Keeping home ownership affordable for families	13.5
Keeping up construction of new schools	12.6
Reducing traffic by expanding roads and highways	12.5
Paying for public improvements as growth occurs	6.9
Protecting property and economic growth	
Limiting government interference with property rights	9.3
Attracting new businesses and jobs	7.1
Unsure/Refused	4.2

Source: 1998 Arizona statewide survey ($N = 807$).

voters who might be persuaded to choose either side (Bailey *et al.* 2000; also see Johnson 2001). Our analysis of a 1998 Arizona state survey shows that about a quarter of the electorate gave its highest priority to managing growth and conserving land (open space and farms); about one-sixth emphasized protection of private property and economic growth.[4] Table 6.2 shows that the big swing vote on land issues in the state, making up close to 50 percent of likely voters, was the group of citizens who expressed concern about quality-of-life issues related to maintaining homes and public goods (housing, traffic, public services, and taxes). These individuals sought a middle ground between no growth and unfettered development, and wanted to manage growth to ensure affordable housing, quality public schools, and efficient roads and highways. They would support growth boundaries if they thought such regulations would support their environmental goals without harming their other community interests. On the other hand, if they felt that growth boundaries would make housing worse, increase traffic, and place excessive pressure on public services, they would be torn between these conflicting goals.

We confirm the ambivalence of those who were concerned about housing and public services by examining their support for the preservation of open space. Table 6.3 shows that this voting bloc supported open-space preservation almost to the same extent as those who placed their highest priority on the environment and land conservation. Therefore, a program

Table 6.3 Support for open-space programs by voter priorities

Support for saving open space	Conserving land and protecting the environment (%)	Maintaining homes and public goods (%)	Protecting property and economic growth (%)
Low	22	29	49
Medium	33	29	26
High	46	42	25
Number of cases	273	367	132

Note: Data are from the 1998 Arizona statewide survey. Entries are column percentages (missing cases on either variable excluded).

focused strictly on saving open space should theoretically have commanded majority support by combining into a single coalition those who were most concerned about conservation and those whose number-one priority was community quality of life. Only citizens who gave top priority to economic growth and private property seemed reluctant to endorse programs aimed at preserving open space.

In contrast to open-space programs, regulatory measures such as growth boundaries create greater ambivalence among voters not only because boundaries are more complex policies, but because the effects of growth boundaries are invariably debated by environmental and building industry interest groups. The strategy of those who favor land regulation is to reduce ambivalence by showing that boundaries are compatible with both environmental and community goals. The strategy employed by opponents of growth boundaries is to create ambivalence by arguing that boundaries protect peripheral lands at the expense of existing communities; in other words, the builders argue that boundaries will save open space by limiting housing choice and forcing existing neighborhoods to accept increased density, traffic, and congestion. To the extent that the building industry succeeds in getting voters to accept its evaluation of the effects of growth boundaries, it drives a wedge between those who are most concerned about the environment and those who want to ensure that they will have access to quality housing and schools and other concrete quality-of-life amenities.

The following analysis illustrates how alternative frames alter voter preferences by heightening ambivalence among swing voters between competing value priorities. Five differently framed questions were posed in the 1998 Arizona statewide survey concerning urban growth boundaries (see table 6.4). The first question provided an objective description of the features of the growth boundary initiative, which emphasized that land outside of designated boundaries would be conserved and public service to these areas would be prohibited. Because there was no explicit reference to any

Table 6.4   Alternative measures of support for CGMI

1. *CGMI (1st ballot test)*
By January 2001, all cities and counties over 2,500 people shall adopt growth management ordinances for voter approval that establish urban growth boundaries no larger than necessary to accommodate ten years of expected population increase. Land outside growth boundaries will not be re-zoned, and extension of water, sewer, or electricity to these areas is prohibited. Re-zoning land will require a four-fifths vote by local government and voter approval is required to re-zone more than twenty acres. Cities and counties will also assess higher fees on development to pay for various public facilities and services. (57.3% yes; 35.6% no)

2. *CGMA vs. higher density*
Here's a statement by a supporter of the Growth Management Initiative. Please tell me if you strongly agree, somewhat agree, somewhat disagree, or strongly disagree: Development in outlying areas should be stopped because it threatens the quality of life. Future developments should be shifted instead to existing communities—even if it requires higher density housing in our neighborhoods and limits where people can live. People must accept higher density housing-like apartments and condominiums to safeguard the environment, preserve the desert, and stop urban sprawl in Arizona. (36.6% agree; 60.5% disagree)

3. *CGMI vs. housing choice*
Smith says we need a state law to stop urban sprawl around Arizona's cities. We should prevent growth in outlying areas and open desert. He says future development of homes and businesses should only be allowed in existing cities next to already built-up neighborhoods.
   Jones says people build homes and businesses in outlying areas because they want to live in single-family homes on good-sized lots that they can afford. He says we shouldn't pass laws that would restrict where people can buy a home or where they choose to live. Which one do you agree with most? (37.9% support Smith; 56.1% support Jones)

4. *CGMI as a radical green plan*
Smith says vote Yes on the Growth Management Initiative to stop sprawl and make developers pay more. He wants growth boundaries to stop development in outlying areas, higher development fees, voter approval of development, and growth restrictions until the plan takes effect in 2001.
   Jones says vote No on the Growth Management Initiative because it's a radical no-growth plan written by the Sierra Club and other environmental extremists. He says the fine print in their plan will hurt our neighborhoods, treat property owners unfairly, and result in frivolous lawsuits that only benefit the lawyers. Which one do you agree with most? (43.0% support Smith; 46.4% support Jones)

5. *CGMI vs. Growing Smarter Act*
Smith says vote Yes on the Growth Management Initiative to stop sprawl and make developers pay more. He wants growth boundaries to stop development in outlying areas, higher development fees, voter approval of development, and growth restrictions until the plan takes effect in 2001.
   Jones says vote No on the Growth Management Initiative because it goes too far. He says it will backfire on our neighborhoods, treat property owners unfairly, and result in phony lawsuits by environmentalists. He supports the "Growing Smarter" alternative that makes developers follow community planning rules and preserves open space from development. Which one do you agree with most? (31.0% support Smith; 61.0% support Jones)

Source: 1998 Arizona statewide survey (*N* = 807).

potential negative consequences of growth boundaries, we would expect that those who placed their highest priority on conserving land *and* those who cared most about maintaining community quality of life (but also supported protecting open space) would join forces in support of this proposal.

The second question, by contrast, raised doubts about the initiative by suggesting that dense neighborhoods would be one of the implications of using growth boundaries to protect the environment. The third question forced a choice between saving outlying areas and the desert, on the one hand, and living in single-family homes on spacious lots, on the other. The fourth and fifth questions presented arguments for and against the initiative and asked respondents to indicate which argument was more persuasive to them. In both cases, the argument in support of growth boundaries outlined the main features of the initiative. Question 4 also presented the counterargument that growth boundaries were unfair to property owners and would result in excessive lawsuits. Question 5 countered by offering a moderate legislative alternative known as the Growing Smarter Act, and suggested that this law would protect open space and strengthen community planning better than CGMI.

CGMI did well in the one-sided, descriptive format, winning a majority vote, but fared rather poorly when framed in contexts that alluded to negative implications or offered an alternative approach. Voters were reluctant, for example, to accept higher density living in exchange for growth boundaries. They also were less likely to support in-fill development when presented with the notion that people want single-family homes on more spacious lots in outlying areas. Voters were least likely to support the initiative when informed about the state's Growing Smarter plans to moderate and control growth.

In general, the most effective frames are able to raise support (or quell opposition) by softening divisions among major groups in the electorate. It is instructive to examine in detail how the coalition for growth boundaries is expanded or shrunk depending on the perceived relationship between the policy and voter priorities. Effective messages are those that increase support across social categories. When preferences on the five items are regressed on attitudes toward growth and government regulation, local priorities, and attitudes toward the Sierra Club (see table 6.5), it is evident that framing of the alternatives alters the coalition of supporters and opponents. Each alternative framing generated a different result depending on the relative strengths of the various frames.

The electorate is broken down in table 6.5 along three dimensions according to (1) priorities for the community; (2) ideal rate of growth; and (3) preferred government approach to growth and development.[5] On each of these dimensions, there was an intermediate group that viewed growth in

Table 6.5 Support for Citizen's Growth Management Initiative (CGMI) against alternatives

Predictor	CGMI (1st vote)	CGMI vs. higher density	CGMI vs. housing choice	CGMI vs. radical green plan	CGMI vs. Growing Smarter	Save open space
Growth priorities						
Conserving land and	0.13**	0.23**	0.20**	0.14**	0.09	0.08**
protecting the environment[a]	(0.04)	(0.04)	(.04)	(.06)	(0.06)	(0.02)
Growth priorities						
Maintaining homes	0.08*	0.06	0.02	0.02	−0.02	0.08**
and public goods[a]	(0.04)	(0.04)	(0.04)	(0.05)	(0.05)	(0.02)
Government regulation	0.10**	0.07	0.21**	0.19**	0.09	0.04*
(stop or restrict growth)[b]	(0.04)	(0.04)	(0.04)	(0.05)	(0.06)	(0.02)
Government regulation	0.09**	0.03	0.08*	0.09*	0.00	0.04**
(planned growth)[b]	(0.03)	(0.03)	(0.03)	(0.04)	(0.04)	(0.02)
Ideal pace of growth	0.13**	0.07*	0.11**	0.11**	0.06	0.02
(slower)[c]	(0.04)	(0.03)	(0.03)	(0.04)	(0.04)	(0.02)
Ideal pace of growth	0.15**	0.10*	0.11**	0.20**	0.06	0.02
(no growth)[c]	(0.04)	(0.04)	(0.04)	(0.05)	(0.06)	(0.02)
Attitude toward Sierra	0.17**	0.21**	0.14**	0.34**	0.14**	0.09**
Club (negative/positive)	(0.04)	(0.04)	(0.04)	(0.06)	(0.06)	(0.02)
Constant	0.24**	0.09**	0.10**	0.08	0.23**	0.62**
	(0.04)	(0.04)	(0.04)	(0.06)	(0.06)	(0.02)
Adjusted R^2	0.14	0.17	0.18	0.28	0.07	0.09
Standard error of estimate	0.30	0.33	0.34	0.31	0.32	0.17
Number of cases	677	675	677	342[d]	335[d]	677

Note: Data are from the 1998 Arizona statewide survey ($N = 807$). See table 6.4 for measurement of the dependent variables. See table 6.2 for measurement of the growth priority variable. See the appendix for measurement of other independent variables. Table entries are unstandardized regression coefficients, with associated standard errors listed in parentheses. All dependent and independent variables have been scored from 0–1 to allow for comparisons across variables. All dependent variables are 5-category ordinal variables that measure degrees of support for CGMI when paired against various alternatives.

**$p \leq .01$; *$p \leq .05$.

[a] The baseline category for growth priorities is the group of respondents who favor "Protecting Property and Economic Growth."

[b] The baseline category for government regulation of growth is the group of respondents who want government to allow people "to use their property as they see fit."

[c] The baseline category for ideal pace of growth is the group of respondents who favor "faster" growth or maintaining the current rate of growth.

[d] The smaller Ns reflect that each of these questions was asked of only half the respondents in the sample.

both positive and negative terms. Citizens who cared most about community services were flanked, on one side, by those who cared most about saving land and, on the other, by those who were most concerned about property and economic prosperity. People who wanted continued growth so long as the pace was moderate fell in between groups that wanted growth either to be curtailed or to continue unabated. With respect to government intervention, about half of the electorate preferred "planned growth" rather than either unregulated growth or severe government restrictions on growth.

Not surprisingly, support for CGMI was greatest when the initiative was presented without counterargument. Each of the three intermediate groups joined with more ardent defenders of the land in supporting CGMI on the first test ballot. Those who wanted both to save land and to obtain quality public services supported CGMI initially to a significantly greater degree than those who wanted foremost to promote economic growth. Similarly, voters who wanted to stop or restrict growth, and those who supported growth but wished to see it managed more carefully, were both significantly more supportive of CGMI than those who wanted the pace of growth to be maintained or accelerated.

Raising the issue of affordable housing and higher density neighborhoods caused a drop in support among respondents who were primarily concerned with homes and public services. Portraying CGMI as a "radical" environmental plan sharpened ideological differences, especially the contrast between supporters and opponents of the Sierra Club; however, this framing also eliminated any significant differences among voters with different priorities for managing growth. Finally, proposing a moderate policy alternative (Growing Smarter) that alluded to the popular goal of open space proved to be the most successful tack for reducing support for CGMI. This framing was so effective in dampening support that it reduced to insignificance the effect of beliefs about the ideal pace of growth and attitudes toward government regulation. Even those whose priority in regulating growth was to save land were no longer significantly more likely than those who wanted to promote growth to support CGMI against the GS alternative. The latter managed to alleviate the ambivalence of those who wanted to manage growth but not stop it by promising to them *both* open space and community planning to regulate growth.

For comparison, the final column of table 6.5 looks at the predictors of support for open-space programs. Unlike support for growth boundaries, support for open space was widespread and brought together the large majority that was interested in saving land and improving local conditions and public services. There were significant differences between supporters and opponents of environmental organizations, but the mean level of support among all groups was considerably higher for open space than for growth boundaries. These results indicate that support for CGMI is maximized when voters focus on the environmental benefits of controlling growth, but minimized when they feel that growth boundaries will compromise other goals pertaining to housing choice and the quality of public services.

The Campaign Against CGMI

The ambivalence of a large segment of the electorate toward urban growth boundaries meant that support for CGMI was vulnerable. ARP was convinced that if it could run a campaign in which it shaped public perceptions of CGMI, it stood an excellent chance of converting public opinion. Specifically, if voters could be offered a more moderate alternative to boundaries, they would probably prefer it. Just as the Sierra Club feared and the legislature intended, the Growing Smarter package provided a safe harbor for voters who became apprehensive about the overall consequences of CGMI.

ARP ran the most expensive initiative campaign in state history, spending over $5 million. Both the CGMI message and its messenger were attacked; the Sierra Club, for example, was painted as an outside, ideologically driven group. ARP spoke about the economic costs of boundaries at the same time that it criticized the unfairness of the CGMI program. The group worked to increase awareness of Growing Smarter and Growing Smarter Plus legislation, in an effort to reassure voters that state leaders were attuned to the issues of growth and doing something about it.

ARP framed the issues early in the campaign by releasing its own studies of the economic impact of Proposition 202, and by publicizing the coalition of individuals and organizations who were opposed to the initiative. The broad base of the ARP coalition was contrasted to the narrow base of the Sierra Club and other environmental groups. Core arguments that ARP used in its campaign were that CGMI:

- treated people unfairly depending on whether they owned land inside or outside of the growth boundaries;
- would lead to higher housing costs and loss of employment;
- would allow a small number of anti-growth zealots to use the lawsuit provision to hold up all development;
- did not accommodate the varied priorities of communities; and
- would channel growth into existing communities and increase housing density, traffic, and pollution.

ARP used extensive direct mailings, mass media, internet communications, and grassroots activism (3,000 volunteers were recruited and mobilized) to transmit its messages about the dangers of CGMI. A massive mailing of campaign brochures was sent 30 days before vote-by-mail began. Because of early voting, ARP made a concerted effort to target the 23 percent of voters who were expected to cast early ballots beginning on October 5, 2000; these individuals were contacted by postcard and telephone and sent an early voter guide.

The electorate was broken down into core supporters, opponents, and swing voters who were up for grabs. Core support for Proposition 202 came from women, Hispanics, and Democrats. The "no" side drew most reliably from men (over the age of 40), Republicans, and rural voters. Upscale, suburban residents, independents, and city dwellers were the key moderate voters in the campaign. Economic and planning arguments were used to solidify the core base of opposition to CGMI, while issues of fairness and process were used to attract support among potential swing voters. The claim that growth boundaries would increase residential density within cities was used to raise concern among CGMI supporters.

Op-ed articles were written and sent to newspapers. ARP issued press releases on the addition of new coalition partners, complete with accompanying photographs. The authors of economic reports on the impact of Proposition 202 made the rounds of the media circuit. Well-prepared speakers appeared in radio and television debates and discussions. Endorsements were central to the ARP effort. Key endorsements by Governor Jane Hull and Senator John McCain, for example, were announced with great fanfare, with the governor being counted on to help persuade women voters. ARP also strived to broaden its coalition significantly beyond the building industry. Prominent Democrats and Hispanics were sought out as part of an effort that ultimately yielded 80 organizational endorsements of ARP's opposition to CGMI.

The opposition had superior resources, popular spokespersons, and effective messages. The combination of these components maximized its capacity to frame issues to its advantage, create doubt in the minds of voters, and persuade ambivalent voters to switch their positions. In the last poll conducted by the homebuilders, on October 23–24, 2000, 88 percent of probable voters had heard something about Proposition 202. Three-quarters of the respondents (76 percent) recalled seeing a television advertisement or hearing a radio message about 202. Importantly, though, almost three times as many people recalled that the ads were opposed to 202 than remembered that the ads were in favor (27 versus 10 percent). Another 27 percent recalled seeing ads both for and against 202, while 12 percent recalled seeing ads but were unsure of their content. Most respondents (59 percent) didn't recall receiving any mailings about 202. But of those who did, almost twice as many (11 versus 6 percent) remembered that the mailing opposed 202. By late October, the Sierra Club's own polls confirmed that CGMI's defeat at the polls was virtually assured.

SUMMARY AND CONCLUSION

The popularity of open-space programs and other measures to manage urban development reflects the growing desire of city and suburban residents to protect their environments and control the future direction of their communities. Conservation groups have used public opinion surveys to identify the most effective ways to frame their arguments for regulating growth and saving open space. Preferences on growth issues are susceptible to framing in part because voters are uncertain about the consequences of restricting growth and ambivalent about the tradeoffs between conservation and development.

Many referendums on open space have been largely uncontested by design. Proponents of open-space programs have often succeeded in arguing for environmental protection and limits on growth without generating ideological and partisan divisions. Among their favorite strategies for minimizing opposition: not attacking anyone, not appearing to harm the interests of any particular group, and generally running a positive rather than a negative campaign. An essential part of this strategy is to gain the cooperation of the building and real estate industries. In many communities, builders and realtors have cooperated with conservation efforts because they recognize that open space is an amenity that increases the sales price of their properties.

Without opposition from the building industry, conservationists often are able to conduct essentially one-sided campaigns in which they remain free to frame the benefits of the policies they promote. Slow growth advocates thus tout the economic *and* environmental benefits of limiting development in order to win the support of both liberal and conservative voters. In particular, they contend that new development generates less tax revenue than the cost of infrastructure needed to support that development. Therefore open-space conservation promises to keep density low while also reducing pressure on property taxes. If so, voter ambivalence about the costs and benefits of growth controls is minimized.

Growth control policies run into trouble, however, when they encounter active opposition and there are conflicting claims about the likely consequences of such policies. A more ambitious approach to land use planning is the establishment of urban growth boundaries. Based on the evidence we have seen at the community level, open space is far easier to defend than urban growth boundaries, even though both concepts typically are able to garner majority support in the abstract. Regulatory measures that seek to impose regional solutions by establishing growth boundaries and imposing impact fees are likely to draw opposition from the business community and to sharpen ideological debate and conflict. Builders are especially opposed to re-zoning regulations that require voter approval.

The Arizona campaign highlights the ambivalence of citizens toward aggressive policies to regulate growth in their communities. People favor open-space programs that do not threaten property rights or raise taxes significantly. Open space is preferred to commercial or residential development by those who already have homes in the community. Urban growth boundaries also have a surface appeal, but cause concern that the economic prosperity of the community may be choked off. Intuitively, people feel that growth boundaries will increase density and perhaps worsen crowding and congestion within the city and in their own neighborhoods. Voters assume that developers have to build somewhere. From this perspective, open-space preservation within the community, combined with development "elsewhere," sufficiently distant from one's own neighborhood, is perhaps the outcome that people most prefer.

In Arizona, two blocs of voters—those who place their highest priority on conservation of open space and the environment, and those who are concerned foremost with sustaining growth and employment—stand on either side of a large plurality group of ambivalent voters who value open space, but also support continued growth so long as public services are maintained and improved on pace with development. This moderate bloc of voters seeks "planned" growth that balances environmental and economic goals rather than no growth, and it represents the swing vote in growth and conservation campaigns. Whichever side in the Arizona campaign could successfully frame the initiative to capture a majority of this bloc would likely prevail at the ballot box.

In their private campaign polling, ARP, the building industry-led coalition opposing Proposition 202, discovered it could prime several negative voter intuitions about the initiative that would turn voters, especially moderates who saw virtue in both growth and conservation, against the specific provisions of CGMI. Many voters were inclined to believe that growth boundaries would increase traffic and density by channeling future growth toward existing neighborhoods. They also found plausible the claim that the lawsuit provision of the initiative might allow a litigious minority to dictate decisions for the majority. Although residents favored local control of urban planning decisions, they questioned whether it was fair that those outside of the boundary would be denied services and lose opportunities to convert their land to commercial use.

ARP exploited these latent negative intuitions in its campaign messages. Although Arizona voters embraced growth boundaries, impact fees, and voter approval of comprehensive local plans in public opinion polls, they withdrew their support at the election polls following a contentious campaign in which many seeds of doubt were successfully planted by an opposition coalition of developers, homebuilders, unions, and politicians. The large pragmatic bloc of voters concerned foremost about managing growth and maintaining public services were persuaded that CGMI was too radical. Ironically, the Sierra Club had designed its initiative with the goal of improving the quality of life in communities by giving residents more control over the pace and location of future growth, but many voters concluded the initiative would harm their communities as well as the state and local economy.

Were voters misled by the building industry's well-financed campaign against CGMI? It is more accurate to say that the intensely fought campaign raised numerous worries among uncertain voters that the coalition in favor of CGMI was unable to dispel. Among political consultants, it is conventional wisdom that the opposition merely has to create doubt and uncertainty in the minds of risk-averse voters to defeat an initiative or referendum.[6] Complex statewide initiatives such as CGMI are especially difficult to pass because they combine several proposals (e.g., growth boundaries, voter approval, citizens' right to sue for noncompliance), each of which can create ambivalence, doubt, and ultimately opposition among voters. Nikolai Ramsey, Director of the Grand Canyon Trust, one of the organizations supporting CGMI, reflected in defeat that perhaps the coalition would have fared better if it had put forth a simple 22-word initiative emphasizing a starker choice between urban sprawl and conservation of the environment.[7] In the end, the multifaceted CGMI may simply have opened too many fronts, leaving itself vulnerable to attack and speculation from too many perspectives.

APPENDIX

The following are question wordings and marginal distributions for items drawn from the 1998 Arizona statewide survey ($N = 807$):

Ideal Pace of Growth. Still thinking about growth and development in your area, which of the following statements comes closest to your own opinion?

	(%)
I want growth to continue at the current pace	15.6
I want growth to continue but the pace is too fast	50.2
I want growth at a faster pace	3.6
I don't want any more growth	21.9
I'm not concerned with how fast or slow growth occurs*	6.3
Unsure*	2.4

Government Regulation of Growth and Development. When it comes to managing growth and development, which one of the following four approaches should government take? [rotated]

	(%)
Government should leave people to use their property as they see fit	23.9
Government should encourage planned growth	50.1

Government should pass laws to restrict growth	19.5
Government should pass laws to stop growth	2.1
Unsure*	3.7

Attitudes toward Sierra Club. All things considered, would you be very likely, somewhat likely, somewhat unlikely, or very unlikely to agree with the recommendations of these organizations and individuals? If you don't consider their advice important, please say so: the Sierra Club.

	(%)
Very likely to agree	7.6
Somewhat likely to agree	25.2
Somewhat unlikely to agree	21.4
Very unlikely to agree	22.6
Don't consider advice important	22.4
Refused*	0.9

Saving Open Space. Recently, the legislature proposed a growth management plan that contains the following parts. Please tell me if you strongly support, somewhat support, somewhat oppose, or strongly oppose these parts of the plan. If you have no opinion, please say so:

1. Local growth management plans must include open-space protection and future growth will be directed to areas close to existing roads, water, and services.

	(%)
Strongly support	38.2
Somewhat support	41.6
Somewhat oppose	7.2
Strongly oppose	4.6
No opinion*	8.3

2. Voters will be asked to approve the use of existing corporate tax revenue over the next ten years to preserve open space.

	(%)
Strongly support	40.6
Somewhat support	34.9
Somewhat oppose	7.3
Strongly oppose	7.4
No opinion*	9.7

3. Some voter-approved money will be used to buy development rights for state trust land so that it will never be built on.

	(%)
Strongly support	37.3
Somewhat support	35.6
Somewhat oppose	10.3
Strongly oppose	8.6
No opinion*	8.2

Answers to these items were combined into a three-item additive scale; "no opinion" responses were treated as a middle category between support and opposition.

Note: Responses marked with an asterisk (*) were treated as missing values in the multivariate analysis presented in table 6.5. For the variable Government Regulation of Growth and Development, "restrict growth" and "stop growth" responses were combined into a single category in that same analysis. For the variable Attitudes toward Sierra Club, "don't consider advice important" was scored as a middle response between those who were likely to agree with that organization's recommendations and those who were not.

NOTES

We thank Dale Vieregge and J. F. Godbout for providing research assistance. We also thank the Trust for Public Land and APCO Worldwide (a communications and public affairs company located in Washington, DC), respectively, for making the TPL national survey and Arizona state survey available to us; however, we alone are responsible for the observations and conclusions drawn from these data. Funding for this research was provided by the Searle Fund. Send correspondence to the authors at Northwestern University, Department of Political Science, 601 University Place, Evanston, Illinois 60208.

1. The Trust for Public Land national telephone survey of registered voters ($N = 800$) was conducted in June 1999 using random-digit dialing (RDD). The primary substantive questions in the survey asked respondents to rate their policy priorities in state and local politics, evaluate the efficiency of government programs, compare alternative policies to combat urban sprawl, and state their preferences for different funding schemes for open-space purchases. The proprietary survey data were made available to us by TPL for this analysis.
2. The CNN/*Time* survey of 1,024 adults was conducted by Luntz Research on January 20–21, 1999; it has a margin of error of ±3 percentage points. The full questionnaire is available at http://nationaljournal.com/members/polltrack.
3. To be sure, the meaning of a "yes" vote is not always clear and does not always signify support for a "smart-growth" measure or idea.
4. This survey was conducted by telephone between April 16 and 22, 1998; a sample of 807 registered voters was collected using RDD without regional quotas. The proprietary data were gathered by APCO Worldwide and made available to us for this analysis.
5. See table 6.2 and the appendix for measurement of these dimensions and the marginal distribution of voters on them.
6. This sentiment was repeated by several political consultants we interviewed in Oregon, Washington State, Washington DC, and California who have coordinated campaigns for conservation ballot measures.
7. Telephone interview conducted on March 27, 2002.

CHAPTER SEVEN

AMBIVALENCE AND ATTITUDES TOWARD CHURCH–STATE RELATIONS

Ted G. Jelen

In the early twenty-first century, relations between church and state have taken center stage in American politics. In late 2003, Alabama Chief Justice Roy Moore was forced to step down from the state bench for his persistent refusal to remove a monument depicting the Ten Commandments from a courthouse in Montgomery (*Washington Post* 2003). In June of 2004, the U.S. Supreme Court declined to hear a case regarding the constitutionality of the phrase "under God" in the Pledge of Allegiance. The latter case involved an appeal from the Ninth Circuit Court of Appeals, which had ruled that using the phrase in public schools violated the "no religious establishment" clause of the First Amendment to the U.S. Constitution (Henderson 2004). Similarly, in the case of *Zelman v. Simmons-Harris*, the Supreme Court ruled that when state governments provide tuition vouchers to the parents of children who attend private schools, their actions do not violate the Establishment Clause, despite the fact that a large majority of private schools are sectarian in nature. The *Zelman* case represents the continuation of an ongoing controversy concerning the proper role of government in religious and public education at the primary and secondary levels.

What stands out about this spate of church–state litigation is that it is absolutely typical of the post–World War II era. Since the Supreme Court "incorporated" the religion clauses of the First Amendment, thereby applying the Establishment and Free Exercise Clauses to the actions of state and local governments, issues of church–state relations have been a central feature of American politics generally, and specifically of jurisprudence in the United States. Perhaps not surprisingly, church–state conflict is often contested within the context of public education. The education of the young is an important function of both church and state, and thus represents an area in which the powers of God and Caesar overlap considerably. Moreover, for the vast majority of Americans, compulsory public education is the most intense and sustained relationship they have with any governmental entity.

The area of church–state relations would seem to be a promising field for investigating the causes and effects of attitudinal ambivalence. At the macro-level, the relationship between the sacred and the secular seems to involve several important societal values. First, the population of the United States exhibits an unusually high level of religious belief, membership, and observance. Relative to other industrialized democracies, Americans are quite likely to believe in God, to belong to religious organizations, and to attend religious services (Wald 2003). Many Americans also seek to enact their religious values into government policy (Witte 1999). Conversely, the principle of "church–state separation" is an important one for people on most sides of specific controversies concerning the public role of religion. While the cases noted earlier indicate that the precise meaning of church–state separation remains contested, there nevertheless appears to exist widespread agreement on the principle itself.

Some analysts have suggested that the independence of religion from government regulation and the high levels of religiosity observed in the United States are, in fact, causally related. Recent developments in the sociology of religion have applied models of economic competition to religious adherence, arguing that competition between religious "firms" in a religious "economy" is conducive to high levels of "consumption" of religious or spiritual goods. According to these models, government efforts to regulate (or, indeed, to support) religious organizations amount to a "restraint of trade," which is believed to discourage innovation and responsiveness to the needs of potential laypeople.[1] Ultimately, the combination of high religiosity plus widespread support for maintaining a separation between God and Caesar suggests that religious politics will continue to animate public discourse in the United States for many years to come. With a highly religious population, we can anticipate that there will always exist a pool of citizens who seek to enact their religious principles into public policy— while commitment to the constitutional value of church–state separation should provide a steady source of opposition to such efforts.

STRUCTURAL AMBIVALENCE: THE CASE OF CHURCH–STATE RELATIONS

It also seems likely, however, that religion, like any issue of constitutional importance, will produce ambivalence at the level of individual attitudes. Those readers of this volume who have taught an introductory course in American government know that the U.S. Constitution creates potential conflict among several core democratic values, such as majority rule versus minority rights, or state sovereignty versus federal supremacy. By the time students in the United States complete high school, they should be quite familiar, and to some extent comfortable, with conflict (or at least tension) between important societal values.

In the case of religion, one such source of tension is that between the Establishment Clause, which represents freedom *from* religion, and the Free Exercise Clause, which provides freedom *of* religion (Davis 1996). In many actual conflicts over church–state relations, one can often arrive at a different (indeed, an opposing) result depending on whether a particular issue is described as involving religious establishment or free exercise. For example, does mandating spoken prayer at a high-school graduation constitute proscribed religious "establishment," or does forbidding such prayer violate the free exercise rights of students who wish to consecrate the occasion with a prayer? Does allowing members of certain religious denominations exemptions from military service (during periods when the law permits people to be drafted) violate their right to religious liberty, or does the provision of such exemptions constitute unlawful favoritism (or establishment) of such creeds (see Choper 1995)?

Further, even if attention is directed solely to the Establishment Clause, constitutionally posed tensions and potential conflicts remain. There exist two general approaches to the Establishment Clause: first, a "separationist" understanding of the clause construes government establishment of religion quite broadly, in that government may not assist religion in any form and must remain neutral between religion and its nonreligious alternatives (Levy 1986, 1988; Jelen 2000). By contrast, an "accommodationist" reading of the Establishment Clause entails a narrower interpretation, involving the belief that a prohibition on religious establishment means only that government may not favor one religion over another; government, however, may legitimately promote religion in general, on a non-preferential basis (Reichley 1985; Neuhaus 1984). A stance of "positive neutrality" is considered by accommodationists to be both legally permissible and politically desirable (Monsma 1993; Monsma and Soper 1997).

In general, the current state of constitutional case law has a separationist tilt. The operative precedent is the 1972 case of *Lemon v. Kurtzman*, in which the Supreme Court set down three criteria by which the constitutionality of government assistance to religious organizations can be assessed: the government program must (1) have a secular purpose; (2) have a secular effect, neither advancing nor inhibiting the free exercise of religion; and (3) avoid "excessive entanglement" between church and state.[2] For present purposes, what is most important here is that *Lemon* makes no distinction between religion in general and particular forms of religion. Although there appears to have been a tendency toward a more accommodationist jurisprudence during the period covering the Rehnquist Court (since the late 1980s), *Lemon* remains the operative precedent and, indeed, it provided the analytic framework for the majority opinion in *Zelman*.

AMBIVALENCE AND ITS ALTERNATIVES

Ambivalence was defined by Alvarez and Brehm (2002: 68) as "strong internalized conflict producing variable opinions." As such, attitudinal ambivalence has two distinct components: an objective (or intersubjective) inconsistency among values and opinions, as well as a subjective aspect, in which the citizen experiences cognitive dissonance as the result of such apparent inconsistency. Alvarez and Brehm (also Albertson, Brehm, and Alvarez 2005) contend that such authentic ambivalence is rather unusual in the American electorate. Unfortunately, it is difficult to measure the second component of ambivalence directly in secondary analyses of survey data. Whether a survey respondent actually experiences cognitive dissonance is an empirical question, which many existing data sources (including the data on which this study is based) are not equipped to answer. It is often necessary to measure ambivalence indirectly—or, perhaps more accurately, incompletely.[3] For some observers, it is the existence of (apparently) inconsistent attitudes that provides the *possibility* of ambivalence.

There are, of course, a number of potential underlying causes for apparently inconsistent or unstable responses in opinion surveys. In one of the earliest formulations, Philip Converse (1964, 1970) proposed that such responses may represent manifestations of non-attitudes; that is, according to Converse, many people lack meaningful opinions about the issues under investigation and, as a result, end up responding more or less randomly to pollsters' questions. Accordingly, his controversial "black-and-white" model[4] portrayed a rather unflattering view of the American electorate. It is not necessary, however, to accept that model in its entirety to attribute apparently inconsistent answers to a lack of sophistication. Alvarez and Brehm (1995) suggested that "domain-specific" information varies across individuals, thereby affecting the relationships between different attitudes that a person holds. In other words, even though survey participants have meaningful attitudes on questions posed by the researcher, they may nevertheless respond in a manner that seems to be inconsistent because they lack important information or because they have "compartmentalized" the values in question. In either case, the apparent inconsistency will not necessarily cause the respondent to feel any psychological discomfort (e.g., see Craig and Martinez 2005; also chapter one in this volume).

An example should help to clarify this last point. In a recent Gallup survey (Newport 2003), 77 percent of respondents disapproved of removing a display of the Ten Commandments from a courthouse in Montgomery, Alabama. In the same survey, only 10 percent endorsed the public display of explicitly Christian symbols in government buildings, while 58 percent approved of displaying symbols of "other religions" along with Christianity. This apparently inconsistent response pattern becomes understandable when one realizes that most respondents do not regard the Ten Commandments as a primarily Christian (or Judeo-Christian) symbol: only 25 percent of respondents in the Gallup Survey believed that the Ten Commandments display gave "special consideration to Jews and Christians," while 73 percent disagreed with that statement. Thus, the response patterns reported by Newport do not seem bereft of political content; for many, though, they lack a crucial piece of information, that is, that the Ten Commandments are specific to the Judeo-Christian tradition and are not universally accepted by believers in other faiths.[5]

Further, and more direct, evidence on the effects of exposure to diversity is also available. In 1993, I conducted a series of focus groups on church–state relations, in which the question of school prayer was discussed extensively. Initially, most participants saw nothing wrong with starting the school day with a nondenominational prayer; moreover, when questioned about the difficulty that might arise in composing such a prayer, most participants did not initially see this as a problem. But after I posed the possibility that atheists, Muslims, and Hindus might be offended, the reactions began to change (the community in question had a large, visible Hindu presence). Although few were bothered by the possibility of offending atheists, and were confident that a nondenominational monotheistic prayer could be composed to satisfy Muslims, the polytheism of the Hindu population became a problem. I suggested some alternatives, including the possibility that the prayer could be rotated with a different student leading the class each day in a prayer from her/his tradition. This was not a popular option, however, and most of the respondents ended up abandoning their earlier support for organized school prayer (Jelen and Wilcox 1995). Again, the point here is that most Americans are not exposed to religious diversity in their everyday lives, and such exposure may produce ambivalence where none had previously existed. More generally, a lack of specific information may reduce cognitive dissonance in the face of apparently inconsistent responses.

Alternatively, citizens may experience genuine ambivalence in the face of competing core values. One of the earliest empirical illustrations of this possibility was the reaction of many Protestant Democrats to the presidential candidacy of John F. Kennedy. The conflict between partisan and religious views was quite salient to many voters despite an absence of public, anti-Catholic cues on the party of the Republican Party or its candidate; it very nearly cost Kennedy an election that he might otherwise have won rather handily (Converse 1966). Other studies of ambivalence have suggested that ambivalence toward legal abortion may result from the tension between religious attitudes and attitudes toward women (Alvarez and Brehm 1995, 2002), and that ambivalence toward gay rights might result from conflict between the values of traditional morality and egalitarianism (Craig *et al.* 2005b).

Finally, McClosky and Zaller (1984; also see Zaller 1992) argued that public responses to controversial issues often depend in part on cues offered by political, media, or (in this case) religious elites. Leaders in the appropriate spheres may define acceptable belief combinations. As Converse (1964) pointed out nearly a generation ago, belief constraint is seldom a matter of strict logic, but is often defined by a process of social construction. Thus, if the application of a core value is contested, opinion leaders may define acceptably "consistent" patterns of beliefs, which would in turn license apparently "inconsistent" beliefs without necessarily inducing cognitive dissonance on the part of ordinary citizens.

To illustrate, imagine an individual who expresses support for the principle of "separation of church and state" while at the same time supporting organized prayer in public schools. Although the U.S. Supreme Court has consistently held that such prayer constituted a violation of the Establishment Clause, leaders from the Christian Right and the House of Representatives have argued that prohibiting such prayers represents a violation of the Free Exercise Clause, and therefore represents government interference with voluntary religious observance (Murley 1988; Jelen 1998, 2000). The fact that the definition of religious establishment is contested at the level of national elites permits the possibility that one may support both church–state separation and school prayer without experiencing any true conflict or psychological discomfort. Similarly, Clyde Wilcox and I have shown in earlier work that religious, political, business, and journalistic leaders often exhibit the same complex attitudes on church–state issues as do ordinary citizens (Jelen and Wilcox 1995). In these cases, an apparent lack of attitudinal constraint does not appear to represent a lack of sophistication or information; rather, it corresponds to distinctions made by presumably well-informed leaders for whom such issues are at least moderately salient.

The purpose of the present study is to investigate the attitudes of citizens who seem to hold inconsistent attitudes on matters of religious establishment. If such apparent inconsistency does indeed represent genuine attitudinal ambivalence, we should find that it is related to conflict among core values underlying alternative interpretations of the Establishment Clause. Further, ambivalence toward church–state relations is predicted to have the effect of reducing the strength of relationships between attitudes toward applications of the Establishment Clause and other predictor variables.

DATA AND MEASURES

Data for this study are from a telephone survey conducted in the greater Washington, DC area in November 1993. The survey was conducted through the auspices of the Department of Government at Georgetown University, using student interviewers who were trained and monitored by a faculty supervisor. The response rate was a very respectable 74 percent, and the interviewing yielded over 600 usable questionnaires. A comparison with census data from the counties in question revealed little racial bias in response rates; in part, this fortunate aspect of the survey can probably be attributed to the popularity of the Georgetown basketball program.[6] The same comparison revealed a response bias in favor of more highly educated respondents, which is rather typical for telephone surveys (Frankfort-Nachmias and Nachmias 2000). To adjust for differential response rates across diverse educational levels, the data are weighted by self-reported educational attainment (see Jelen and Wilcox 1995, 1997 for additional details).[7]

For purposes of the following analysis, ambivalence is measured by combining answers to two questions relating to the Establishment Clause.[8] Survey participants were presented with the following Likert-type items:

- We should maintain a high wall of separation between Church and State.
- The government should protect our Judeo-Christian heritage.

Responses were recoded into *separationist* (agree with the first, disagree with the second) and *accommodationist* (disagree with the first, agree with the second) categories.

ESTIMATING CHURCH–STATE AMBIVALENCE

The simplest approach to studying ambivalence regarding the values embodied in the Establishment Clause is to define "ambivalents" as individuals who offer a separationist response to one of the above items, and an accommodationist response to the other. The frequency of such ambivalent (or perhaps just inconsistent) responses is shown in table 7.1, which is a simple cross-tabulation of the two religious establishment measures. The upper-left quadrant of the table (yes to a high wall of separation, no to government protection of

Table 7.1 Cross-tabulation of Church–State items

High wall of separation between Church and State	Government should protect Judeo-Christian heritage		Total
	No (Separationist)	Yes (Accommodationist)	
Yes (Separationist)	35.4% (150)	43.6% (185)	79.0% (335)
No (Accommodationist)	5.7% (24)	15.3% (65)	21.0% (89)
Total	41.0% (174)	59.0% (250)	N = 424

Note: Data are from the 1993 DC-area survey. Entries are percentages based on the total number of observations in the table, with cell frequencies in parentheses.

the Judeo-Christian heritage) contains respondents who might be considered *consistent separationists*; while those in the lower-right quadrant (no to a high wall, yes to government protection) can be viewed as *consistent accommodationists*. In contrast, respondents in the lower-left and upper-right quadrants gave apparently inconsistent answers to the establishment items and may therefore be described as ambivalent. Accordingly, those who inhabit either inconsistent cell in table 7.1 are referred to as "general" church–state ambivalents in the discussion that follows.

It is, however, possible to make distinctions between types of ambivalent responses. If attention is directed to the plurality of respondents who favor a high wall of separation between church and state *and* government protection of our Judeo-Christian heritage (upper-right quadrant), it might be hypothesized that such responses are not ambivalent or inconsistent at all but, rather, that they represent a particular, coherent view of church–state relations. Some leaders of conservative Christian movements insist that while separation of church and state is a desirable goal, the wall of separation has in fact been breached by government. Their argument is that government, by promoting policies such as permitting legal abortion, mandating the teaching of creationism in public schools, prohibiting school prayer, and legislating against employment or housing discrimination against gays, has interfered with the free exercise rights of citizens who oppose such "secular" policies. As Ralph Reed (1994: 18, 41), former executive director of Christian Coalition, explained:

> The [Christian Right] movement is best understood as an essentially defensive struggle by people seeking to sustain their faith and their values. . . . Presumably all of us want freedom to practice our religion, to enjoy the rights of free speech guaranteed by the First Amendment, and to fully participate in our

duties of citizenship. Yet intolerance towards religion has reached disturbing levels, threatening civility and undermining a basic sense of fairness (Reed 1994: 18, 41).

In the language of the schoolyard, "They started it." Because government is believed to have violated the separation of church and state, protection *by* government of our Judeo-Christian heritage is considered necessary to correct the wrongs that have been wrought (see also Carter 1993).

It seems unlikely that all, or even most, of the respondents who endorsed a high wall of separation along with government protection of the country's Judeo-Christian heritage would be able to articulate such coherent rationales reconciling the two statements. Indeed, the fact that a plurality of respondents in table 7.1 (43.6 percent) support this very combination suggests that overcoming the apparent inconsistency between these two items is not cognitively demanding. Nevertheless, although such a response pattern clearly could represent one of several possible non-ambivalent positions, more likely is that the idea of church–state separation is a powerful rhetorical symbol in the United States that draws support even from people who favor a number of different government accommodations of religious belief and practice. Accordingly, individuals exhibiting this particular combination of attitudes on the religious establishment items will be considered as *symbolic ambivalents*.

I term the remaining respondents (a mere 5.7 percent in table 7.1), who reject both a high wall of separation and government protection of the Judeo-Christian heritage, *sophisticated ambivalents*. The positive label "sophisticated" is used because a thoughtful rationale for this combination would likely involve the belief that not all religions practiced in the United States are part of the Judeo-Christian heritage, and, therefore, that constitutionally valid promotion of religion on the part of government would necessarily require that mainstream religions, including Christianity and Judaism, be denied special treatment. Stephen Monsma (1993) described the argument here as one of "positive neutrality," and suggested that such a posture involves a very narrow reading of the Establishment Clause. Simply put, a thoughtful rationale for the combination of beliefs that comprise the sophisticated ambivalent category might well involve the accommodationist belief that the Establishment Clause *only* proscribes government support for, or endorsement of, a *particular* religion. However, this standard accommodationist position may be tempered with the recognition that even broadly defined religious traditions, supported by large majorities of the American people, constitute a "particular" religion for purposes of interpreting the meaning of religious establishment. In other words, the American religious mosaic is sufficiently diverse as to exclude preferential treatment for Christians or Jews.

Again, it is not clear that those who responded negatively to both religious establishment items would endorse the line of reasoning described earlier. Indeed, such responses may indicate nothing more than measurement error or the expression of non-attitudes. Conversely, such patterns could represent the cognitive dissonance with which one would associate genuine ambivalence.[9] More generally, for purposes of this study, the working hypothesis is that people who are not consistent separationists or accommodationists are, in some sense, ambivalent about issues of church–state relations. Ultimately, the question of whether such response patterns are rooted in attitudinal ambivalence or something else is an empirical question, to which attention is now turned.

CHURCH–STATE AMBIVALENCE AND CORE VALUES

Accounts of attitudinal ambivalence typically distinguish that response from a lack of constraint by suggesting that genuine ambivalence is the result of conflict between core values that relate, in opposite directions, to the policy question under consideration. Actual conflict between competing values, rather than simple confusion, is considered to be the defining characteristic of authentic attitudinal ambivalence.[10] It is, however, no easy matter to discern the core values that might underlie ambivalence on issues relating to religious establishment—a problem that is exacerbated when the data being utilized were not collected for that purpose. After some experimentation, the analysis here proceeds under the assumption that the core values underlying church–state ambivalence are *religiosity* (measured by frequency of church attendance) and *ideological liberalism* (measured by respondent self-placement on a liberal-conservative scale).

While neither of these is ideal from a conceptual or methodological standpoint, each has a certain plausibility. While some separationists undoubtedly are highly religious and motivated by theological motives, it seems likely that accommodationists are the more likely of the two groups to have a positive view regarding the public role of religion and to exhibit relatively high levels of personal religiosity. Thus, it might be expected that greater religious intensity will exert an accommodationist effect on attitudes toward church–state relations.

Similarly, while liberal Christian groups, such as Sojourners and Pax Christi, do exist, there appears to be no mobilized "Christian Left" in the United States that corresponds to the Christian Right at the level of the mass public.[11] In contemporary political discourse, accommodationist attitudes toward issues of church–state separation tend to be associated with the Republican Party, and more generally with the political right.[12] Although there is no logical reason why liberals should be less supportive of the public expression of religious values than conservatives, a socially constructed "consistency" among attitudes (see Converse 1964) suggests that ideological liberalism and church–state accommodationism are at least potentially conflictual. Consequently, we might anticipate that ambivalence toward matters of religious establishment will be more pronounced among frequent church attenders who identify with the political left, and among infrequent attenders who consider themselves political conservatives.

The effects of these core values are presented in table 7.2, which contains a multivariate model for all three variations of church–state ambivalence described earlier. In addition to core values and an interaction term that captures conflict between them, each model contains measures of the respondent's education, denominational affiliation as a Roman Catholic or evangelical Protestant, view of the Bible, and a separate indicator of religious non-affiliation.[13] As the data show, both core values (religiosity and ideological self-placement) make independent contributions toward what we identified as sophisticated church–state ambivalence in the preceding section; that is, frequent church attenders are significantly *less* likely to exhibit sophisticated ambivalence, while self-identified liberals tend to be significantly *more* ambivalent in this particular sense. Neither core value is associated with general or symbolic ambivalence, however, and the interaction between them does not attain statistical significance in any of the three models.

The overall pattern of results (including the fact that the explanatory power of the third model depicted in table 7.2 is considerably greater than that associated with the other two) provides some evidence of the validity of this measure of symbolic ambivalence, at least when compared with the general and symbolic ambivalence variables. Conversely, the latter seem to be tapping something, albeit with an apparent lack of precision. If one is willing to reject the null hypothesis when $p < .10$, a respondent's view of the Bible is significantly (and negatively) related to all three measures of ambivalence; that is, people who regard the Bible as an authoritative source are significantly less likely than others to exhibit ambivalent response patterns in any of the three senses considered here.[14] Also, Roman Catholicism is related to general and symbolic (but not sophisticated) ambivalence at $p < .10$, while membership in an evangelical denomination is significantly related only to symbolic ambivalence.

Overall, the analysis of church–state ambivalence as a dependent variable is somewhat difficult to interpret. It would appear that the sophisticated measure comes closest to capturing true ambivalence, in that sophisticated ambivalence alone is related to core values in the expected direction: highly religious people tend to be less ambivalent about the proper relationship between church and state, whereas self-identified liberals are

Table 7.2 Multivariate models of Church–State ambivalence

Variable	Model 1 general		Model 2 symbolic		Model 3 sophisticated	
	b	S.E.	b	S.E.	b	S.E.
Church attendance	−0.34	0.27	−0.13	0.27	−1.60*	0.78
Biblical authority	−0.41**	0.15	−0.30†	0.15	−0.56†	0.31
Education	−0.17	0.14	−0.09	0.14	−0.26	0.29
Liberal-conservative identification	0.28	0.26	0.08	0.26	1.45*	0.73
Catholic	−0.53†	0.28	−0.56†	0.28	0.41	0.72
Evangelical denomination	−0.49	0.36	−0.77*	0.37	0.97	0.73
No religion	−0.18	0.53	−0.55	0.56	1.21	0.95
Church attendance × Liberal-conservative ID	−0.11	0.08	−0.07	0.08	−0.31	0.20
Constant	2.83*	1.15	1.78	1.15	1.43	2.39
Pseudo R^2 (Nagelkerke)	0.070		0.057		0.204	
Percent classified correctly	60.1		62.9		94.0	
−2 log likelihood	416.314		410.434		117.622	
Number of cases	316		303		304	

Note: Data are from the 1993 DC-area survey. Entries are unstandardized logistic regression coefficients with associated standard errors.

$**p \le .01$; $*p \le .05$; $†p \le .10$.

more ambivalent.[15] Surprisingly, however, the interaction between religiosity and political liberalism (which is intended to represent value *conflict*) was found to be unrelated to any of the three measures of ambivalence. This suggests that respondents simply do not experience cognitive dissonance when attempting to reconcile the two values.[16] Although scholarly observers may perceive inconsistency among respondents who reject the "wall of separation" between church and state, and who simultaneously reject government protection of "our Judeo-Christian heritage," individuals who are supposedly conflicted between the core values underlying church–state relations do not appear any more ambivalent than those who are not.

The Attitudinal Effects of Church–State Ambivalence

Ultimately, of course, the value of the ambivalence concept depends upon its ability to help explain differences in citizens' policy attitudes, in this case, their attitudes about church–state relations. Accordingly, we turn now to an examination of the effects of church–state ambivalence on attitudes toward applications of religious establishment. Following Craig and his colleagues (2005b), it is hypothesized that ambivalence will moderate the effects of other predictor variables on respondents' answers to two Likert-type questions in the DC-area survey: (1) Public schools should set aside a moment of silence each day for students to pray if they want to; and (2) It's good for sporting events at public high schools to begin with a public prayer.

Each of these items taps attitudes toward specific church–state controversies that were matters of intense public attention at the time the survey was conducted. The practice of mandating a moment of silence in public schools, during which students could pray or meditate on their own, was declared unconstitutional by the Supreme Court in 1985, in the case of *Wallace v. Jaffre*. This was held to violate the "secular purpose" and "secular effects" prongs of the *Lemon* test and, consequently, to constitute a violation of the Establishment Clause. The issue was revisited in our 1993 survey after several legislative bodies at different levels subsequently enacted measures permitting some form of school prayer, and a constitutional amendment in the same vein was introduced in the U.S. House of Representatives (Jelen 1998; Murley 1988). In light of these actions, it seems reasonable to assume that the issue remained salient to at least a portion of the general public.

Similarly, the question of public prayer at high-school football games also was prominent during the period of the survey. During the early 1990s, a number of school districts (generally located in the state of Texas) had mandated a public prayer, broadcast over the public address system, prior to school-sponsored athletic contests. When the parents of a number of Roman Catholic and Mormon students complained, the district superintendent at Santa Fe High School, located approximately one hundred miles southwest of Houston, modified the policy in 1995 to permit "voluntary," student-led, public prayer, which was to be "nonsectarian," and "nonproselytizing." This policy was ultimately held unconstitutional by the U.S. Supreme Court in the 2000 case of *Santa Fe Independent School District v Doe*.

Thus, the survey included measures of attitudes toward two public policies that were (1) quite popular among members of the mass public; (2) objects of heated public discussion during the late 1980s and early to middle 1990s; and (3) invalidated by the Supreme Court as violations of the Establishment Clause. For each issue, three multivariate models were estimated. Model 1 includes most of the same variables that were used to predict the various forms of church–state ambivalence in table 7.2; notable changes in specification from the earlier table are that (1) the core values interaction between liberal/conservative self-placement and church attendance is omitted;[17] and (2) two dummy variables are added, representing agreement with the "high wall of separation" and "protect our Judeo-Christian heritage" questions. Model 2 is more complex, utilizing all of the independent variables in Model 1 plus the interaction of Biblical authority and sophisticated ambivalence. Finally, Model 3 is identical to Model 2 except that sophisticated ambivalence is replaced by symbolic ambivalence in calculating the interaction term. To the extent that ambivalence toward matters of church and state are substantively meaningful in explaining attitudes toward concrete applications of the Establishment Clause, it is anticipated that including the interactions will serve to moderate (indeed, will reduce) the effects of other independent variables—specifically, in this instance, the effect of views about Biblical authority.

The Model 1 results shown in table 7.3 exhibit some expected patterns. Education and the desire to protect America's Judeo-Christian heritage are, for example, strong predictors of attitudes toward both applications of the

Table 7.3 Multivariate models of concrete Church–State issues

Variable	Moment of silence			Prayer at sporting events		
	Model 1	Model 2	Model 3	Model 1	Model 2	Model 3
Church attendance	0.19**	0.13**	0.13**	0.10*	0.10*	0.07†
	(0.04)	(0.04)	(0.05)	(0.04)	(0.04)	(0.04)
Biblical authority	0.01	−0.22	0.00	0.29**	0.31*	0.37**
	(0.08)	(0.15)	(0.08)	(0.08)	(0.15)	(0.09)
Education	−0.29**	−0.29**	−0.29**	−0.31**	−0.33**	−0.38**
	(0.06)	(0.06)	(0.06)	(0.06)	(0.06)	(0.06)
Liberal-conservative ID	−0.19**	−0.19**	−0.18**	−0.09†	−0.10†	−0.10†
	(0.06)	(0.06)	(0.06)	(0.06)	(0.06)	(0.06)
Catholic	−0.22	−0.24†	−0.22†	−0.00	−0.00	−0.00
	(0.13)	(0.13)	(0.13)	(0.12)	(0.12)	(0.13)
Evangelical denomination	0.01	0.01	0.00	−0.17	−0.17	−0.19
	(0.12)	(0.17)	(0.17)	(0.16)	(0.16)	(0.16)
Age	0.00	0.00	0.00	0.01†	0.01†	0.01
	(0.00)	(0.00)	(0.00)	(0.00)	(0.00)	(0.00)
Protect Judeo-Christian heritage	0.34**	0.44**	0.01	0.48**	0.47**	0.75**
	(0.12)	(0.13)	(0.23)	(0.12)	(0.13)	(0.22)
High wall of separation	−0.19	0.00	−0.34†	−0.00	−0.01	0.13
	(0.15)	(0.17)	(0.19)	(0.14)	(0.16)	(0.18)
Biblical authority × Sophisticated ambivalence	n/a	0.28*	n/a	n/a	0.00	n/a
		(0.13)			(0.13)	
Biblical authority × Symbolic ambivalence	n/a	n/a	0.12	n/a	n/a	−0.13
			(0.09)			(0.09)
Constant	2.92**	2.92**	2.74**	2.09**	2.09**	2.78**
	(0.45)	(0.45)	(0.48)	(0.44)	(0.43)	(0.45)
Adjusted R²	0.208	0.218	0.209	0.364	0.362	0.367
Number of cases	297	297	297	286	286	286

Note: Data are from the 1993 DC-area study. Entries are unstandardized OLS regression coefficients, with standard errors in parentheses.

$**p \le .01$; $*p \le .05$; $^\dagger p \le .10$.

Establishment Clause considered here. People with higher levels of education, and those who do not favor special protection for a presumably shared religious tradition, are much less likely than others to favor permitting mandated moments of silence or public prayer at school-sponsored sporting events. More frequent church attendance and conservative ideological identification also are significantly associated (the latter at $p < .10$) with support for both the moment of silence and high-school prayer proposals, while Biblical authority is significant for attitudes toward prayer at sporting events.

Once again, it is hypothesized that ambivalence will moderate the effect of other predictor variables. Models 2 and 3 provide tests of that hypothesis with respect to the Biblical authority question: the interaction between sophisticated ambivalence and respondent views about Biblical authority does, in fact, have a significant effect on attitudes toward the moment of silence, but not on support for public prayer at sporting events. In the former case, it is particularly noteworthy that the coefficient is of the opposite sign from the main effect for Biblical authority, that is, the effects of Biblical literalism among sophisticated ambivalents are very nearly zero (as evidenced by the sum of the main effect of Biblical authority and the interaction term). By contrast, the interaction between Biblical authority and symbolic ambivalence has no discernible impact on either dependent variable.

These findings provide a possible explanation for why simple attitudes toward the Bible are such strong predictors of support for prayer at high-school sporting events, but are not related to attitudes toward moments of silence in public schools. Supporters of public prayer (at football games or elsewhere) may be skeptical of the possibility of a religiously neutral, non-sectarian prayer and, indeed, may not desire such a general expression of religious affirmation. Supporters of such public prayers may in fact desire the affirmation of beliefs associated with very specific faith traditions. After all, the plaintiffs in *Santa Fe* were not atheists or non-Christians, but were members of the Roman Catholic Church and the Church of Latter-Day Saints. While it seems unlikely that many mass publics were informed to this extent, it is clear that the neutrality of public prayers at high-school football games might be problematic. By contrast, the moment of silence may be perceived as an authentic attempt to provide a "positively neutral" means of acknowledging the sacred publicly, while not endorsing or favoring particular doctrines or denominations. If symbolic ambivalence is regarded as representing actual cognitive dissonance, many supporters of a mandated moment of silence appear genuinely ambivalent, and seem concerned about both the core values of Christian religiosity and individual autonomy with regard to the sacred.

CONCLUSION

As noted earlier, it is difficult to measure attitudinal ambivalence directly in secondary analyses of survey data. Moreover, genuine ambivalence may be fairly uncommon in instances where the contestation of constitutional principles in the U.S. Supreme Court raises the salience of political issues among the mass public to unusually high levels. The present study has shown that only about one-half of respondents in the 1993 DC-area survey can be described as consistent separationists or consistent accommodationists. It is, however, premature to conclude either that those who are neither consistent separationists nor consistent accommodationists lack cognitive sophistication, or that they experience true ambivalence due to a conflict between competing core values. Rather, what initially appears to be ambivalent responses may, for some people, reflect nuanced attitudes toward aspects of the Establishment Clause.

As I have suggested, much of the inconsistency (or ambivalence) documented here may actually represent attitudes of religious non-preferentialism. In other words, citizens may oppose a high wall of separation between church and state because they believe it to be desirable for government to offer assistance to religion on a non-discriminatory basis; these individuals do not favor government support for "our Judeo-Christian heritage" because they recognize that genuine neutrality would involve support for religious organizations within and outside the dominant religious tradition. Similarly, respondents who are characterized as sophisticated ambivalents in this study may favor a separation of church and state but regard government attempts to restrict public religious observance as violations of that principle. By such restrictions, government is thought to violate the rights of religious free exercise, and (therefore) the doctrine of church–state separation. Of course, such speculations extend well beyond the limits permitted by the available data. Nevertheless, the results of this study show that apparently inconsistent responses to general questions about church–state relations are not necessarily the result of conflicting values, but instead may represent coherent responses to the practical difficulties of maintaining a secular government in a highly religious population.

NOTES

1. See especially Finke and Stark (1992), Stark and Finke (2000). For an overview of the market model of religious competition and of its critics, see Jelen (2002).
2. In *Agostini v. Felton* (1997), Justice Sandra Day O'Connor suggested merging the purpose and effects tests into a single "non-endorsement" of religion standard.
3. But see Craig, Martinez, and Kane (2002; also Craig, Martinez, and Kane 2005a; Craig *et al.* 2005b, and chapter four in this volume).

4. The model specifically posits that there are two types of survey respondents: those who have coherent and stable attitudes about an issue, and those who have no real attitude and are simply answering questions randomly. See Converse (1964, 1970).

5. For an account of the effects of exposure to religious diversity on public attitudes toward church–state relations, see Wilcox, Goldberg, and Jelen (2002).

6. The Georgetown basketball team was led at the time of the survey by the highly successful John Thompson, who was the first African-American coach to win a Division I NCAA national championship in that sport. His popularity may have made African Americans more willing to participate in a university-sponsored survey.

7. Although Frankfort-Nachmias and Nachmias (2000) reported that the class and educational bias in telephone surveys has become less severe in recent years, a comparison of marginal distributions from our survey with census data from the same region prompted the decision to weight our data.

8. The survey also included two statements that tapped general attitudes toward religious free exercise: "People have the right to practice their religion as they see fit, even if their practices seem strange to most Americans," and "It is important for people to obey the law, even if it means limiting their religious freedom." I do not analyze these items here since they are virtual constants among this particular population. Over 93 percent gave libertarian responses (agree) to the first item, and nearly 80 percent gave communalist responses (agree) to the second. Crosstabulation of the two items reveals that 77.4 percent of respondents would be considered "ambivalent" in the sense used in this study.

9. The treatment of ambivalence here is different and, in some senses, much simpler than that suggested by Kaplan (1972) and refined by Craig and his colleagues (2002, 2005b). Unfortunately, the data from the DC-area survey do not permit direct measurement of polarity except as estimated by extreme scores on the Likert scales from which ambivalence scores computed. At the same time, however, an advantage of the approach used here is that it permits a distinction between types of apparent ambivalence, which is substantively important for purposes of this study.

10. Empirical support for this proposition is, to say the least, mixed (e.g., see Craig *et al.* 2005b, as well as chapter five in the current volume).

11. For nearly two decades, approximately one American in six (about 15 percent) has expressed support for the religious right (Wilcox, Goldberg, and Jelen 2002).

12. Less impressionistic considerations can also be brought to bear on this question. Among respondents to the DC-area survey, church attendance was not significantly related to liberal self-identification among any of the major religious traditions (Evangelical Protestant, Mainline Protestant, Roman Catholic, and Jewish). Overall, the correlation between attendance at religious services and liberal/conservative self-placement is a moderate, but statistically significant, 0.17.

13. Evangelical denominations include Baptists of all varieties, Assemblies of God and other Pentecostal denominations, the Church of God and other churches from the Holiness tradition, Missouri Synod Lutheran, as well as some Reformed Churches. This list was adapted from Kellstedt and Green (1993).

The Bible item was worded as follows: "Which comes closest to your views of the Bible? (1) The Bible is the inspired Word of God and is literally true,

144 / TED JELEN

word for word; (2) The Bible is the inspired Word of God and has no errors, but some of it is meant to be taken figuratively; (3) The Bible is inspired by God, but contains human errors; (4) The Bible is not the Word of God." Several studies (Jelen 1989; Jelen, Smidt, and Wilcox 1990) have shown that responses to such items are generally insensitive to variations in question wording.

For purposes of this study, "no religion" is defined quite stringently as including only those who profess no denominational affiliation *and* who attend religious services "never" or "a few times a year." This approach is occasioned by the growing number of nondenominational churches in the United States (Kellstedt and Green 2003).

14. Despite the relatively robust relationships between one's view of the Bible and all three types of church–state ambivalence, scriptural authority is not conceptualized here as a "core value." Doing so would bias the analysis in the direction of Evangelical Protestantism, since in many other traditions (such as Roman Catholicism and Mainline Protestantism) the Bible is regarded as an important, but not necessarily authoritative, source (Jelen 1993).

15. This result is more intelligible if one assumes that very few Americans (including self-identified liberals) are actually hostile to the public expression of religious values. Contrary to the pronouncements of some Christian Right leaders, genuine antireligious sentiment is quite rare in the United States (Wald 2003).

16. The results here are quite robust across model specifications. In particular, they are substantially unchanged when a simplified model is used with only church attendance, ideology, and the interaction between the two are used as independent variables.

17. Inclusion of the interaction term makes no measurable difference to the results reported here.

CHAPTER EIGHT

ATTITUDINAL AMBIVALENCE AND POLITICAL OPINION: REVIEW AND AVENUES FOR FURTHER RESEARCH

Christopher J. Armitage and Mark Conner

Most people are not strongly committed to a specific ideology, meaning that in principle they are open to messages advocating opposite sides of any given issue. Especially in the United States, where just two political parties dominate political discourse, it is common for citizens to receive conflicting messages. Such factors create ideal conditions for the induction of attitudinal ambivalence and make politics an important testbed for exploring the bidimensional conceptualization of attitudes that ambivalence implies. The chapters that make up the current volume and its companion, *Ambivalence and the Structure of Political Opinion* (Craig and Martinez 2005), draw together psychologists and political scientists of various persuasions to provide a timely update on the current state of research on the subject. These chapters cover a broad range of basic and applied work, from current understandings regarding the conceptualization, operationalization, and antecedents of ambivalence to the consequences of ambivalence in relation to topics as diverse as national institutions, legal abortion, the United States as a nation, and voter behavior. In the pages that follow, we provide an overview of the key contributions made by each chapter and draw together some fundamental themes that run through them. We go on to assess the current state of the science of ambivalence before outlining what we regard as promising avenues for further research.

KEY CONTRIBUTIONS

Albertson, Brehm, and Alvarez (2005) begin *Ambivalence and the Structure of Political Opinion* by providing a valuable conceptual analysis of attitudinal ambivalence, teasing apart several different uses of the term. The authors draw particular attention to numerous instances where conflict has been erroneously confounded with ambivalence. The most obvious of these relates to lay discussion. Analogous to the manner in which the term *schizophrenic* is often misused, *ambivalence* has frequently been employed to describe public opinion as a whole rather than the attitudes of individual citizens. Accordingly, Albertson and her colleagues point out that when half the public supports a policy that the other half opposes, such a division indicates a conflicted nation rather than a nation of conflicted individuals. More generally, Albertson, Brehm, and Alvarez argue that ambivalence does not exist simply because a person has two distinct thoughts or feelings about an object, as these thoughts or feelings can be uniform; instead, it is necessary that ambivalence reflect a specific choice or specific evaluation of the attitude object.

The approach in Albertson, Brehm, and Alvarez emphasizes that serial experience of positive and negative evaluations is not sufficient to infer ambivalence because both must be experienced simultaneously. This clearly discriminates ambivalence from concepts that have sometimes been confused with ambivalence—most notably attitudinal variability, which taps temporal oscillations in attitudes rather than simultaneous positive and negative evaluations. Such a distinction maps closely onto earlier distinctions between synchronic and diachronic ambivalence (Conner and Sparks 2002; Stocker 1990), as well as Lavine and Steenbergen's view (see chapter one in this volume) that also highlights *internalized conflict* about a specific political choice. The latter study posits three conditions that are necessary and sufficient to produce ambivalence; these conditions refer to (1) the *relevance* of competing considerations, which should be equal if ambivalence is to occur; (2) the *dominance* of competing considerations over other considerations such as self-interest; and (3) the *inhibition of choice*, with support for two competing considerations undermining political decision-making. This conceptualization of ambivalence is referred to explicitly and implicitly throughout the preceding seven chapters and in Craig and Martinez (2005).

Albertson, Brehm, and Alvarez strongly advocate an inferential approach to measuring ambivalence. Briefly, the method they use involves the examination of patterns of error variance in heteroskedastic probit models of binary choice; their analyses simultaneously examine several policy areas, and show that value conflict and additional information tend to increase response variability and alterations to the choices made by survey respondents in only one of these (flexible admissions standards). Although such an approach can only be used to estimate levels of ambivalence in a population rather than the individual differences in ambivalence that have tended to preoccupy social psychologists, it may prove to be an important tool for political campaigns that wish to target ambivalent voters. We return to this issue later.

Newby-Clark, McGregor, and Zanna (2005) examine two direct means of measuring ambivalence: the "felt" approach asks people to infer and self-report their ambivalence, while the "potential" approach derives a measure of ambivalence from the attitude judgment process or its outcomes.[1] Interestingly the two are generally found to be only moderately related ($r = .45$ in a recent meta-analysis; see Riketta 2004). Consistent with the idea that mere conflict is not sufficient to infer ambivalence, Newby-Clark, McGregor, and Zanna contend that accessibility is an important moderator of ambivalence effects that might explain why felt ambivalence is not more strongly correlated with potential ambivalence. More specifically, the authors go beyond the idea that the accessibility of attitudes *per se* is an important determinant of action and suggest, instead, that simultaneous accessibility of the positive and negative poles associated with an attitude object is a key moderator of the relationship between felt ambivalence and potential ambivalence. This line of research taps into cognitive dissonance theory by showing that awareness of conflicted attitudes creates aversive emotional states that people try to reduce or eliminate through processes such as suppression, distraction, or compensatory conviction. Newby-Clark and his colleagues prefer the idea of self-distraction to resolution of the conflict because, in their view, changing attitudes to value-related topics such as abortion or capital punishment is likely to involve greater cognitive resources than people are likely to be willing to allocate.

Holbrook and Krosnick (2005) extend this work by examining the structural properties of measures of felt and potential ambivalence and their consequences in the domains of abortion and capital punishment. In general, Holbrook and Krosnick's work shows that indices designed to tap potential and felt ambivalence represent distinct constructs and, more importantly, that the two indices have different consequences for cognition and behavior. For example, whereas felt ambivalence was related to less reported interest in learning issue-relevant information, a stronger false consensus effect, and less perceived hostile media bias, greater potential ambivalence was uniquely associated with increased reports of general activism. On the other hand, felt and potential ambivalence shared two consequences in common: both were negatively related to resistance to persuasion and were associated with a reduced tendency to use candidates' issue positions to evaluate them.

This pattern of findings was interpreted as evidence for two distinct routes by which felt and potential ambivalence exert their effects. First, discomfort and the desire to reduce discomfort were hypothesized to underpin the effects of felt ambivalence. Accordingly, Holbrook and Krosnick provide evidence to suggest that people who score high in felt ambivalence tend to avoid stimuli that bring their discomfort to mind. In contrast, the perception of attitude-relevant information was posited as the means by which potential ambivalence works. More specifically, Holbrook and Krosnick argue that because people with high levels of potential ambivalence are aware of a range of positively and negatively valenced information, persuasive communications are likely to be interpreted as consistent with previously held attitudes, thus making their overall attitude on the issue more susceptible to change.

With accumulated research suggesting that potential ambivalence may exist without conscious awareness of it, one might plausibly assume that potential ambivalence causes felt ambivalence. Holbrook and Krosnick test this hypothesis and find that felt ambivalence fails to mediate fully the effects of potential ambivalence on resistance to persuasion, activism, information gathering, perceived consensus, perceived media bias, contents of candidate evaluations, and false consensus effect. The implication is that the effects of felt and potential ambivalence are independent and that both may have different antecedents. From a theoretical perspective, more work is needed to identify the antecedents of potential and felt ambivalence; from an applied perspective, researchers need to be cognizant of these differences between potential and felt ambivalence when choosing measures for their studies.

Temporal stability is regarded as one of the sufficient conditions to infer that an attitude is "strong" (Krosnick and Petty 1995). Using a panel survey of Florida voters from 1999, Craig, Martinez, and Kane (2005) investigate the effects of ambivalence on the temporal stability of attitudes toward abortion. Consistent with the idea that attitudinal ambivalence is an index of attitude strength, univalent attitudes are found to exhibit greater temporal stability than ambivalent attitudes. Importantly, these effects remain even when the effects of other dimensions of attitude strength, including importance, certainty, intensity, and commitment, are statistically controlled. Craig and his colleagues also show that framing exerts powerful effects on attitudes toward legal abortion. That is, both attitudes and attitudinal ambivalence associated with legal abortion are dependent on whether the procedure is presented as being *elective* (e.g., the woman does not want more children) or sought under more *traumatic* circumstances (e.g., rape, birth defect). In effect, presenting abortion as either elective or traumatic produces different attitudes and patterns of ambivalence with relatively little overlap. Even people with stable attitudes about abortion in traumatic circumstances do not necessarily have stable attitudes toward abortion in elective conditions, and *vice versa*. Accordingly, Craig *et al.* recommend that future research dealing with attitudes on abortion specify the circumstances in advance—a recommendation that should be heeded by researchers in other areas where context is likely to be an important determinant of political attitudes.

Consistent with Craig *et al.*'s (2005a) conclusion that the effects of ambivalence on attitude stability are consistent across contexts, if not within individuals, Fournier (see chapter two in this volume) assesses the role of ambivalence across a variety of political contexts and in several election years. Specifically, Fournier examines the effect of ambivalence on temporal stability for 11 decisions, measured in 9 surveys conducted in the United States, Britain, and Canada. Even controlling for the effects of variables such as strength of opinion and issue importance, the findings are remarkably consistent: the voting preferences of individuals who are ambivalent tend to be less predictable than those of individuals holding univalent attitudes. The generalizability of these results is further enhanced by the fact that the magnitude of the effects is replicated across different decisions, surveys, and countries.

Of particular note, Fournier's results are obtained using a novel measure of what the author calls *actual ambivalence*. The measure is computed by first taking the considerations relevant to voting intentions, which are operationalized as significant correlates of voting intentions. Once identified, these considerations are then coded as being consistent, neutral, or inconsistent with the respondent's initial position. For example, an intention to vote for John Kerry might be determined by party identification; in this case, identification with the Democrats would be coded consistent, identification with the Republicans as inconsistent, and identification as an Independent or with other parties would be coded neutral. Actual ambivalence is then computed from the difference between the proportion of inconsistent considerations and the proportion of consistent considerations. Although, as Fournier acknowledges, the nature of the data do not allow a full psychometric evaluation, the findings are encouraging. It would be valuable, however, to conduct further work on this measure to address the potential problem of a confound between the antecedents of intention and the measure of ambivalence, and to account for the fact that different considerations might be held with different levels of intensity.

McGraw and Bartels's (2005) reanalysis of the 1997 American National Election Study Pilot Study is designed to explore the extent of Americans' ambivalence about the institutions of national government (Congress, president, Supreme Court), and to examine the consequences of ambivalence for trust, efficacy, and support for the democratic process. This study, which is the first to look at this particular subject matter, reveals considerable levels of ambivalence overall but more so toward Congress than the other institutions. In addition, an examination of the antecedents of ambivalence indicates that only one factor (political efficacy) underpins ambivalence toward Congress, the president, *and* the Court, that is, the sources of ambivalence are relatively unique to each institution. Further analyses by the authors focus on two classes of variables: attitudes and cognitions. Results show that ambivalence toward both the president and the Supreme Court is associated with more negative evaluations of the institution (or individual leader) in question, but ambivalence toward Congress has no significant effect on evaluations.

McGraw and Bartels interpret these differences between Congress on the one hand, and the president and Supreme Court on the other, in terms of the "default" (or baseline) opinions that citizens hold toward the various institutions. At the time of data collection, in 1997, prevailing attitudes toward Congress were generally negative, while attitudes toward the president and Supreme Court were more positive. In the case of Congress, this supposedly led to ambivalence being associated with more *positive* beliefs; initially positive attitudes toward the president and Supreme Court, however, resulted in *negative* beliefs being more closely linked to ambivalence about those institutions. In contrast, the effects of ambivalence toward Congress on cognition are more marked than those of presidential and Supreme Court ambivalence. Specifically, ambivalence toward Congress is associated with greater propensity to seek out political information, less uncertainty about the ideological orientation of Congress, and the tendency to differentiate between evaluations of Congress as an institution and of one's own representative, while ambivalence about the president and Supreme Court has few effects on cognition. These findings are interpreted by McGraw and Bartels as providing further evidence for the effects of ambivalence on information processing; they are important because the initial valence of prevailing attitudes has rarely been taken into account in work of this kind.

Citrin and Luks's (2005) work provides a novel approach to the study of ambivalence: whereas there has been a tendency to focus on cognitive ambivalence (mixed thoughts), these authors focus on Americans' emotional reactions toward their own country. Using the 1996 General Social Survey, Citrin and Luks compute and evaluate citizens' emotional ambivalence toward the United States. They present four key findings. First, many more people report experiencing emotional ambivalence toward the United States than expected, given the prevailing backdrop of patriotic feelings. Second, emotional ambivalence does not differ greatly across demographic lines, as people of different political persuasions, genders, ages, income levels, and ethnicities exhibit similar levels of ambivalence. Third, even Americans who report identifying strongly with their country sometimes also feel emotional ambivalence; as a result, the national identity–ambivalence correlation is fairly modest. Fourth, although ambivalence is negatively related to patriotism, once again the strength of the relationship is not terribly strong. Interestingly, emotional ambivalence does not appear to generate either negative attitudes toward foreigners or in-group favoritism.

However, the Citrin and Luks study also raises a number of methodological issues. The most important of these stems from the fact that the authors control for nonrandom measurement error. Explicit in the conceptualization of ambivalence is the idea that the positive and negative poles used in responding to attitude objects are empirically distinct. Yet controlling for the effects of nonrandom measurement error fails to confirm this assumption: positive and negative reactions (even within participants) remain associated with global attitude in predictable ways. Citrin and Luks conclude that the assumption of bipolarity must be tested on a case-by-case basis, and they recommend that multiple indicators of attitudinal ambivalence be used wherever possible.

Economic policy and economic performance are regarded as key determinants of voter behavior, especially in the United States, and yet there has been a dearth of research examining voter ambivalence that might underpin attitudes toward such policies. Jacoby's (2005) analysis of the 1992 American National Election Study explains an apparent contradiction in that many people express negative attitudes toward the increasing power of the central government while simultaneously holding positive attitudes toward public expenditures. These seemingly conflicting opinions are not, however, attributable to ambivalence concerning the role of government in modern society. According to Jacoby, the nature of the expenditure is important. Whereas attitudes toward "welfare spending" are strongly influenced by factors such as symbolic racism, party identification, and self-interest, the effects of those variables on "non-welfare spending" are substantially weaker. Thus, the apparent contradiction between attitudes toward central government and public spending might be attributable to people's tendency to equate government spending with welfare spending, which remains a divisive issue in American politics. On the other hand, attitudes toward spending on non-welfare programs appear to reflect a consensual belief that the government is responsible for supporting education, science, and broad-based social insurance programs.

In chapter one of the present volume, Lavine and Steenbergen contend that American public opinion is often rooted in attitudes toward particular social groups that are associated with either liberal or conservative ideals. Using data from the 2000 American National Election Study, these authors derive a measure of group ambivalence from expressed feelings toward both liberal groups (e.g., labor unions, Democrats) and conservative groups (e.g., Christian Fundamentalists, big business). In analyses that control for a range of variables, including the effects of ambivalence toward political parties and candidates, Lavine and Steenbergen report that ambivalence toward social groups does indeed affect voters' choices involving policies, political predispositions, and candidates.

Perhaps more importantly, group ambivalence is also associated with differences in variables more closely related to voter behavior. For example, even controlling for the effects of ambivalence toward the candidates, people who score high in group ambivalence make later voting decisions, possess less stable attitudes toward candidates, and are more likely to vote for different parties for president and Congress. The implication is that individuals with opposed (and thereby "consistent") attitudes toward liberal and conservative groups tend to behave in a more predictable fashion, while those who like (or dislike) social groups on both the left *and* right make up their minds later, have unstable attitudes regarding the candidates, and rely less on relevant issues in making their voting decision. Consistent with Albertson, Brehm, and Alvarez (2005), Lavine and Steenbergen note that specific political choice is the level at which to analyze the effects of ambivalence, as opposed to other apparent conflicts that might be more accurately characterized as inconsistency.

From an applied perspective, the analysis by Martinez, Craig, Kane, and Gainous of attitudes toward abortion and gay rights (see chapter four in this volume) suggests that public opinion on controversial issues may not be as polarized as is often assumed. Perhaps as a function of the publicity afforded extreme views in these particular topic areas, general public opinion turns out to be surprisingly complex, with many people making subtle distinctions based on situational and other contextual factors. For example, pro-choice voters are found to be more ambivalent about elective abortions whereas pro-life voters tend to be more ambivalent about abortions obtained in traumatic circumstances. Ambivalence is thus shown not to generalize across topics, implying that the observed patterns are not attributable to people who happen to be chronically ambivalent. Martinez *et al.*'s analyses also indicate that ambivalence is at least partly related to value conflict and that conflict among core values may cause ambivalence.

Finally, Martinez and his colleagues hypothesize that ambivalence might account for instances where apparent majorities can be overcome by issue-specific minorities: because individuals with ambivalent attitudes are engaged in both sides of an argument, they are likely to share certain attitudes in common and therefore partially sympathize with minority groups. This speculation provides an interesting parallel with social psychological research on minority influence, which has emphasized the impact of diachronic and synchronic consistency on the influence exerted by minority groups (Moscovici 1976; Phillips 2003).

Building on the idea that the relationship between ideological conservatism and racial ambivalence among white Americans is mediated by the conflict that often exists between individualistic and humanitarian values, Federico (see chapter five in this volume) explores the possibility that these effects are moderated by cognitive sophistication (operationalized in terms of whether or not one is college-educated). Using data from the 1991 National Race and Politics Study, Federico shows that (1) the conservatism–racial ambivalence relationship is stronger among whites who are more cognitively sophisticated; and (2) the effect of the conservatism × cognitive sophistication interaction is mediated, as hypothesized, through conflict between individualistic and humanitarian values. In other words, it seems that cognitive sophistication may actually intensify conflict that exists between humanitarianism and individualism among conservatives, ultimately leading to greater ambivalence. Federico further argues that higher education might serve to amplify value conflict.

This research also highlights the importance of specificity in understanding value conflict. Although the work of Katz and colleagues (e.g., Katz and Hass 1988) suggests that value conflict need only occur at a very general level, it is the specific conflict between individualistic and humanitarian concerns in the domain of race relations that exerts a powerful effect in Federico's data. The findings here show that values work at a specific level—that is, at the level of beliefs about how those values relate to particular social groups, which is consistent with research indicating that for example, generalized individualism is less consequential than the specific belief that blacks lack individualistic values (e.g., Kinder and Mendelberg 2000).

Whereas Federico contrasts individualism with humanitarian concerns, Gainous and Martinez (see chapter three in this volume) examine potential conflict between the values of individualism and egalitarianism. The authors also examine some additional predictors of ambivalence about social welfare policy, namely, value importance and policy preferences, which have hitherto been measured in separate studies but have not yet been observed within a single study. The importance that people place on values is of particular interest here because values are typically organized in terms of hierarchies, which are likely to affect the extent to which they truly conflict (Schwartz 1992).

Based on data collected specifically for their study, Gainous and Martinez identify value conflict, value importance, policy preference, and race as significant predictors of ambivalence about social welfare policy. Interestingly, race is the dominant predictor, with blacks being significantly less ambivalent about social welfare policy than whites even when controlling for the effects of value conflict, value importance, and policy preference. The implication is that value conflict is one of a *range* of predictors of ambivalence about social welfare policy, and that the importance that one ascribes to particular values is likely to determine levels of ambivalence about policy issues. In addition, it is clear that additional variables (such as political identity; see chapter three) need to be tested as potential mediators of the effects of race on ambivalence. We return to this issue later.

Chong and Wolinsky-Nahmias (see chapter six in this volume) discuss the exploitation of ambivalence to meet political ends, using a 2000 Arizona referendum known as the Citizen's Growth Management Initiative (a piece of legislation proposed to regulate open-space planning) as a case study. Typically, if there is no opposition from the building industry, advocates of environmentally friendly policies are free to emphasize the economic and environmental benefits of limiting development in order to appeal to liberals and conservatives alike. Psychologically, Chong and Wolinsky-Nahmias argue, this limits the amount of ambivalence experienced by voters. Thus, although on the face of it, a vote on the Citizen's Growth Management Initiative would be expected to split along traditional liberal versus conservative lines (open space versus economic growth), supporters of both political parties often profess similar positive attitudes about such measures. Indeed, Arizona voters generally held positive attitudes toward many aspects of the initiative.

In this instance, however, a targeted campaign waged by a key opposition group, Arizonans for Responsible Planning (a building industry-led coalition) helped to undermine public support. The Citizen's Growth Management Initiative included many elements such as growth boundaries and the right of citizens to sue for noncompliance that were revealed as areas of concern for voters. For example, people believed that growth boundaries meant that future growth would be focused in existing neighborhoods, that the people who chose to exercise the lawsuit provision could hold other residents to ransom, and that local control of urban planning decisions would create disputes along the edges of the growth boundaries. The principal opposition group (Arizonans for Responsible Planning) used these negative beliefs to design the campaign that ultimately led to a "no" vote on election day. Thus, Chong and Wolinsky-Nahmias identify the exploitation of value conflicts between growth and conservation as a key means by which ambivalence was created, and also demonstrate the power of ambivalence for generating change in voter decisions.

The relationship between church and state has been a central feature of political thought for centuries. Jelen (see chapter seven in this volume) provides a novel insight into this area by conducting a secondary analysis of data on citizens' attitudes toward that relationship. Using two elements—one tapping the extent to which people feel there should be a high wall between church and state, the other their beliefs about whether government should protect the Judeo-Christian heritage—Jelen identifies four distinct groups of respondents: consistent separationists, consistent accommodationists, symbolic ambivalents, and sophisticated ambivalents. It is the latter two groups on which his analyses center. Symbolic ambivalents endorse both the idea that government should protect the Judeo-Christian heritage *and* the notion that there should be a high wall between church and state; sophisticated ambivalents, on the other hand, do not believe that government should protect the Judeo-Christian heritage *or* that there should be a high wall between church and state. Interestingly, sophisticated ambivalence is predicted by the core values of religiosity (operationalized as church attendance) and ideological self-placement (liberal versus conservative), such that lower levels of religiosity and identification as a liberal are associated with greater sophisticated ambivalence. Although this suggests that the measure of sophisticated ambivalence most accurately reflects common operationalizations of ambivalence, the interaction between religiosity and ideology is nonsignificant; the latter finding would seem to imply a lack of value conflict and, hence, felt ambivalence.

Jelen goes on to argue that the apparently conflicting responses do not reflect value conflict, but rather that they represent pragmatic responses to the need for reconciling a relatively religious population with secular government. Sophisticated ambivalents may, for example, oppose a high wall of separation between church and state because they believe it to be desirable for government to offer assistance to religion on a nondiscriminatory basis. In sum, ambivalence is not aroused in the absence of conflicting values and so apparent contradictions tend to be resolved in a pragmatic way. This discussion has important implications for our understanding of the nature of value conflict.

Summary of the Key Contributions

The research reviewed above represents a wealth of valuable insights into the concept of ambivalence and consists of major original contributions by political scientists and social psychologists alike. At the risk of foreshadowing one of our eventual conclusions, in many respects this body of research is remarkably consistent, particularly with respect to the consequences of attitudinal ambivalence. In contrast, research into the antecedents of ambivalence has produced more mixed findings. The following section draws together a number of the emerging themes.

EMERGING THEMES

Conceptualization of Ambivalence

The idea that attitudinal ambivalence is a reconceptualization of a unidimensional view of attitudes has led to a number of ambiguities in the literature, many of which are elucidated in the essay by Albertson, Brehm, and Alvarez (2005). The most obvious ambiguity concerns usage of the term "ambivalence" in lay discussions of political attitudes. As we noted at the outset of the chapter, ambivalence has frequently been used to describe public opinion as a whole rather than the attitudes of individual citizens. To repeat, when half the public supports a policy that the other half opposes, such a division indicates a conflicted nation rather than a nation of conflicted individuals.

Ambiguities have arisen in the academic literature as well. In social psychology, for example, the concepts of attitude uncertainty and attitude variability also reflect inconsistencies in attitudes (e.g., Sparks, Hedderley, and Shepherd 1992). Unlike ambivalence, however, uncertainty and variability capture temporal instability in attitudes reflecting possible alternating positive and negative evaluations of objects, but do not tap the simultaneous conflict in evaluations that is implied by ambivalence. In political science, ambivalence has sometimes been used interchangeably with the notion of "value conflict." For example, Feldman and Zaller (1992) reported that liberals are more ambivalent about social welfare issues than conservatives because they must reconcile pro-welfare views with their support for the broader principles of individualism and limited government. Yet even though these values may indeed conflict for many people, this does not necessarily result in the sort of internalized conflict associated with ambivalence. We return to the issue of value conflict as a possible antecedent of ambivalence later in the chapter.

The consensus reached by a majority of contributors to both this and the previous volume (Craig and Martinez 2005) maps on to the two defining characteristics of ambivalence identified by Conner and Sparks (2002), and encapsulated in the widely employed formula proposed by Thompson, Zanna, and Griffin (1995). Briefly, ambivalence is viewed as a function of (1) the extent to which positive and negative evaluations of the same object are similar; and (2) the intensity associated with those positive and negative evaluations. This conceptualization is captured in Thompson, Zanna, and Griffin's (1995: 367) definition of ambivalence as an individual's inclination "to give [an attitude object] equivalently strong positive and negative evaluations." In the same vein, Albertson, Brehm, and Alvarez (2005) define ambivalence as strong internalized conflict experienced at the moment of an interviewer's question, implying that there is a threshold underpinning ambivalence (cf. Priester and Petty 1996).

Operationalization of Ambivalence

The chapters presented here and in Craig and Martinez (2005) reflect a current lack of agreement regarding the best means to measure ambivalence. Three broad approaches are found in the literature. First, ambivalence has been inferred from in-depth interviews, responses to open-ended survey questions, and patterns of error variance in heteroskedastic probit models of binary choice (Albertson, Brehm, and Alvarez 2005; Chong and Wolinsky-Nahmias 2005). Second, direct measures of ambivalence have been taken by asking people to make meta-judgments about their own levels of ambivalence; for example, Priester and Petty (1996) asked participants to rate their subjective ("felt") ambivalence on 11-point scales anchored at either end by *feel no conflict at all* ($= 0$) and *feel maximum conflict* ($= 10$). Third, measures of potential ambivalence have employed separate assessments of positive and negative thoughts, feelings, or beliefs; these positive and negative reactions are then combined to yield a continuous index of ambivalence (Thompson, Zanna, and Griffin 1995).

Each approach has both strengths and weaknesses. Although inferring ambivalence from people's responses to survey questions reduces possible experimenter bias, for example, a judgment is required as to whether the phenomenon under investigation reflects ambivalence or some third variable that is not amenable to experimentation. Direct measures of ambivalence avoid this potential ambiguity, and may also be useful for tapping the extent to which ambivalence is experienced as unpleasant (similar to the idea of cognitive dissonance, high levels of felt ambivalence may motivate individuals to try and resolve the conflict; see Festinger 1957). In general, though, such measures appear to be more open to extraneous influences that can undermine their validity (Bassili 1996). For example, Newby-Clark, McGregor, and Zanna (2002) discovered that the relationship between felt and potential ambivalence is dependent upon the extent to which the opposing poles are salient. Thus, someone's felt ambivalence can be affected by extraneous influences, and (with the exception of studies that deliberately manipulate salience) it is not clear whether the information upon which one might form judgments of felt ambivalence are ordinarily available to consciousness.

Measures of potential ambivalence possess some similarity to Bassili's (1996) operative indices of attitude strength. Such indices are derived from the attitude judgment process or its outcomes (e.g., response latency) and are generally preferred to the extent that they do not require the respondent to combine positive and negative evaluations in a biased manner. Nevertheless, the term "potential ambivalence" is appropriate because high scores may not reflect higher levels of experienced ambivalence unless both positive and negative evaluations upon which the potential ambivalence is based are both similarly accessible (Conner and Sparks 2002; Newby-Clark, McGregor, and Zanna 2002). Moreover, given that potential and felt ambivalence seem to have different consequences (Holbrook and Krosnick 2005), it would be worthwhile for researchers to measure both types and, ideally, to manipulate each form of ambivalence independently.

One area where there does appear to be consensus concerns the combination of positive and negative poles in direct measures of potential ambivalence. Although several formulae have been proposed to combine positive and negative evaluations, the Thompson–Zanna–Griffin index (Thompson, Zanna, and Griffin 1995) seems to be the formula of choice. This is probably because the index captures both the intensity of positive and negative evaluations as well as the level of similarity between the two:

$$\text{Ambivalence} = \frac{\text{positive} + \text{negative}}{2} - |\text{positive} - \text{negative}|$$

This formula has been used throughout the two volumes (also see Craig and Martinez 2005), including a modified version employed by Lavine and Steenbergen in chapter one of this book to assess group ambivalence. Interestingly, both Riketta (2000) and Priester and Petty (1996) found Thompson–Zanna–Griffin to be more closely correlated ($r = .62$ and $.44$, respectively) with experienced ambivalence than are alternative measures of potential (felt) ambivalence.

It is also worth noting that there is an increasing body of literature distinguishing between felt and potential ambivalence in terms of antecedents and consequences. Priester and Petty (2001), for example, reported that intra-individual attitude conflict was an antecedent of felt but not of potential ambivalence. In a similar vein, Conner (2004a) found higher levels of potential ambivalence to be associated with attitude *in*stability while higher levels of felt ambivalence are associated with *more* stable attitudes. Thus, although it would appear that potential ambivalence is similar to attitude strength (with higher ambivalence equating to weaker attitudes), measures of felt ambivalence exhibit more complex patterns. Clearly, this has important implications for studying ambivalence in relation to political opinion.

Antecedents of Ambivalence

Top-down processes. Value conflict has often been presented as an antecedent of ambivalence, and this is reflected in several of the chapters here and in Craig and Martinez (2005). Values are general beliefs about desirable ends around which specific attitudes can be structured and, it is argued, our values often conflict with one another. For example, Schwartz (1992) regarded values as potentially falling along two dimensions that range between openness to change and conservation on the one hand, and between self-enhancement and self-transcendence on the other. In other words, people need (1) stimulation yet crave stability; and (2) to achieve yet be benevolent. According to Schwartz, there is chronic conflict across these dimensions and, accordingly, scholars have frequently posited a causal link between value conflict and ambivalence (e.g., Alvarez and Brehm 1995; Katz and Hass 1988; Zaller 1992).

Until the present volumes, however, there has been little research exploring these proposed effects. We would argue that clear evidence in support of value conflict causing ambivalence is still lacking. For example, Craig *et al.* (2005b) reported virtually no zero–order relationship between value conflict and ambivalence about gay rights and, even when controlling for a range of factors from religious guidance to age, multivariate analyses revealed statistically significant associations but small effect sizes. Comparable findings are reported by Gainous and Martinez (see chapter three in this volume), who found that value conflict is the weakest statistically significant predictor of social welfare ambivalence and that it fails to mediate the effects of race. In addition, Federico (see chapter five) discovered that value conflict predicts racial ambivalence only when such conflict is highly specified and therefore does not conform to most definitions of values as overarching structures (also see Jelen's analysis in chapter seven). Given the strong theoretical arguments for the idea that value conflict underpins attitudinal ambivalence, we should begin to explore the reasons why the proposed association is so weak empirically. The following section explores some of these grounds.

One difficulty associated with the concept of value conflict is that values may conflict but not be diametrically opposed. Analogous with research on the mechanisms underpinning approach/avoidance responses (i.e., where *failing to approach* an object is not the equivalent of *avoiding* that object, e.g., Coats, Janoff-Bulman, and Alpert 1996), pro-welfare values are not diametrically opposed to pro-individuality values. Thus, although values may be inconsistent with one another, they are unlikely to be diametrically opposed and, consequently, to generate the internalized conflict that characterizes true ambivalence (cf. Albertson, Brehm, and Alvarez 2005). At the very least, this should serve to limit the frequency with which ambivalence is aroused by the presence of seemingly contradictory values.

Perhaps more importantly, researchers have rarely taken the intensity and/or personal importance associated with values into account. This means that even if values truly clash with one another, yet they are not held with conviction, not held at similar levels of intensity, or are regarded as unimportant by the individual, value conflict is unlikely to result. For example, while actual voter turnout in the United States is consistently around the 50-percent mark, self-reports of turnout are consistently higher, suggesting that although most Americans endorse democratic values they seem not to be consistently acted upon (e.g., Silver, Abramson, and Anderson 1986). Gainous and Martinez's work (see chapter three) shows that three indices of value importance are better predictors of ambivalence than is value conflict *per se.*

In fact, one strand of research suggests that values are rarely held with any level of intensity and are not generally regarded as important except to justify attitudes toward value-relevant issues. More specifically, Maio and Olson (1998) have argued that values act as truisms, used in society to provide support for one's attitudes, but until recently they have not been the subject of debate in their own right. For example, although the value of openness to change might be cited as justification for introducing same sex marriage into the Anglican Church, how important is the value of openness to change *per se*?

Maio and Olson (1998) noted that for values to act as truisms they must be both widely endorsed and lack cognitive support. These authors examined the values of helpfulness, honesty, forgiveness, and equality and found a high degree of endorsement in each instance. Interestingly, there was significantly greater agreement with these values than there was agreement with known truisms measured at the same time (e.g., that penicillin has been a boon to humankind). Yet despite this apparent consensus, Maio and Olson demonstrated that people often struggle to generate a rationale for their beliefs; in fact, participants were able to state just two reasons (on average) underpinning their values—but five reasons (on average) for their like or dislike of popular beverages. This implies an absence of cognitive support consistent with the idea that values may be vacuous and act as truisms for many individuals. Given the pivotal role ascribed to values, particularly in relation to ambivalence, the lack of cognitive support shown by Maio and Olson is potentially problematic.

A second strand of evidence further supports the conclusion that values are vacuous: Maio and Olson (1998) found that asking people to analyze the reasons why they held particular values sometimes changed their propensity to endorse those values. This finding is once again consistent with the notion that values lack cognitive support, and it suggests that responses to the values questions may have been created on the spot (cf. Wilson and Hodges 1992). The implication is that even though people use values to support their attitudes toward different issues, they rarely understand the reasoning behind them (Maio and Olson 1998).

The theoretical account of values-as-truisms (Bernard, Maio, and Olson 2003; Maio and Olson 1998) suggests that even if there is an apparent conflict between values, both values may be lacking in cognitive support and therefore highly malleable; as a result, value conflict will be experienced at the level of the individual less often than one might expect. This account, coupled with the lack of empirical evidence reported here and in Craig and Martinez (2005), suggests in turn that value conflict may not be at the root of ambivalence after all. Even if pro-welfare values logically conflict with pro-individualist values, for example, it seems likely that the manner in which they are experienced by individuals engenders relatively little internalized conflict or ambivalence. Nevertheless, more recent work shows that it is possible to inoculate against these effects by exposure to attacking arguments and encouraging refutation of those arguments (e.g., Bernard, Maio, and Olson 2003). Thus, although it is possible that making two conflicting values non-truistic could lead to ambivalence, it seems less likely that value conflict will cause ambivalence without such direct intervention. Such inoculation techniques might, however, prove useful in generating ambivalence, and it would be valuable to explore this idea in future work.

Similar to the results for value conflict, there is very little evidence showing that other chronic influences, such as personality types, affect feelings of ambivalence (Craig *et al.* 2005b; Thompson and Zanna 1995; also see chapter four in this volume). The implication is that other top-down processes need to be identified. One possible source of ambivalence might be conflicts in the bases of attitudes. Many of the chapters presented in these two volumes begin with a working definition of attitudes, describing them as consisting of affective, behavioral, cognitive, and evaluative responses to attitude objects. In other words, people respond to attitude objects by making evaluations, expressing feelings, or by cognitively processing aspects of the object. However, it is notable that these bases of attitudes are often not discussed further. Although the measures of ambivalence are typically described as being either primarily affective or primarily cognitive, the implications of attitude base are seldom taken into account. This is important because conflicts *between* affect and cognition are stronger than conflicts *within* affect and cognition, for the reason that the two are underpinned by different neural mechanisms (LeDoux 2000). Again, it would be valuable to explore the potential role of attitude base on ambivalence in future research.

Bottom-up processes. In contrast to the mixed findings associated with the impact of value conflict in generating ambivalence, there is an emerging body of evidence that points to bottom-up processes driving ambivalent reactions. For example, presentation of evaluatively consistent or evaluatively inconsistent messages has been shown to cause ambivalence (Conner 2004b; Jonas, Diehl, and Brömer 1997). Moreover, Jonas and his colleagues (1997) found that attitudinal ambivalence was associated with increased systematic information processing. The question then arises as to whether some people are more susceptible than others to these kinds of information effects. Presumably, a great deal depends upon how personally salient the evaluatively inconsistent information is to the individual (Newby-Clark, McGregor, and Zanna 2005), and whether they have the ability and motivation to process the incoming message (Petty and Cacioppo 1986). For individuals who do have this ability and motivation, inconsistent information should lead to greater elaboration of relevant information than a consistent message

(Maheswaran and Chaiken 1991). In such a case, a message that presents inconsistent information may actually lead to the strengthening of an attitude (and perhaps reducing of ambivalence). Alternatively, where ability or motivation for processing are lacking, an inconsistent message can result in heightened ambivalence and a weakening of the attitude (see also Sengupta and Johar 2002).

The idea of bottom-up processing information to create attitudes has been expanded in Wilson and Hodges's (1992) attitudes-as-constructions model (see also Erber, Hodges, and Wilson 1995; Zaller and Feldman 1992). According to this model, attitudes are temporary constructs that are constructed on the spot, as and when they are needed (e.g., for decision-making). Thus, attitudes are likely to be univalent to the degree that similarly valenced information is retrieved each time an attitude is constructed. It would therefore be valuable to examine further the basic processes by which ambivalent attitudes are formed. For example, what are the elements of a persuasive message in terms of quality, quantity, and extremity that maximize the induction of ambivalence? In addition, the impacts on potential versus felt ambivalence need to be explored.

Consequences of Ambivalence

In contrast with research that examines the antecedents of ambivalence, research on the consequences of attitudinal ambivalence is relatively clear. The evidence reported here and in Craig and Martinez (2005) demonstrates an association between ambivalence and information seeking, temporal stability of attitudes, engaging in attitude-relevant behaviors (e.g., political activism), and resistance to persuasion. Overall, there is strong support for the idea that univalent attitudes are stronger than ambivalent attitudes (Krosnick and Petty 1995). There are, however, some limitations in the data collected to date that limit the ability to generalize these findings and to gauge the potential effectiveness of ambivalence to make changes in the real world. For example, there is relatively little evidence to suggest that ambivalence affects objectively measured behavior. Although we have developed a better understanding of the ambivalence that underpins people's attitudes to certain political candidates, it is the behavior associated with those candidates that is important (including whether to vote for them). If "thinking is for doing" as Fiske (1992) proposes, then it is important to determine whether the ambivalence that people experience in relation to a range of political issues translates into behavior.

Similarly, it would be beneficial to control for a greater range of potential confounding variables, most notably other indices of attitude strength. Although, as we have noted, there are ambiguities regarding the conceptualization of ambivalence found in the literature, it may be that these ambiguities reflect logically related constructs. The range of alternative indices that have been examined to date are welcome additions to the literature, but their differences make direct comparisons between studies more difficult. Finally, as alluded to earlier, the consequences of ambivalence are more clear-cut for measures of potential than of felt ambivalence. While in the former case there is good reason to consider high levels of ambivalence as reflecting a weaker attitude, the evidence is less consistent for felt ambivalence. Indeed, high levels of felt ambivalence sometimes exhibit properties of a strong attitude, perhaps through prompting elaboration around the attitude object in order to tackle the "discomfort" individuals may feel over the conflicting evaluations expressed in such a judgment. We note some further concerns about the current state of research on ambivalence in the following section.

Addressing Limitations

In our view, potential difficulties associated with a lack of objective measures of behavior and the need to control for a greater range of potential confounds referred to in the preceding section are the result of an overreliance on analysis of existing datasets of public opinion. Although the benefits associated with archival techniques are well known, it is worth revisiting three of their limitations to demonstrate how they might have affected accumulated knowledge in the science of ambivalence. First, the most common limitation highlighted by the authors of these chapters is that the measures included in the datasets were not originally designed to tap ambivalence, nor were they designed with the researchers' specific hypotheses in mind. Despite the controversy regarding the best means of assessing ambivalence, the analysis of existing datasets has led to the use of several idiosyncratic operationalizations of ambivalence due to necessary compromises being made using available measures. Similarly, there is often a lack of correspondence or specificity between measures and, in some cases, measures have to be treated as contemporaneous when they have in fact been assessed months and even years apart. At best, these compromises are likely to undermine the size of reported effects; at worst, they will lead to a potentially misleading body of evidence. Clearly, then, there is a need for research that is set up to examine ambivalence *per se*, rather than trying to divine ambivalence from other types of indicators. The research presented in these volumes highlights the importance of ambivalence in the political domain, but more needs to be done in terms of establishing a coherent body of work in this field.

A second limitation associated with the use of archival sources is that the studies are most often cross-sectional and rarely if ever experimental, meaning that cause-and-effect relations cannot be inferred. Of course, the equally valid counterpoint to this is that experimental studies are most often conducted on samples of undergraduate students, whose attitudes toward political issues are likely to be unrepresentative of the general population and whose attitudes are likely to be less stable (Sears 1986). It would therefore be helpful to conduct more experimental work on public opinion, but also to broaden the pool of participants with whom such work is carried out.

The final limitation we wish to note stems from the possibility that work based on large electoral surveys may be overpowered. This is important because although larger samples make it easier to detect statistically significant effects, there is a tendency to overlook the size of those effects. Given that the associated dependent variables are often "soft"—that is, typically based on self-reported cognition rather than more objective measures of behavior—it is disappointing that, more often than not, the reported effect sizes are fairly modest (Cohen 1992). The most obvious way to address these limitations would be for political scientists to be allowed greater input into election and public opinion surveys, and to be granted control over them over periods of time. This is an important issue because systematically conducted surveys would increase confidence in the conclusions drawn, and allow the science of ambivalence to progress in a more even fashion. We hope that the chapters collected together to form these two volumes represent a case for inferential work, rather than descriptive work, to be conducted on electoral surveys.

Practical Implications

There are several practical implications of the findings presented in the preceding chapters and in Craig and Martinez (2005). It appears, for example, that ambivalent voters take longer to decide whom to vote for, have attitudes that are relatively unstable, are more receptive to persuasive information, and are more inclined to seek and process relevant information. The question then arises as to how these insights can be used to change public opinion. Approaches are likely to depend upon whether preexisting attitudes are mostly univalent or ambivalent.

For people with univalent attitudes, it would be valuable to identify the most effective means by which ambivalence is evoked. We pointed out earlier that value conflict might be aroused by providing arguments and refutations to attacks on core values, and that the presentation of inconsistent information can induce ambivalence (Bernard, Maio, and Olson 2003; Conner 2004b). However, can these manipulations work on a general level without alienating one's core constituency? Perhaps more importantly, can these techniques be used to persuade univalent nonvoters to exercise their constitutional right to vote? Regardless, the prospects of changing strong, univalent attitudes is likely to prove a difficult but worthwhile avenue for further research.

Perhaps a more achievable goal in the short term would be to focus on examining the impact of election campaigns on people who hold ambivalent attitudes. The challenge in this case would be to frame campaigns so as to accommodate the positive beliefs of those who are ambivalent. An important question for future research therefore concerns the ways in which cues are effective in changing ambivalent attitudes. Given that individuals with ambivalent attitudes are likely to be responsive to credible campaign influences, such as debates and news coverage, this would seem like a sensible place to start. The implication is that campaign messages can be tailored to persuade those who are ambivalent and then targeted at ambivalent groups. Thus, it would be important to know the distribution of people with ambivalent attitudes on key issues in the general population. In contrast to many of the other variables (such as age and gender) by which audiences are segmented, however, the identification of ambivalent persons will likely prove difficult and costly, not least because people seem to be ambivalent with respect to isolated issues (Craig et al., 2005a). This area of inquiry is where inferential techniques may ultimately come into their own (Albertson, Brehm, and Alvarez 2005).

More generally, because ambivalent attitudes contain evaluations that are consistent with multiple viewpoints, the challenge is to develop messages that maintain one's core support while resolving inconsistencies in possible converts. There is also a potential paradox: while changing ambivalent attitudes seems relatively straightforward, the challenge shifts to not just creating new attitudes that are univalent, but creating attitudes that are univalent *and* temporally stable. The question then arises as to whether there are constructs beyond values that might draw together constellations of attitudes. One approach that might prove fruitful in this regard centers around the idea of belief homogeneity (Armitage 2003). Belief homogeneity concerns the interrelationships between beliefs about a particular topic, and reflects the extent to which the database from which one's attitude is formed is consistent (Armitage 2003; cf. Erber, Hodges, and Wilson 1995). Thus, whereas ambivalent individuals might simultaneously evaluate a politician both positively and negatively, people with heterogeneous belief sets might hold beliefs of different valence with different levels of intensity. A politician, for example, might be perceived as very honest, slightly trustworthy, not at all engaging, but highly believable. The evidence to date shows that belief homogeneity can be manipulated and that it affects people's decisions and actions (Armitage 2003), and one possible avenue for further research would be to see if these effects can be replicated in the political domain.

CONCLUSIONS

In sum, the research reported here and in Craig and Martinez (2005) covers a breadth of work that is both diverse and yet consistent in many respects. First, ambivalence seems to arise in response to all of the various attitude objects examined—from public expenditure to the institutions of national government to liberal, conservative, or race-based social groups. This is important because it implies that the bi-dimensional conceptualization of attitudes captured in the concept of ambivalence supersedes the traditional view that positive and negative attitudes toward the same object are perfectly negatively correlated. Second, the consequences of ambivalence are remarkably consistent across diverse populations, topics, and measurement, and even controlling for several alternative indices of attitude strength. It is therefore clear that ambivalence represents an important aspect of attitude strength. The challenges for future research include (among others) identifying means by which ambivalence might be induced, or by which existing ambivalence might be changed most effectively; and ensuring that future election surveys are designed not simply to describe the attitudes of the population, but also to address key basic research questions.

NOTE

1. Note that throughout this chapter, we refer to a distinction between felt and potential ambivalence. Elsewhere, measures of felt ambivalence have been described as "subjective," "meta-psychological," and "direct," while measures of potential ambivalence have been labeled as "objective," "operative," and "indirect," respectively.

REFERENCES

Abelson, Robert P., Donald R. Kinder, Mark D. Peters, and Susan T. Fiske. 1982. "Affective and Semantic Components in Political Perception." *Journal of Personality and Social Psychology* 42: 619–630.

Abramowitz, Alan I. 1995. "It's Abortion, Stupid: Policy Voting in the 1992 Presidential Election." *Journal of Politics* 57: 176–186.

Achen, Christopher H. 1975. "Mass Political Attitudes and the Survey Response." *American Political Science Review* 69: 1218–1231.

Adams, Greg D. 1997. "Abortion: Evidence of an Issue Evolution." *American Journal of Political Science* 41: 718–737.

Aiken, Leona S., and Stephen G. West. 1991. *Multiple Regression: Testing and Interpreting Interactions*. Newbury Park, CA: Sage.

Albertson, Bethany, John Brehm, and R. Michael Alvarez. 2005. "Ambivalence as Internal Conflict." Pp. 15–32 in *Ambivalence and the Structure of Political Opinion*, eds. Stephen C. Craig and Michael D. Martinez. New York: Palgrave Macmillan.

Albrecht, Don E., Gordon Bultena, and Eric Hoiberg. 1986. "Constituency of the Antigrowth Movement: A Comparison of the Growth Orientations of Urban Status Groups." *Urban Studies Quarterly* 21: 607–616.

Aldrich, John H., and Forrest D. Nelson. 1984. *Linear Probability, Logit, and Probit Models*. Beverly Hills: Sage.

Alvarez, R. Michael, and John Brehm. 1995. "American Ambivalence Towards Abortion Policy: Development of a Heteroskedastic Probit Model of Competing Values." *American Journal of Political Science* 39: 1055–1082.

———. 1997. "Are Americans Ambivalent Towards Racial Policies?" *American Journal of Political Science* 41: 345–374.

———. 1998. "Speaking in Two Voices: American Equivocation About the Internal Revenue Service." *American Journal of Political Science* 42: 418–452.

———. 2002. *Hard Choices, Easy Answers: Values, Information, and American Public Opinion*. Princeton, NJ: Princeton University Press.

Alvarez, R. Michael, and Lisa García Bedolla. 2003. "The Foundations of Latino Voter Partisanship: Evidence from the 2000 Election." *Journal of Politics* 65: 31–49.

American Institute of Architects. 1999. "Survey of State and Local Communities on Livable Communities." Report prepared by Frederick Schneiders Reseach, July 1999.

Ansolabehere, Stephen, James M. Snyder, Jr., and Charles Stewart III. 2001. "The Effects of Party and Preferences on Congressional Roll-Call Voting." *Legislative Studies Quarterly* 26: 533–572.

Armitage, Christopher J. 2003. "Beyond Attitudinal Ambivalence: Effects of Belief Homogeneity on Attitude–Intention–Behaviour Relations." *European Journal of Social Psychology* 33: 551–563.

Armitage, Christopher J., and Mark Conner. 2000. "Attitudinal Ambivalence: A Test of Three Key Hypotheses." *Personality and Social Psychology Bulletin* 26: 1421–1432.

Bailey, Michael A., Ronald A. Faucheux, Paul S. Herrnson, and Clyde Wilcox, eds. 2000. *Campaigns and Elections: Contemporary Case Studies.* Washington, DC: CQ Press.

Baldassare, Mark. 1985. "The Suburban Movement to Limit Growth: Reasons for Support in Orange County." *Policy Studies Review* 4: 613–625.

———.1990. "Suburban Support for No-Growth Parties: Implications for the Growth Revolt." *Journal of Urban Affairs* 12: 197–206.

Bardes, Barbara A., and Robert W. Olendick. 2003. *Public Opinion: Measuring the American Mind.* Belmont, CA: Thomson Wadsworth.

Bargh, John A., Shelley Chaiken, Rajen Govender, and Felicia Pratto. 1992. "The Generality of the Automatic Attitude Activation Effect." *Journal of Personality and Social Psychology* 62: 893–912.

Baron, Reuben M., and David A. Kenny. 1986. "The Moderator-Mediator Variable Distinction in Social Psychological Research: Conceptual, Strategic, and Statistical Considerations." *Journal of Personality and Social Psychology* 51: 1173–1182.

Barrett, Edith J., and Fay Lomax Cook. 1991. "Congressional Attitudes and Voting Behavior: An Examination of Support for Social Welfare." *Legislative Studies Quarterly* 16: 375–392.

Basinger, Scott, and Howard Lavine. 2005. "Ambivalence, Information, and Electoral Choice." *American Political Science Review* (in press).

Bassili, John N. 1996. "Meta-Judgmental Versus Operative Indexes of Psychological Attributes: The Case of Measures of Attitude Strength." *Journal of Personality and Social Psychology* 71: 637–653.

Berelson, Bernard R., Paul F. Lazarsfeld, and William N. McPhee. 1954. *Voting: A Study of Opinion Formation in a Presidential Campaign.* Chicago: University of Chicago Press.

Bernard, Mark M., Gregory R. Maio, and James M. Olson. 2003. "The Vulnerability of Values to Attack: Inoculation of Values and Value-Relevant Attitudes." *Personality and Social Psychology Bulletin* 29: 63–75.

Bobo, Lawrence, and James R. Kluegel. 1993. "Opposition to Race Targeting: Self-Interest, Stratification Ideology, or Racial Attitudes?" *American Sociological Review* 58: 443–464.

Brady, Henry E. 1985. "The Perils of Survey Research: Inter-Personally Incomparable Responses." *Political Methodology* 11: 269–291.

Brady, Henry E., and Paul M. Sniderman. 1985. "Attitude Attribution: A Group Basis for Political Reasoning." *American Political Science Review* 79: 1061–1978.

Breckler, Steven J. 1994. "A Comparison of Numerical Indexes for Measuring Attitudinal Ambivalence." *Educational and Psychological Measurement* 54: 350–365.

Brewer, Paul R. 2003. "The Shifting Foundations of Public Opinion about Gay Rights." *Journal of Politics* 65: 1208–1220.

Cacioppo, John T., and Gary G. Berntson. 1994. "Relationship between Attitudes and Evaluative Space: A Critical Review, with Emphasis on the Separability of Positive and Negative Substrates." *Psychological Bulletin* 115: 401–423.

Cacioppo, John T., Wendi L. Gardner, and Gary G. Berntson. 1999. "The Affect System Has Parallel and Integrative Processing Components: Form Follows Function." *Journal of Personality and Social Psychology* 76: 839–855.

Campbell, Angus, Philip E. Converse, Warren E. Miller, and Donald E. Stokes. 1960. *The American Voter.* New York: John Wiley and Sons.

Cantril, Albert H., and Susan Davis Cantril. 1999. *Reading Mixed Signals: Ambivalence in American Public Opinion about Government.* Washington, DC: Woodrow Wilson Center Press.

Carmines, Edward G., and James A. Stimson. 1980. "The Two Faces of Issue Voting." *American Political Science Review* 74: 78–91.

Carter, Stephen L. 1993. *The Culture of Disbelief: How American Law and Politics Trivialize Religious Devotion.* New York: Basic Books.

Chong, Dennis. 1996. "Creating Common Frames of Reference on Political Issues." Pp. 195–224 in *Political Persuasion and Attitude Change*, eds. Diana C. Mutz, Paul M. Sniderman, and Richard A. Brody. Ann Arbor: University of Michigan Press.

Chong, Dennis, and Yael Wolinsky-Nahmias. 2001. "Public Opinion toward Saving Open Space." Paper presented at the 2001 Annual Meetings of the American Political Science Association, San Francisco, CA.

Choper, Jesse H. 1995. *Securing Religious Liberty: Principles for Judicial Interpretation of the Religion Clauses.* Chicago: University of Chicago Press.

Citrin, Jack, and Samantha Luks. 2005. "Patriotic to the Core? American Ambivalence about America." Pp. 127–148 in *Ambivalence and the Structure of Public Opinion*, eds. Stephen C. Craig and Michael D. Martinez. New York: Palgrave Macmillan.

Coats, Erik J., Ronnie Janoff-Bulman, and Nancy Alpert. 1996. "Approach Versus Avoidance Goals: Differences in Self-Evaluation and Well-Being." *Personality and Social Psychology Bulletin* 22: 1057–1067.

Cobb, Michael D., and James H. Kuklinski. 1997. "Changing Minds: Political Arguments and Political Persuasion." *American Journal of Political Science* 41: 88–121.

Cohen, Jacob. 1992. "A Power Primer." *Psychological Bulletin* 112: 155–159.

Conner, Mark. 2004a. "Potential and Felt Attitudinal Ambivalence: Implications for Attitude Stability." Unpublished manuscript.

———. 2004b. "Attitudinal Ambivalence and the Attitude–Intention–Behaviour Relationship." Unpublished manuscript.

Conner, Mark, and Paul Sparks. 2002. "Ambivalence and Attitudes." *European Review of Social Psychology* 12: 37–70.

Conner, Mark, Paul Sparks, Rachel Povey, Rhiannon James, Richard Shepherd, and Christopher J. Armitage. 2002. "Moderator Effects of Attitudinal Ambivalence on Attitude–Behaviour Relationships." *European Journal of Social Psychology* 32: 705–718.

Connerly, Charles E., and James E. Frank. 1986. "Predicting Support for Local Growth Controls." *Social Science Quarterly* 67: 572–586.

Conover, Pamela Johnston. 1984. "The Influence of Group Identifications on Political Perception and Evaluation." *Journal of Politics* 46: 760–785.

Conover, Pamela Johnston. 1988. "The Role of Social Groups in Political Thinking." *British Journal of Political Science* 18: 51–76.

Conover, Pamela Johnston, and Stanley Feldman. 1981. "The Origins and Meaning of Liberal/Conservative Self-Identifications." *American Journal of Political Science* 25: 617–645.

Converse, Philip E. 1964. "The Nature of Belief Systems in Mass Publics." Pp. 206–261 in *Ideology and Discontent*, ed. David E. Apter. New York: The Free Press.

———. 1966. "Religion and Politics: The 1960 Election." Pp. 96–124 in *Elections and the Political Order*, eds. Angus Campbell, Philip E. Converse, Warren E. Miller, and Donald E. Stokes. New York: Wiley.

———.1970. "Attitudes and Non-Attitudes: Continuation of a Dialogue." Pp. 168–189 in *The Quantitative Analysis of Social Problems*, ed. Edward R. Tufte. Reading, MA: Addison-Wesley.

Cook, Elizabeth Adell, Ted G. Jelen, and Clyde Wilcox. 1992. *Between Two Absolutes: Public Opinion and the Politics of Abortion*. Boulder CO: Westview.

Cook, Fay Lomax, and Edith J. Barrett. 1992. *Support for the American Welfare State: The Views of Congress and the Public*. New York: Columbia University Press.

Craig, Stephen C., Michael D. Martinez, and James G. Kane. 1999. "The Structure of Political Competition: Dimensions of Candidate and Group Evaluation Revisited." *Political Behavior* 21: 283–304.

———. 2002. "Sometimes You Feel Like a Nut, Sometimes You Don't: Citizens' Ambivalence about Abortion." *Political Psychology* 23: 285–301.

———. 2005a. "Ambivalence and Response Instability: A Panel Study." Pp. 55–71 in *Ambivalence and the Structure of Political Opinion*, eds. Stephen C. Craig and Michael D. Martinez. New York: Palgrave Macmillan.

Craig, Stephen C., and Michael D. Martinez, eds. 2005. *Ambivalence and the Structure of Political Opinion*. New York: Palgrave Macmillan.

Craig, Stephen C., Michael D. Martinez, James G. Kane, and Jason Gainous. 2005b. "Core Values, Value Conflict, and Citizens' Ambivalence about Gay Rights." *Political Research Quarterly* 58: 5–17

Cunningham, William A., Marcia K. Johnson, J. Chris Gatenby, John C. Gore, and Mahzarin R. Banaji. 2003. "Neural Components of Social Evaluation." *Journal of Personality and Social Psychology* 85: 639–649.

Davis, Derek H. 1996. "Resolving Not to Resolve the Tension Between the Establishment and Free Exercise Clauses." *Journal of Church and State* 38: 245–259.

de la Garza, Rodolfo, O., Angelo Falcon, and F. Chris Garcia. 1996. "Will the Real Americans Please Stand Up: Anglo and Mexican-American Support of Core American Political Values." *American Journal of Political Science* 40: 335–351.

de la Garza, Rodolfo, O., Louis DeSipio, F. Chris Garcia, and Angelo Falcon. 1992. *Latino Voices: Mexican, Puerto Rican, and Cuban Perspectives on American Politics*. Boulder, CO: Westview.

Delli Carpini, Michael X., and Scott Keeter. 1993. "Measuring Political Knowledge: Putting First Things First." *American Journal of Political Science* 37: 1179–1206.

———. 1996. *What Americans Know about Politics and Why It Matters*. New Haven, CT: Yale University Press.

D'Emilio, John. 2000. "Cycles of Change, Questions of Strategy: The Gay and Lesbian Movement after Fifty Years." Pp. 31–53 in *The Politics of Gay Rights*, eds. Craig A. Rimmerman, Kenneth D. Wald, and Clyde Wilcox. Chicago: University of Chicago Press.

DeSipio, Louis. 1996. *Counting on the Latino Vote: Latinos as a New Electorate.* Charlottesville, VA: University Press of Virginia.

Diamond, Henry L., and Patrick F. Noonan, eds. 1996. *Land Use in America.* Washington, DC: Island Press.

Domke, David, Dhavan V. Shah, and Daniel B. Wackman. 1998. " 'Moral Referendums': Values, News Media, and the Process of Candidate Choice." *Political Communication* 15: 301–321.

Downs, Anthony. 1994. *New Visions for Metropolitan America.* Washington, DC: Brookings Institution.

———. 2000. "Dealing Effectively With Fast Growth." Policy brief prepared for The Brookings Institution, Washington, DC, November 2000.

Druckman, James N. 2001. "The Implications of Framing Effects for Citizen Competence." *Political Behavior* 23: 225–256.

Druckman, James N., and Kjersten R. Nelson. 2003. "Framing and Deliberation: How Citizens' Conversations Limit Elite Influence." *American Journal of Political Science* 47: 729–745.

Dunlap, Riley E. 1995. "Public Opinion and Environmental Policy." Pp. 63–114 in *Environmental Politics and Policy*, 2nd edition, ed. James P. Lester. Durham, NC: Duke University Press.

Dunlap, Riley E., and Rik Scarce. 1991. "Poll Trends: Environmental Problems and Protection." *Public Opinion Quarterly* 55: 651–672.

Eagly, Alice H., and Shelly Chaiken. 1975. "An Attribution Analysis of the Effect of Communicator Characteristics on Opinion Change: The Case of Communicator Attractiveness." *Journal of Personality and Social Psychology* 32: 136–144.

———. 1993. *The Psychology of Attitudes.* Fort Worth: Harcourt Brace.

Erber, Maureen Wang, Sara D. Hodges, and Timothy D. Wilson. 1995. "Attitude Strength, Attitude Stability, and the Effects of Analyzing Reasons." Pp. 433–454, in *Attitude Strength: Antecedents and Consequences*, eds. Richard E. Petty and Jon A. Krosnick. Mahwah, NJ: Lawrence Erlbaum.

Feather, N. T. 2004. "Value Correlates of Ambivalent Attitudes toward Gender Relations." *Personality and Social Psychology Bulletin* 30: 3–12.

Federico, Christopher M. 2004. "Ideology and the Affective Structure of Whites' Racial Perceptions." Paper presented at the 2004 Annual Meetings of the Midwest Political Science Association, Chicago, IL.

Federico, Christopher M., and Jim Sidanius. 2002a. "Racism, Ideology, and Affirmative Action Revisited: The Antecedents and Consequences of 'Principled Objections' to Affirmative Action." *Journal of Personality and Social Psychology* 82: 488–502.

———. 2002b. "Sophistication and the Antecedents of Whites' Racial Policy Attitudes: Racism, Ideology, and Affirmative Action in America." *Public Opinion Quarterly* 66: 145–176.

Feldman, Stanley. 1988. "Structure and Consistency in Public Opinion: The Role of Core Beliefs and Values." *American Journal of Political Science* 32: 416–440.

Feldman, Stanley. 1995. "Answering Survey Questions." Pp. 249–270 in *Political Judgment: Structure and Process*, eds. Milton Lodge and Kathleen M. McGraw. Ann Arbor, MI: University of Michigan Press.

Feldman, Stanley. 2003. "Values, Ideology, and the Structure of Political Attitudes." Pp. 477–510 in *Oxford Handbook of Political Psychology*, eds. David O. Sears, Leonie Huddy, and Robert Jervis. New York: Oxford University Press.

Feldman, Stanley, and John Zaller. 1992. "The Political Culture of Ambivalence: Ideological Responses to the Welfare State." *American Journal of Political Science* 36: 268–307.

Feldman, Stanley, and Marco R. Steenbergen. 2001. "The Humanitarian Foundation of Public Support for Social Welfare." *American Journal of Political Science* 45: 658–677.

Festinger, Leon. 1957. *A Theory of Cognitive Dissonance*. Palo Alto, CA: Stanford University Press.

Finke, Roger, and Rodney Stark. 1992. *The Churching of America, 1776–1990: Winners and Losers in Our Religious Economy*. New Brunswick, NJ: Rutgers University Press.

Fishbein, Martin. 1967. *Readings in Attitude Theory and Measurement*. New York: Wiley.

Fishbein, Martin, and Icek Ajzen. 1975. *Belief, Attitude, Intention, and Behavior: An Introduction to Theory and Research*. Reading, MA: Addison-Wesley.

Fiske, Susan T. 1992. "Thinking Is for Doing: Portraits of Social Cognition from Daguerreotype to Laserphoto." *Journal of Personality and Social Psychology* 63: 877–889.

Fiske, Susan T., Richard R. Lau, and Richard A. Smith. 1990. "On the Varieties and Utilities of Political Expertise." *Social Cognition* 8: 31–48.

Fournier, Patrick. 2000. *Heterogeneity in Political Decision-Making: The Nature, Sources, Extent, Dynamics, and Consequences of Interpersonal Differences in Coefficient Strength*. Unpublished Ph.D. Dissertation, University of British Columbia.

———. 2002. "The Uninformed Canadian Voter." Pp. 92–109 in *Citizen Politics: Research and Theory in Canadian Political Behaviour*, eds. Joanna Everitt and Brenda O'Neill. Oxford: Oxford University Press.

———. 2003. "The Individual Determinants of Political Persuasion." Paper presented at the 2003 Annual Meetings of the American Association for Public Opinion Research, Nashville, TN.

Frankfort-Nachmias, Chava, and David Nachmias. 2000. *Research Methods in the Social Sciences*, 6th edition. New York: Worth.

Frankovic, Kathleen A., and Monika L. McDermott. 2001. "Public Opinion in the 2000 Election: The Ambivalent Electorate." Pp. 73–91 in *The Election of 2000: Reports and Interpretations*, by Gerald M. Pomper *et al.* New York: Chatham House.

Free, Lloyd A., and Hadley Cantril. 1967. *The Political Beliefs of Americans: A Study of Public Opinion*. New Brunswick, NJ: Rutgers University Press.

Fulton, William, Paul Shigley, Alicia Harrison, and Peter Sezzi. 2000. "Trends in Local Land Use Ballot Measures, 1986–2000: An Analysis of City, County and Statewide Trends." Report prepared by the Solimar Research Group, Inc., Ventura, CA, December 2000.

Fulton, William, Rolf Pendall, Mai Nguyen, and Alicia Harrison. 2001. "Who Sprawls Most? How Growth Patterns Differ Across the U.S." Report prepared for The Brookings Institution Center on Urban and Metropolitan Policy, Washington, DC, July 2001.

Gamson, William A. 1992. *Talking Politics*. New York: Cambridge University Press.

Gilens, Martin. 1988. "Gender and Support for Reagan: A Comprehensive Model of Presidential Approval." *American Journal of Political Science* 32: 19–49.

———. 1995. "Racial Attitudes and Opposition to Welfare." *Journal of Politics* 57: 994–1014.

Goren, Paul. 2001. "Core Principles and Policy Reasoning in Mass Publics: A Test of Two Theories." *British Journal of Political Science* 31: 159–177.

Gottdiener, Mark, and Max Nieman. 1981. "Characteristics of Support for Local Growth Control." *Urban Affairs Quarterly* 17: 55–73.

Green, Donald Philip. 1988. "On the Dimensionality of Public Sentiment toward Partisan and Ideological Groups." *American Journal of Political Science* 32: 758–780.

Green, Donald Philip, and Jack Citrin. 1994. "Measurement Error and the Structure of Attitudes: Are Positive and Negative Judgment Opposites?" *American Journal of Political Science* 38: 256–281.

Green, Donald Philip, Bradley Palmquist, and Eric Schickler. 2002. *Partisan Hearts and Minds: Political Parties and the Social Identities of Voters*. New Haven, CT: Yale University Press.

Green, John C. 2000. "Antigay: Varieties of Opposition to Gay Rights." Pp. 121–138 in *The Politics of Gay Rights*, eds. Craig A. Rimmerman, Kenneth D. Wald, and Clyde Wilcox. Chicago: University of Chicago Press.

Greenberg, Stanley B. 2004. *The Two Americas: Our Current Political Deadlock and How to Break It*. New York: Thomas Dunne.

Guge, Michael, and Michael F. Meffert. 1998. "The Political Consequences of Attitude Ambivalence." Paper presented at the 1998 Annual Meetings of the Midwest Political Science Association, Chicago, IL.

Haddock, Geoffrey. 2003. "Making a Party Leader Less of a Party Member: The Impact of Ambivalence on Assimilation and Contrast Effects in Political Party Attitudes." *Political Psychology* 24: 769–780.

Haeberle, Steven H. 1999. "Gay and Lesbian Rights: Emerging Trends in Public Opinion and Voting Behavior." Pp. 146–169 in *Gays and Lesbians in the Democratic Process: Public Policy, Public Opinion, and Political Representation*, eds. Ellen D. B. Riggle and Barry L. Tadlock. New York: Columbia University Press.

Hagle, Timothy M., and Glenn E. Mitchell II. 1992. "Goodness-of-Fit Measures for Probit and Logit." *American Journal of Political Science* 36: 762–784.

Harvey, A. C. 1976. "Estimating Regression Models With Multiplicative Heteroscedasticity." *Econometrica* 44: 461–465.

Hass, R. Glen, Irwin Katz, Nina Rizzo, Joanne Bailey, and Lynn Moore. 1992. "When Racial Ambivalence Evokes Negative Affect: Using a Disguised Measure of Mood." *Personality and Social Psychology Bulletin* 18: 786–797.

Henderson, Steve. 2004. "Justices Duck Fight over 'Under God.' " *St. Louis Post-Dispatch*. June 15: A1.

Herek, Gregory M. 2002. "Gender Gaps in Public Opinion about Lesbians and Gay Men." *Public Opinion Quarterly* 66: 40–66.

Hill, Jennifer L., and Hanspeter Kriesi. 2001. "An Extension and Test of Converse's 'Black-and-White' Model of Response Stability." *American Political Science Review* 95: 397–413.

Hochschild, Jennifer L. 1981. *What's Fair? American Beliefs about Distributive Justice*. Cambridge, MA: Harvard University Press.

Hodson, Gordon, Gregory R. Maio, and Victoria M. Esses. 2001. "The Role of Attitudinal Ambivalence in Susceptibility to Consensus Information." *Basic and Applied Social Psychology* 23: 197–205.

Holbrook, Allyson L., and Jon A. Krosnick. 2005. "Meta-Psychological Versus Operative Measures of Ambivalence: Differentiating the Consequences of Perceived Intra-Psychic Conflict and Real Intra-Psychic Conflict." Pp. 73–103 in *Ambivalence and the Structure of Political Opinion*, eds. Stephen C. Craig and Michael D. Martinez. New York: Palgrave Macmillan.

Hollis, Linda E., and William Fulton. 2002. "Open Space Protection: Conservation Meets Growth Management." Discussion paper prepared for The Brookings Institution Center for Urban and Metropolitan Policy, Washington, DC, April 2002.

Hollis, Linda E., Douglas R. Porter, and Paul S. Tischler. 2000. "Livability and Affordability: Open Space Preservation and Land Supply." Paper presented at Fannie Mae Foundation Conference on Fair Growth, Atlanta, GA.

Horton, Nicholas J., and Stuart R. Lipsitz. 2001. "Multiple Imputation in Practice: Comparison of Software Packages for Regression Models with Missing Variables." *The American Statistician* 55: 244–254.

Hovland, Carl I., and Irving L. Janis, eds. 1959. *Personality and Persuasibility*. New Haven, CT: Yale University Press.

Hovland, Carl I., Irving L. Janis, and Harold H. Kelly. 1953. *Communication and Persuasion: Psychological Studies of Opinion Change*. New Haven, CT: Yale University Press.

Huckfeldt, Robert, and John Sprague. 2000. "Political Consequences of Inconsistency: The Accessibility and Stability of Abortion Attitudes." *Political Psychology* 21: 57–79.

Iyengar, Shanto, and Donald R. Kinder. 1987. *News That Matters: Television and American Opinion*. Chicago: University of Chicago Press.

Iyengar, Shanto, Mark D. Peters, and Donald R. Kinder. 1982. "Experimental Demonstrations of the 'Not-So-Minimal' Consequences of Television News Programs." *American Political Science Review* 76: 848–858.

Jacobs, Lawrence R., and Robert Y. Shapiro. 2000. *Politicians Don't Pander: Political Manipulation and the Loss of Democratic Responsiveness*. Chicago: University of Chicago Press.

Jacoby, William G. 1991. "Ideological Identification and Issue Attitudes." *American Journal of Political Science* 35: 178–205.

———. 2002. "Core Values and Political Attitudes." Pp. 177–201 in *Understanding Public Opinion*, 2nd edition, eds. Barbara Norrander and Clyde Wilcox. Washington, DC: CQ Press.

———. 2005. "Is It Really Ambivalence? Public Opinion Toward Government Spending." Pp. 149–172 in *Ambivalence and the Structure of Political Opinion*, eds. Stephen C. Craig and Michael D. Martinez. New York: Palgrave Macmillan.

Jelen, Ted G. 1989. "Biblical Literalism and Inerrancy: Does the Difference Make a Difference?" *Sociological Analysis* 49: 421–429.

———. 1993. *The Political World of the Clergy*. Westport, CT: Praeger.

———. 1998. "God or Country: Debating Religion in Public Life." Pp. 135–163 in *Moral Controversies in American Politics: Cases in Social Regulatory Policy*, eds. Raymond Tatalovich and Byron W. Daynes. Armonk, NY: M. E. Sharpe.

————. 2000. *To Serve God and Mammon: Church-State Relations in American Politics.* Boulder, CO: Westview.

————, ed. 2002. *Sacred Markets, Sacred Canopies: Essays on Religious Markets and Religious Pluralism.* Lanham, MD: Rowman and Littlefield.

Jelen, Ted G., and Clyde Wilcox. 1995. *Public Attitudes toward Church and State.* Armonk, NY: M. E. Sharpe.

————. 1997. "Conscientious Objectors in the Culture War?: A Typology of Attitudes Toward Church-State Relations." *Sociology of Religion* 58: 277–287.

Jelen, Ted G., Corwin E. Smidt, and Clyde Wilcox. 1990. "Biblical Literalism and Inerrancy: A Methodological Investigation." *Sociological Analysis* 51: 307–313.

Jewell, Robert D. 2003. "The Effects of Deadline Pressure on Attitudinal Ambivalence." *Marketing Letters* 14: 83–95.

Johnson, Dennis W. 2001. *No Place for Amateurs: How Political Consultants Are Reshaping American Democracy.* New York: Routledge.

Jonas, Klaus, Michael Diehl, and Philip Brömer. 1997. "Effects of Attitudinal Ambivalence on Information Processing and Attitude–Intention Consistency." *Journal of Experimental Social Psychology* 33: 190–210.

Judd, Charles M., and James W. Downing. 1990. "Political Expertise and the Development of Attitude Consistency." *Social Cognition* 8: 104–124.

Judd, Charles M., and Jon A. Krosnick. 1989. "The Structural Bases of Consistency Among Political Attitudes: Effects of Expertise and Attitude Importance." Pp. 99–128 in *Attitude Structure and Function*, eds. Anthony R. Pratkanis, Steven J. Breckler, and Anthony G. Greenwald. Hillsdale, NJ: Erlbaum.

Judd, Charles M., and Michael A. Milburn. 1980. "The Structure of Attitude Systems in the General Public: Comparisons of a Structural Equation Model." *American Sociological Review* 45: 627–643.

Kaplan, Kalman J. 1972. "On the Ambivalence–Indifference Problem in Attitude Theory and Measurement: A Suggested Modification of the Semantic Differential Technique." *Psychological Bulletin* 77: 361–372.

Katz, Bruce, and Jennifer Bradley. 1999. "Divided We Sprawl." *Atlantic Monthly* December: 26–42.

Katz, Elihu, and Paul F. Lazarsfeld. 1955. *Personal Influence: The Part Played by People in the Flow of Mass Communications.* New York: Free Press.

Katz, Irwin, and R. Glen Hass. 1988. "Racial Ambivalence and American Value Conflict: Correlational and Priming Studies of Dual Cognitive Structures." *Journal of Personality and Social Psychology* 55: 893–905.

Katz, Irwin, Joyce Wackenhut, and R. Glen Hass. 1986. "Racial Ambivalence, Value Duality, and Behavior." Pp. 35–59 in *Prejudice, Discrimination, and Racism*, eds. John F. Dovidio and Samuel L. Gaertner. Orlando, FL: Academic Press.

Kaufmann, Karen M., and John R. Petrocik. 1999. "The Changing Politics of American Men: Understanding the Sources of the Gender Gap." *American Journal of Political Science* 43: 864–887.

Kellstedt, Lyman A., and John C. Green. 1993. "Knowing God's Many People: Denominational Preference and Political Behavior." Pp. 53–71 in *Rediscovering the Religious Factor in American Politics*, eds. David C. Leege and Lyman A. Kellstedt. Armonk, NY: M. E. Sharpe.

————. 2003. "The Politics of the Willow Creek Association Pastors." *Journal for the Scientific Study of Religion* 42: 547–561.

Kelly, Margaret, and Mattew Zieper. 2000. "Financing for the Future: The Economic Benefits of Parks and Open Space." *Government Finance Review* 16: 23–26.

Kerlinger, Fred N. 1967. "Social Attitudes and Their Criterial Referents." *Psychological Review* 74: 110–122.

Kinder, Donald R., and Tali Mendelberg. 2000. "Individualism Reconsidered: Principles and Prejudice in Contemporary American Opinion." Pp. 44–74 in *Racialized Politics: The Debate about Racism in America*, eds. David O. Sears, Jim Sidanius, and Lawrence Bobo. Chicago: University of Chicago Press.

Kinder, Donald R., and Lynn M. Sanders. 1990. "Mimicking Political Debate with Survey Questions." *Social Cognition* 8: 73–103.

———. 1996. *Divided by Color: Racial Politics and Democratic Ideals*. Chicago: University of Chicago Press.

Kinder, Donald R., and David O. Sears. 1985. "Public Opinion and Political Action." Pp. 659–741 in *Handbook of Social Psychology*, 3rd edition, eds. Gardner Lindzey and Elliot Aronson. New York: Random House.

Kinder, Donald R., and Nicholas Winter. 2001. "Exploring the Racial Divide: Blacks, Whites, and Opinion on National Policy." *American Journal of Political Science* 45: 439–456.

Klopfer, Frederick J., and Thomas J. Madden. 1980. "The Middlemost Choice on Attitude Items: Ambivalence, Neutrality, or Uncertainty?" *Personality and Social Psychology Bulletin* 6: 97–101.

Koch, Jeffrey W. 1998. "Political Rhetoric and Political Persuasion: The Changing Structure of Citizens' Preferences on Health Insurance during Policy Debate." *Public Opinion Quarterly* 62: 209–229.

Krosnick, Jon A. 1988. "The Role of Attitude Importance in Social Evaluation: A Study of Policy Preferences, Presidential Candidate Evaluations, and Voting Behavior." *Journal of Personality and Social Psychology* 55: 196–210.

———. 1990. "Government Policy and Citizen Passion: A Study of Issue Publics in Contemporary America." *Political Behavior* 12: 59–92.

Krosnick, Jon A., and Donald R. Kinder. 1990. "Altering the Foundations of Support for the President through Priming." *American Political Science Review* 84: 497–512.

Krosnick, Jon A., and Laura A. Brannon. 1993. "The Impact of the Gulf War on the Ingredients of Presidential Evaluations: Multidimensional Effects of Political Involvement." *American Political Science Review* 87: 963–975.

Krosnick, Jon A., and Richard E. Petty. 1995. "Attitude Strength: An Overview." Pp. 1–24 in *Attitude Strength: Antecedents and Consequences*, eds. Richard E. Petty and Jon A. Krosnick. Mahwah, NJ: Lawrence Erlbaum.

Lavine, Howard. 2001. "The Electoral Consequences of Ambivalence toward Presidential Candidates." *American Journal of Political Science* 45: 915–929.

Lavine, Howard, Cynthia J. Thomsen, and Marti Hope Gonzales. 1997. "The Development of Interattitudinal Consistency: The Shared-Consequences Model." *Journal of Personality and Social Psychology* 72: 735–749.

Lavine, Howard, Eugene Borgida, and John L. Sullivan. 2000. "On the Relationship between Attitude Involvement and Attitude Accessibility: Toward a Cognitive-Motivational Model of Political Information Processing." *Political Psychology* 21: 81–106.

Lavine, Howard, Joseph W. Huff, Stephen H. Wagner, and Donna Sweeney. 1998. "The Moderating Influence of Attitude Strength on the Susceptibility to

Context Effects in Attitude Surveys." *Journal of Personality and Social Psychology* 75: 359–373.

Layman, Geoffrey C., and Thomas M. Carsey. 2002. "Party Polarization and 'Conflict Extension' in the American Electorate." *American Journal of Political Science* 46: 786–802.

Lazarsfeld, Paul, Bernard Berelson, and Hazel Gaudet. 1944. *The People's Choice: How the Voter Makes Up His Mind in a Presidential Campaign.* New York: Columbia University Press.

LeDoux, Joseph E. 2000. "Emotion Circuits in the Brain." *Annual Review of Neuroscience* 23: 155–184.

Leege, David C., Kenneth D. Wald, Brian S. Krueger and Paul D. Mueller. 2002. *The Politics of Cultural Differences: Social Change and Voter Mobilization Strategies in the Post–New Deal Period.* Princeton, NJ: Princeton University Press.

Levine, Jeffrey, Edward G. Carmines, and Paul M. Sniderman. 1999. "The Empirical Dimensionality of Racial Stereotypes." *Public Opinion Quarterly* 63: 371–384.

Levy, Leonard W. 1986. *The Establishment Clause: Religion and the First Amendment.* New York: Macmillan.

Levy, Leonard W. 1988. *Original Intent and the Framers' Constitution.* New York: Macmillan.

Lewis, Gregory B., and Marc A. Rogers. 1999. "Does the Public Support Equal Employment Rights for Gays and Lesbians?" Pp. 118–145 in *Gays and Lesbians in the Democratic Process: Public Policy, Public Opinion, and Political Representation,* eds. Ellen D. B. Riggle and Barry L. Tadlock. New York: Columbia University Press.

Liberman, Akiva, and Shelly Chaiken. 1991. "Value Conflict and Thought-Induced Attitude Change." *Journal of Experimental Social Psychology* 27: 203–216.

Lindaman, Kara, and Donald P. Haider-Markel. 2002. "Issue Evolution, Political Parties, and the Culture Wars." *Political Research Quarterly* 55: 91–110.

Lipset, Seymour M., and William Schneider. 1978. "The Bakke Case: How Would It Be Decided at the Bar of Public Opinion?" *Public Opinion* 1: 38–44.

Lodge, Milton, Kathleen M. McGraw, and Patrick Stroh. 1989. "An Impression-Driven Model of Candidate Evaluation." *American Political Science Review* 83: 399–419.

Lodge, Milton, Marco R. Steenbergen, and Shawn Brau. 1995. "The Responsive Voter: Campaign Information and the Dynamics of Candidate Evaluation." *American Political Science Review* 89: 309–326.

Long, J. Scott, and Laurie H. Ervin. 2000. "Using Heteroscedasticity Consistent Standard Errors in the Linear Regression Model." *American Statistician* 54: 217–234.

Luker, Kristin. 1984. *Abortion and the Politics of Motherhood.* Berkeley: University of California Press.

Luskin, Robert C. 1987. "Measuring Political Sophistication." *American Journal of Political Science* 31: 856–899.

———. 1990. "Explaining Political Sophistication." *Political Behavior* 12: 331–361.

Luskin, Robert C., and Joseph Ten Barge. 1995. "Education, Intelligence, and Political Sophistication." Paper presented at the 1995 Annual Meetings of the Midwest Political Science Association, Chicago, IL.

Maheswaran, Durairaj, and Shelly Chaiken. 1991. "Promoting Systematic Processing in Low-Motivation Settings: Effect of Incongruent Information on Processing and Judgment." *Journal of Personality and Social Psychology* 61: 13–25.

Maio, Gregory R., and James M. Olson. 1998. "Values as Truisms: Evidence and Implications." *Journal of Personality and Social Psychology* 74: 294–311.

McCann, James A. 1997. "Electoral Choices and Core Value Change: The 1992 Presidential Campaign." *American Journal of Political Science* 41: 564–583.

McClosky, Herbert, and John Zaller. 1984. *The American Ethos: Public Attitudes toward Capitalism and Democracy.* Cambridge, MA: Harvard University Press.

McGraw, Kathleen M., and Brandon Bartels. 2005. "Ambivalence Toward American Political Institutions: Sources and Consequences." Pp. 105–126 in *Ambivalence and the Structure of Public Opinion*, eds. Stephen C. Craig and Michael D. Martinez. New York: Palgrave Macmillan.

McGraw, Kathleen M., and Marco Steenbergen. 1995. "Pictures in the Head: Memory Representations of Political Candidates." Pp. 15–41 in *Political Judgment: Structure and Process*, eds. Milton Lodge and Kathleen M. McGraw. Ann Arbor: University of Michigan Press.

McGraw, Kathleen M., and Neil Pinney. 1990. "The Effects of General and Domain-Specific Expertise on Political Memory and Judgment." *Social Cognition* 8: 9–30.

McGraw, Kathleen M., Edward Hasecke, and Kimberly Conger. 2003. "Ambivalence, Uncertainty, and Processes of Candidate Evaluation." *Political Psychology* 24: 421–448.

McGraw, Kathleen M., Milton Lodge, and Patrick Stroh. 1990. "On-Line Processing in Candidate Evaluation: The Effects of Issue Order, Issue Importance, and Sophistication." *Political Behavior* 12: 41–58.

Meffert, Michael F., Michael Guge, and Milton Lodge. 2000. "Good, Bad, Indifferent and Ambivalent: The Consequences of Multidimensional Political Attitudes." Pp. 60–100 in *The Issue of Belief: Essays in the Intersection of Non-Attitudes and Attitude Change*, eds. Willem E. Saris and Paul M. Sniderman. Amsterdam: The Amsterdam School of Communication Research, Universiteit van Amsterdam, The Netherlands.

Miller, Arthur H., Christopher Wlezien, and Anne Hildreth. 1991. "A Reference Group Theory of Partisan Coalitions." *Journal of Politics* 53: 1134–1149.

Miller, Joanne M., and Jon A. Krosnick. 1996. "News Media Impact on the Ingredients of Presidential Evaluations: A Program of Research on the Priming Hypothesis." Pp. 79–99 in *Political Persuasion and Attitude Change*, eds. Diana C. Mutz and Paul M. Sniderman. Ann Arbor: University of Michigan Press.

———. 2000. "News Media Impact on the Ingredients of Presidential Evaluations: Politically Knowledgeable Citizens Are Guided by a Trusted Source." *American Journal of Political Science* 44: 301–315.

Monsma, Stephen V. 1993. *Positive Neutrality: Letting Religious Freedom Ring.* Westport, CT: Greenwood Press.

Monsma, Stephen V., and J. Christopher Soper. 1997. *The Challenge of Pluralism: Church and State in Five Democracies.* Lanham, MD: Rowman and Littlefield.

Monteith, Margo J. 1996. "Contemporary Forms of Prejudice-Related Conflict: In Search of a Nutshell." *Personality and Social Psychology Bulletin* 22: 461–473.

Morrison Institute for Public Policy. 2001. *Hits and Misses: Fast Growth in Metropolitan Phoenix*. Tempe, AZ: Arizona State University.

Moscovici, Serge. 1976. *Social Influence and Social Change*. London: Academic Press.

Murley, John A. 1988. "School Prayer: Free Exercise of Religion or Establishment of Religion?" Pp. 5–40 in *Social Regulatory Policy: Moral Controversies in American Politics*, eds. Raymond Tatalovich and Byron W. Danes. Boulder, CO: Westview.

Mutz, Diana C., Paul M. Sniderman, and Richard A. Brody, eds. 1996. *Political Persuasion and Attitude Change*. Ann Arbor: University of Michigan Press.

Myers, Phyllis. 1999. "Livability at the Ballot Box: State and Local Referenda on Parks, Conservation, and Smarter Growth, Election Day 1998." Discussion paper prepared for The Brookings Institution Center on Urban and Metropolitan Policy, Washington, DC, January.

Myers, Phyllis, and Robert Puentes. 2001. "Growth at the Ballot Box: Electing the Shape of Communities in November 2000." Discussion paper prepared for The Brookings Institution Center on Urban and Metropolitan Policy, Washington, DC, February.

Nadeau, Richard, and Christopher Fleury. 1994. "Cross-Pressured Nationalists and the Sovereignty Decision: Evidence from the Quebec Case." Paper presented at the 1994 Annual Meetings of the American Political Science Association, New York.

Nelson, Thomas E., and Donald R. Kinder. 1996. "Issue Frames and Group-Centrism in American Public Opinion." *Journal of Politics* 58: 1055–1078.

Nelson, Thomas E., Rosalee A. Clawson, and Zoe M. Oxley. 1997. "Media Framing of a Civil Liberties Conflict and Its Effect on Tolerance." *American Political Science Review* 91: 567–583.

Neuhaus, Richard John. 1984. *The Naked Public Square: Religion and Democracy in America*. Grand Rapids, MI: Eerdmans.

Newby-Clark, Ian R., Ian McGregor, and Mark P. Zanna. 2002. "Thinking and Caring about Cognitive Inconsistency: When and for Whom Does Attitudinal Ambivalence Feel Uncomfortable?" *Journal of Personality and Social Psychology* 82: 157–166.

———. 2005. "Ambivalence and Accessibility: The Consequences of Accessible Ambivalence." Pp. 33–53 in *Ambivalence and the Structure of Public Opinion*, eds. Stephen C. Craig and Michael D. Martinez. New York: Palgrave Macmillan.

Newport, Frank. 2003. "Americans Approve of Public Displays of Religious Symbols." *Gallup Poll News Services* (www.gallup.com). October 3.

Nisbett, Richard E., and Timothy DeCamp Wilson. 1977. "Telling More Than We Can Know: Verbal Reports on Mental Processes." *Psychological Review* 84: 231–259.

O'Keefe, Daniel J. 1990. *Persuasion: Theory and Research*. Newbury Park, CA: Sage.

Orfield, Myron. 1997. *Metropolitics: A Regional Agenda for Community and Stability*, revised edition. Washington, DC: Brookings Institution.

Orfield, Myron. 2002. *American Metropolitics: The New Suburban Reality*. Washington, DC: Brookings Institution.

Osgood, Charles E., George J. Suci, and Percy H. Tannenbaum. 1957. *The Measurement of Meaning*. Urbana: University of Illinois Press.

Patchen, Martin, Gerhard Hofmann, and James D. Davidson. 1976. "Interracial Perceptions Among High School Students." *Sociometry* 39: 341–354.

Peffley, Mark A., Pia Knigge, and Jon Hurwitz. 2001. "A Multiple Values Model of Political Tolerance." *Political Research Quarterly* 54: 379–406.

Petty, Richard E., and John T. Cacioppo. 1986. *Communication and Persuasion: Central and Peripheral Routes to Attitude Change.* New York: Springer-Verlag.

Petty, Richard E., and Jon A. Krosnick, eds. 1995. *Attitude Strength: Antecedents and Consequences.* Mahwah, NJ: Lawrence Erlbaum.

Phillips, Katherine W. 2003. "The Effects of Categorically Based Expectations on Minority Influence: The Importance of Congruence." *Personality and Social Psychology Bulletin* 29: 3–13.

Press, Daniel. 1999. "Local Open Space Preservation in California." Pp. 153–180 in *Toward Sustainable Communities*, eds. Daniel A. Mazmanian and Michael E. Kraft. Cambridge, MA: MIT Press.

———. 2002. *Saving Open Space: The Politics of Local Preservation in California.* Berkeley: University of California Press.

Priester, Joseph R., and Richard E. Petty. 1996. "The Gradual Threshold Model of Ambivalence: Relating the Positive and Negative Bases of Attitudes to Subjective Ambivalence." *Journal of Personality and Social Psychology* 71: 431–449.

———. 2001. "Extending the Bases of Subjective Attitudinal Ambivalence: Interpersonal and Intrapersonal Antecedents of Evaluative Tension." *Journal of Personality and Social Psychology* 80: 19–34.

Protash, William, and Mark Baldassare. 1983. "Growth Policies and Community Status: A Test and Modification of Logan's Theory." *Urban Affairs Quarterly* 18: 397–412.

Rahn, Wendy M., Jon A. Krosnick, and Marijke Breuning. 1994. "Rationalization and Derivation Processes in Survey Studies of Political Candidate Evaluation." *American Journal of Political Science* 38: 582–600.

Reed, Ralph. 1994. *Politically Incorrect: The Emerging Faith Factor in American Politics.* Dallas, TX: Word Publishing.

Reichley, A. James. 1985. *Religion in American Public Life.* Washington, DC: Brookings Institution.

Riketta, Michael. 2000. "Discriminative Validation of Numerical Indices of Attitude Ambivalence." *Current Research in Social Psychology* 5: 1–9.

———. 2004. "Convergence of Direct and Indirect Measures of Attitudinal Ambivalence." Unpublished manuscript.

Rokeach, Milton. 1973. *The Nature of Human Values.* New York: Free Press.

Schnell, Frauke. 1993. "The Foundations of Abortion Attitudes: The Role of Values and Value Conflict." Pp. 23–43 in *Understanding the New Politics of Abortion*, ed. Malcolm L. Goggin. Newbury Park, CA: Sage.

Schuman, Howard, Charlotte Steeh, Lawrence Bobo, and Maria Krysan. 1997. *Racial Attitudes in America: Trends and Interpretations*, revised edition. Cambridge, MA: Harvard University Press.

Schwartz, Norbert, and Herbert Bless. 1992. "Constructing Reality and Its Alternatives: An Inclusion/Exclusion model of Assimilation and Contrast Effects in Social Judgments." Pp. 217–245 in *The Construction of Social Judgments*, eds. Leonard L. Martin and Abraham Tesser. Hillsdale, NJ: Erlbaum.

Schwartz, Shalom H. 1992. "Universals in the Content of Structure of Values: Theoretical Advances and Empirical Tests in 20 Countries." Pp. 1–65 in

Advances in Experimental Social Psychology, vol. 25, ed. Mark P. Zanna. Orlando, FL: Academic Press.

Schwartz, Shalom H., and Wolfgang Bilsky. 1987. "Toward a Universal Psychological Structure of Human Values." *Journal of Personality and Social Psychology* 53: 550–562.

Scott, William A. 1969. "Structure of Natural Cognitions." *Journal of Personality and Social Psychology* 12: 261–278.

Sears, David O. 1986. "College Sophomores in the Laboratory: Influences of a Narrow Data Base on Social Psychology's View of Human Nature." *Journal of Personality and Social Psychology* 51: 515–530.

———. 1988. "Symbolic Racism." Pp. 53–84 in *Eliminating Racism: Profiles in Controversy*, eds. Phyllis A. Katz and Dalmas A. Taylor. New York: Plenum.

Sears, David O., and Jack Citrin. 1985. *Tax Revolt: Something for Nothing in California*, enlarged edition. Cambridge, MA: Harvard University Press.

Sears, David O., and P. J. Henry. 2003. "The Origins of Symbolic Racism." *Journal of Personality and Social Psychology* 85: 259–275.

Sears, David O., Carl P. Hensler, and Leslie K. Speer. 1979. "Whites' Opposition to 'Busing': Self-Interest or Symbolic Politics?" *American Political Science Review* 73: 369–384.

Sengupta, Jaideep, and Gita Venkataramani Johar. 2002. "Effects of Inconsistent Attribute Information on the Predictive Value of Product Attitudes: Toward a Resolution of Opposing Perspectives. *Journal of Consumer Research* 29: 39–56.

Sherif, Carolyn W., Muzafer Sherif, and Roger E. Nebergall. 1965. *Attitude and Attitude Change: The Social Judgment–Involvement Approach*. Philadelphia, PA: Saunders.

Sherrill, Kenneth, and Alan Yang. 2000. "From Outlaws to In-Laws." *Public Perspective*. 11: 20–23.

Sidanius, James, and Felicia Pratto. 1999. *Social Dominance: An Intergroup Theory of Social Hierarchy and Oppression*. New York: Cambridge University Press.

Sidanius, Jim, Felicia Pratto, and Lawrence Bobo. 1996. "Racism, Conservatism, Affirmative Action, and Intellectual Sophistication: A Matter of Principled Conservatism or Group Dominance?" *Journal of Personality and Social Psychology* 70: 476–490.

Sidanius, Jim, Pam Singh, John J. Hetts, and Chris Federico. 2000. "It's Not Affirmative Action, It's The Blacks: The Continuing Relevance of Race in American Politics." Pp. 183–219 in *Racialized Politics: The Debate About Racism in America*, eds. David O. Sears, Jim Sidanius, and Lawrence Bobo. Chicago: University of Chicago Press.

Sierra Club. 1998. "Sprawl Costs Us All." Report issued by the Grand Canyon Chapter of the Sierra Club in conjunction with the Sierra Club Southwest Office.

Silver, Brian D., Paul R. Abramson, and Barbara A. Anderson. 1986. "The Presence of Others and Overreporting of Voting in American National Elections. *Public Opinion Quarterly* 50: 228–239.

Sinclair, Barbara Deckard. 1978. "The Policy Consequences of Party Realignment—Social Welfare Legislation in the House of Representatives, 1933–1954." *American Journal of Political Science* 22: 83–105.

Smith, Eric R. A. N. 1989. *The Unchanging American Voter*. Berkeley: University of California Press.

Sniderman, Paul M., and Edward G. Carmines. 1997. *Reaching Beyond Race*. Cambridge, MA: Harvard University Press.

Sniderman, Paul M., and Thomas Piazza. 1993. *The Scar of Race*. Cambridge, MA: Harvard University Press.

Sniderman, Paul M., Gretchen C. Crosby, and William G. Howell. 2000. "The Politics of Race." Pp. 236–279 in *Racialized Politics: The Debate about Racism in America*, eds. David O. Sears, Jim Sidanius, and Lawrence Bobo. Chicago: University of Chicago Press.

Sniderman, Paul M., Richard A. Brody, and Philip E. Tetlock. 1991. *Reasoning and Choice: Explorations in Political Psychology*. New York: Cambridge University Press.

Sparks, Paul, Duncan Hedderley, and Richard Shepherd. 1992. "An Investigation into the Relationship between Perceived Control, Attitude Variability, and the Consumption of Two Common Foods." *European Journal of Social Psychology* 22: 55–71.

Sparks, Paul, Mark Conner, Rhiannon James, Richard Shepherd, and Rachel Povey. 2001. "Ambivalence about Health-Related Behaviours: An Exploration in the Domain of Food Choice." *British Journal of Health Psychology* 6: 53–68.

Stark, Rodney, and Roger Finke. 2000. *Acts of Faith: Explaining the Human Side of Religion*. Berkeley: University of California Press.

Steenbergen, Marco R., and Paul R. Brewer. 2000. "The Not-So-Ambivalent Public: Policy Attitudes in the Political Culture of Ambivalence." Pp. 101–142 in *The Issue of Belief: Essays in the Intersection of Non-Attitudes and Attitude Change*, eds. Willem E. Saris and Paul M. Sniderman. Amsterdam: The Amsterdam School of Communication Research, Universiteit van Amsterdam, The Netherlands.

Stimson, James A. 1975. "Belief Systems: Constraint, Complexity, and the 1972 Election." *American Journal of Political Science* 19: 393–417.

Stocker, Michael. 1990. *Plural and Conflicting Values*. New York: Oxford University Press.

Stonecash, Jeffrey M. 2000. *Class and Party in American Politics*. Boulder, CO: Westview.

Tate, Katherine. 1994. *From Protest to Politics: The New Black Voters in American Elections*. Cambridge, MA: Harvard University Press.

Tesser, Abraham. 1978. "Self-Generated Attitude Change." Pp. 290–338 in *Advances in Experimental Social Psychology*, vol. 2, ed. Leonard Berkowitz. New York: Academic Press.

Tetlock, Philip E. 1986. "A Value Pluralism Model of Ideological Reasoning." *Journal of Personality and Social Psychology* 50: 819–827.

Thompson, Megan M., and Mark P. Zanna. 1995. "The Conflicted Individual: Personality-Based and Domain-Specific Antecedents of Ambivalent Social Attitudes." *Journal of Personality* 63: 259–288.

Thompson, Megan, Mark P. Zanna, and Dale W. Griffin. 1995. "Let's Not Be Indifferent About (Attitudinal) Ambivalence." Pp. 361–386 in *Attitude Strength: Antecedents and Consequences*, eds. Richard E. Petty and Jon A. Krosnick. Mahwah, NJ: Lawrence Erlbaum.

Thurstone, Louis L. 1928. "Attitudes Can Be Measured." *American Journal of Sociology* 33: 529–554.

Thurstone, Louis L., and Edward J. Chave. 1929. *The Measurement of Attitude.* Chicago: University of Chicago Press.

Tourangeau, Roger, and Kenneth A. Rasinski. 1988. "Cognitive Processes Underlying Contest Effects in Attitude Measurement." *Psychological Bulletin* 103: 299–314.

Tourangeau, Roger, Kenneth A. Rasinski, Norman Bradburn, and Roy D'Andrade. 1989a. "Belief Accessibility and Context Effects in Attitude Measurement." *Journal of Experimental Social Psychology* 25: 401–421.

Tourangeau, Roger, Kenneth A. Rasinki, Norman Bradburn, and Roy D'Andrade. 1989b. "Carryover Effects in Attitude Surveys." *Public Opinion Quarterly* 53: 495–524.

Tourangeau, Roger, Lance J. Rips, and Kenneth A. Rasinski. 2000. *The Psychology of Survey Response.* New York: Cambridge University Press.

The Trust for Public Land and Land Trust Alliance. 2002. "LandVote 2001: Americans Invest in Parks and Open Space." San Francisco, CA.

Tygart, C. E. 2000. "Genetic Causation Attribution and Public Support of Gay Rights." *International Journal of Public Opinion Research* 12: 259–275.

Uhlaner, Carole J., Mark M. Gray, and F. Chris Garcia. 2000. "Ideology, Issues, and Partisanship among Latinos." Paper presented at the 2000 Annual Meetings of the Western Political Science Association, San Jose, CA.

van der Maas, Han L. J., Rogier Kolstein, and Joop van der Pligt. 2003. "Sudden Transitions in Attitudes." *Sociological Methods and Research* 32: 125–152.

Wald, Kenneth D. 2000. "The Context of Gay Politics." Pp. 1–28 in *The Politics of Gay Rights*, eds. Craig A. Rimmerman, Kenneth D. Wald, and Clyde Wilcox. Chicago: University of Chicago Press.

Wald, Kenneth D. 2003. *Religion and Politics in the United States*, 4th edition. Lanham, MD: Rowman and Littlefield.

Washington Post. 2003. "Justices Won't Hear Ten Commandments Appeal from Alabama." November 4: A3.

Wegener, Duane T., and Leandre R. Fabrigar. 2000. "Analysis and Design for Nonexperimental Data: Addressing Causal and Noncausal Hypotheses." Pp. 412–450 in *Handbook of Research Methods in Social and Personality Psychology*, eds. Harry T. Reis and Charles M. Judd. New York: Cambridge University Press.

Weisberg, Herbert F. 1980. "A Multidimensional Conceptualization of Party Identification." *Political Behavior* 2: 33–60.

Weisberg, Herbert F., Audrey A. Haynes, and Jon A. Krosnick. 1995. "Social-Group Polarization in 1992." Pp. 241–259 in *Democracy's Feast: Elections in America*, ed. Herbert F. Weisberg. Chatham, NJ: Chatham House.

Welch, Susan. 1985. "The 'More for Less' Paradox: Public Attitudes on Taxing and Spending." *Public Opinion Quarterly* 49: 310–316.

Welch, Susan, and Lee Sigelman. 1993. "The Politics of Hispanic Americans: Insights from National Surveys, 1980–1988." *Social Science Quarterly* 74: 76–94.

Whitley, Bernard E., and Sarah E. Lee. 2000. "The Relationship of Authoritarianism and Related Constructs to Attitudes Toward Homosexuality." *Journal of Applied Social Psychology* 30: 144–170.

Wilcox, Clyde, and Barbara Norrander. 2002. "Of Moods and Morals: The Dynamics of Opinion on Abortion and Gay Rights." Pp. 121–147 in

Understanding Public Opinion, 2nd edition, eds. Barbara Norrander and Clyde Wilcox. Washington, DC: CQ Press.

Wilcox, Clyde, and Robin Wolpert. 2000. "Gay Rights in the Public Sphere: Public Opinion on Gay and Lesbian Equality." Pp. 409–432 in *The Politics of Gay Rights*, eds. Craig A. Rimmerman, Kenneth D. Wald, and Clyde Wilcox. Chicago: University of Chicago Press.

Wilcox, Clyde, Lee Sigelmen, and Elizabeth Cook. 1989. "Some Like It Hot: Individual Differences in Responses to Group Feeling Thermometers." *Public Opinion Quarterly* 53: 246–257.

Wilcox, Clyde, Rachel Goldberg, and Ted G. Jelen. 2002. "Public Attitudes on Church and State: Coexistence or Conflict?" Pp. 221–233 in *Piety, Politics, and Pluralism: Religion, the Courts, and the 2000 Election*, ed. Mary C. Segers. Lanham, MD: Rowman and Littlefield.

Wilson, Timothy D., and Sara D. Hodges. 1992. "Attitudes as Temporary Constructions." Pp. 37–65 in *The Construction of Social Judgments*, eds. Leonard L. Martin and Abraham Tesser. Hillsdale, NJ: Lawrence Erlbaum.

Winter, Nicholas, and Adam Berinsky. 1999. "What's Your Temperature? Thermometer Ratings and Political Analysis." Paper presented at the 1999 Annual Meetings of the American Political Science Association, Atlanta, GA.

Witte, John, Jr. 1999. *Religion and the American Constitutional Experiment: Essential Rights and Liberties*. Boulder, CO: Westview.

Yang, Alan S. 1997. "Attitudes toward Homosexuality." *Public Opinion Quarterly* 61: 477–507.

Zaller, John. 1990. "Political Awareness, Elite Opinion Leadership, and the Mass Survey Response." *Social Cognition* 8: 125–153.

———. 1992. *The Nature and Origins of Mass Opinion*. Cambridge: Cambridge University Press.

———. 1996. "The Myth of Massive Media Impact Revived: New Support for a Discredited Idea." Pp. 17–78 in *Political Persuasion and Attitude Change*, eds. Diana C. Mutz, Paul M. Sniderman, and Richard A. Brody. Ann Arbor: University of Michigan Press.

Zaller, John, and Stanley Feldman. 1992. "A Simple Theory of the Survey Response: Answering Questions versus Revealing Preferences." *American Journal of Political Science* 36: 579–616.

Zucker, Gail S. 1999. "Attributional and Symbolic Predictors of Abortion Attitudes." *Journal of Applied Social Psychology* 29: 1218–1245.

INDEX

Accessibility, 2–3, 10–11, 30, 147, 157
Activism, 47, 64, 119, 147–148, 162
Actual ambivalence, 33–44, 149
Albertson, Bethany, 145–146, 152, 155–6
Alvarez, R. Michael, 2, 4, 5, 25n, 65–66, 130, 145–146, 152, 155–156
Ambivalence and the Structure of Political Opinion, xv, xviii, 63, 145
Armitage, Christopher, xviii
Attitude conflict, 29, 158
Attitudinal
  importance (or salience), 28–30, 74, 85, 99, 106, 132, 142, 148–149, 157, 161
  polarity, 25n, 84–85, 96, 143, 151
  stability, 1–3, 10–12, 19–20, 22–24, 27–46, 130, 143n, 148–149, 152, 156, 158, 162, 164–165
  strength, 3, 35–37, 41, 45, 148–149, 157, 158, 162, 166

Bartels, Brandon, 149–150
Basinger, Scott, 2
Belief homogeneity, 165
Belief systems, 1, 7, 31, 86–89, 100
Brady, Henry, 7
Brehm, John, 2, 4, 5, 25n, 65–66, 130, 145–146, 152, 155–156
Brewer, Paul, 50
Brody, Richard, 9, 25n, 28
Brömer, Philip, 161

Candidate ambivalence, xvi, 1–26
Candidate evaluation, 10, 12, 19–21, 148
Cantril, Albert, 6, 13, 48–49
Cantril, Susan, 6, 13, 48–49
Carmines, Edward, 63
Chong, Dennis, xvii, 154
Citrin, Jack, 150–151
Cognitive dissonance, 28, 130–132, 136, 138, 141, 147, 157
Cognitive sophistication, 86–100, 130, 132, 142, 153; *see also* political sophistication
Conflict amplification, 97
Conger, Kimberly, 3
Conner, Mark, xviii, 156, 158
Conover, Pamela, 8, 9
Consistency of attitudes, 4–5, 10, 14, 18–20, 23–24, 29, 31, 50, 130, 132, 135, 137–138, 142, 152, 156, 165
Converse, Philip, 7, 130, 132
Cook, Elizabeth, 68
Counterargument, 29, 42, 116, 118
Craig, Stephen, xvii, 46n, 53, 138, 143n, 148, 152

Davidson, James, 84
Diehl, Michael, 161
Distraction, 147

Economic retrospection, 14–15
Efficacy, 149
Ego-involvement, 28

Elaboration, 161, 163
Emotions, 147, 150
Ervin, Laurie, 91

False consensus effect, 147–148
Federalist 10, xv
Federico, Christopher, xvii, 99,
    152–153, 159
Feldman, Stanley, 4, 8, 9, 50, 51, 53,
    59, 61n, 65, 156
Finke, Roger, 142n
Fiske, Susan, 162
Florida Voter survey organization, 53,
    61n, 62n, 66, 79n
Fournier, Patrick, xvi, 149
Framing, 31, 79, 104–107, 116, 118,
    121, 148
Frankfort-Nachmias, Chava, 143n
Extremity, 13–14, 17, 19–22, 64,
    152, 162
Free, Lloyd, 6

Gainous, Jason, xvi, xvii, 53, 138,
    143n, 152, 153, 159
Goldberg, Rachel, 143n
Government spending, 56, 58–60,
    61n, 62n, 151
Green, Donald, 9–10, 25n
Green, John, 143n
Griffin, Dale, 11, 12, 25n, 35, 54, 61n,
    68, 90, 156, 158
Group ambivalence, xvi, 1–26,
    151–152, 158
Group polarity, 8–10
Group salience, 7, 10, 11
Growth management (including
    conservation and environmental
    policy), 103–126, 154, 158

Haider-Markel, Donald, 79n
Hasecke, Edward, 3
Hass, R. Glen, 84, 85, 153
Haynes, Audrey, 9, 25n

Hodges, Sara, 162
Hofmann, Gerhard, 84
Holbrook, Allyson, 147–148
Hurwitz, Jon, 65

Ideology, 3, 4, 6–10, 14–24, 25n, 26n,
    31, 33, 34, 44, 64, 79n, 83–101,
    102n, 105, 110, 121, 136–137,
    141, 144n, 145, 152, 155
Indifference, 24, 28, 30, 33, 34, 36,
    38–41, 44
Inferential measure of ambivalence,
    146, 157, 165
Information seeking, 162
Information processing, 31, 150, 161
Information gathering, 148
Intensity, 30, 35, 57, 69, 80n, 90, 136,
    148–149, 156, 158–160, 165
Internalized conflict, 1, 4, 5, 10, 23,
    24, 27, 29, 33, 37, 68, 130, 146,
    156, 159, 161
Issue proximity, 2, 14–15, 20–22

Jacoby, William, 49–50, 52,
    61n, 151
Jelen, Ted, xviii, 68, 132, 142n,
    143n, 154–145, 159
Jonas, Klaus, 161

Kane, James, xvii, 46n, 53, 138, 142n,
    143n, 148–149, 152, 159
Kaplan, Kalman, 61n, 80n, 143n
Katz, Irwin, 84, 85, 153
Kerlinger, Fred, 8
Knigge, Pia, 65
Krosnick, Jon, 9, 25n, 30, 147–148

Lavine, Howard, xvi, 146, 151–152, 158
Learning, 27, 127
Lindaman, Kara, 79n
Lipset, Seymour, 85
Long, J. Scott, 91
Luks, Samantha, 150–151

Maio, Gregory, 160
Martinez, Michael, xvi, xvii, 46n, 53,
    61n, 138, 142n, 143n, 148–149,
    152, 153, 159
McClosky, Herbert, 132
McGraw, Kathleen, 3, 149–150
McGregor, Ian, 147, 157
Measurement error, 9, 136, 151
Media bias, 147–148
Memory, 1, 3, 30
Modern racism, 25n
Monsma, Stephen, 135
Multiple imputation, 61n, 81n
Mutz, Diana, 28

Nachmias, David, 143n
National identity, 150
Newby-Clark, Ian, 147, 157
Newport, Frank, 131
Non-attitudes, 130, 136

Objective ambivalence, 33, 35–37, 41,
    43, 65, 81–82n, 130, 166n
Olson, James, 160

Party ambivalence, xvi, 1–26
Party identification, 3, 14–22, 26n,
    27–28, 31, 33–41, 43–45,
    105, 151
Patchen, Martin, 84
Patriotism, 150
Peffley, Mark, 65
Persuasion, 2, 26n, 28–31, 37, 42,
    106–108, 113, 116, 120, 123,
    147–148, 162, 164–165
Petty, Richard, 46n, 157–158
Political information, 17, 20, 24, 35,
    36, 38–41, 45, 46n, 150
Political interest, 14, 17–19, 22, 41
Political knowledge, 35, 37, 39, 45,
    91–92, 94, 101
Political sophistication, 3, 28, 31, 35,
    46n; see also cognitive sophistication

Potential ambivalence, 147–148,
    157–158, 166
Prejudice, 5
Priester, Joseph, 46n, 157–158
Priming, 27, 31

Racial ambivalence, xvii, 83–102,
    152–153, 159
Reed, Ralph, 134
Religion, xviii, 2, 73, 127–144, 155
Religiosity, 44, 128, 136–138,
    141, 155
Resistance to persuasion, 31, 146,
    148, 162
Response latency, 157

Schnieder, William, 85
Schwartz, Shalom, 158
Self-interest, 2, 23, 109, 146, 151
Size of government, 48
Sniderman, Paul, 7, 9, 25n, 28
Social differentiation, 8
Social welfare ambivalence, 47–62,
    151, 153, 159
Social welfare policy (including welfare
    issues and welfare spending), 2,
    47–62, 151, 153, 156
Sophisticated ambivalence, 135,
    137–142, 154–155
Sparks, Paul, 156
Split ticket voting, 10, 19, 22–24, 25n
Stark, Rodney, 142n
Steenbergen, Marco, xvi, 50, 61n, 146,
    151, 152–158
Stimson, James, 63
Subjective (felt) ambivalence, 33–37,
    41, 43, 65, 74, 81–82n, 130,
    147–148, 155, 157–158,
    162–163, 166, 166n
Suppression, 147
Symbolic ambivalence, xviii, 135,
    137–141, 154
Symbolic racism, 98, 151

Tetlock, Philip, 9, 25n
Thompson, John, 143n
Thompson, Megan, 11, 12, 25n, 35, 54, 61n, 68, 90, 102n, 156, 158

Uncertainty, 20, 24, 103, 106, 123, 150, 156

Value conflict, xvii, 12–21, 26n, 48, 50–60, 63–79, 81n, 82n, 87–89, 94–100, 106, 138, 146, 152, 153–156, 158–161, 164
Value hierarchies, 52, 61, 153
Value importance (or salience), 47, 50–53, 55, 58–60, 62n, 153, 159
Values, 2, 4, 6, 13, 16, 17, 25n, 27, 29, 30, 33, 47–61, 62n, 65, 70–79, 80n, 85–7, 98, 104, 106, 112–118, 128–133, 136–138, 144n, 158–161, 164–165
Values, core, xvi, xvii, 4, 6, 47, 51–54, 58, 63, 65–66, 72–78, 81n, 99, 131, 136–142, 152–156

Wackenhut, Joyce, 85
Weisberg, Herbert, 9, 25n
Wilcox, Clyde, 68, 132
Wilson, Timothy, 162
Wolinsky-Nahmias, Yael, xvii, 154

Zaller, John, 4, 31, 39, 50–51, 53, 59, 132, 156
Zanna, Mark, 11, 12, 25n, 35, 54, 61n, 68, 90, 102n, 147, 156, 157, 158